"In these difficult years ahead, this book wil[...] leaders." —**Nelson Lim**, executive director, Fels Institute of Government, University of Pennsylvania

"When the ideas to achieve high performance in governmental agencies are written down in such an accessible and practical way, there is no reason for public sector organizations to not use this book to achieve the high performance status." —**André de Waal**, author of *What Makes A High Performance Organization*

"If you are working in the public sector in the United States, the UK, or the UN, anywhere, you have to be interested in improving performance and so you have to read this book." —**Duncan Brown**, head of HR Research and Consultancy, Institute for Employment Studies

"Drawing on more than 40 years of experience, Risher and Wilder have produced a compelling and valuable resource for everyone interested in good and effective government." —**Max Stier**, president and chief executive officer, The Partnership for Public Service

"[The authors'] approach to performance management recognizes the importance of metrics and structured systems but shifts the principal focus to managers and, as the authors use the phrase, day-to-day "people management" to improve government processes and services." —**David N. Ammons**, University of North Carolina at Chapel Hill

"This book is long overdue and it is recommended that governments throughout the world that want to improve their efficiency and effectiveness follow the valuable recommendations contained in the book." —**Neil Reichenberg**, executive director, International Public Management Association for Human Resources

"Whether you want big government or small, everyone wants one that is well led, well managed, and well served by the thousands of public employees who work for it. That's why this book is so important. It not only provides HR professionals with an invaluable overview of the state-of-the-art in public sector HR practices, but it will be even more valuable to those front-line executives and managers who actually make the day-to-day people decisions in government; they're the ones who really make or break an agency's performance. This work ought to be required reading for them." —**Ron Sanders**, vice president and fellow, Booz Allen Hamilton

"Delivering quality public service requires labor and management to find the best ways to engage the workforce and to effectively solve workplace issues. By putting in practice the strategies proposed by Risher and Wilder, the public's confidence in government can be restored." —**Michael B. Filler**, National Council on Federal Labor-Management Relations

It's Time for High-Performance Government

It's Time for High-Performance Government

Winning Strategies to Engage and Energize the Public Sector Workforce

Howard Risher and
William Wilder

ROWMAN & LITTLEFIELD
Lanham • Boulder • New York • London

Published by Rowman & Littlefield
A wholly owned subsidiary of The Rowman & Littlefield Publishing Group, Inc.
4501 Forbes Boulevard, Suite 200, Lanham, Maryland 20706
www.rowman.com

Unit A, Whitacre Mews, 26-34 Stannary Street, London SE11 4AB

British Library Cataloguing in Publication Information Available

Library of Congress Cataloging-in-Publication Data Available

978-1-4422-6122-8 (cloth)
978-1-4422-6150-1 (paper)
978-1-4422-6123-5 (ebook)

♾™ The paper used in this publication meets the minimum requirements of American National Standard for Information Sciences—Permanence of Paper for Printed Library Materials, ANSI/NISO Z39.48-1992.

Printed in the United States of America

Contents

Foreword

The pressure on organizations to become more effective has built over time, in part because of resource constraints—the need to do more with less—but also because of the growing realization of the remarkable variation in performance across what we might think of as otherwise similar organizations. That variation is easy to see in business, where we look at differences in profitability, but we can see it in areas where profits are not necessarily an outcome, such as health care, where we now measure patient outcomes, or in schools, where student performance can be compared.

What makes some organizations more effective than others? Observers of organizations have long noted that there isn't much of anything to them except for people and the way they are managed. Certainly little else differentiates high-performing organizations from poor ones in the same field.

The public sector and the administrative functions within government have been among the last to feel this pressure. One reason, which spans the private sector as well, is that it is quite difficult to measure administrative performance. Another reason, much more unique to government, is that outcomes are not the only concern here. The process through which they are achieved is of special concern when taxpayer dollars are being considered. Issues of fairness become paramount in this environment: Do constituents get a say in decisions, do they have time to ponder those decisions, are the processes open to all, and so forth. In that context, some solutions that might lead to better outcomes might not clear all the fairness hurdles. Those that do may also take more time to execute.

Nevertheless, the pressures to improve government functions have certainly been building and have created the need to rethink some of the ways that we have operated in the past, perhaps to make different trade-offs on some criteria than were made previously. A good way to begin that rethinking process is to see what we can learn from practices elsewhere. The logical place to look is to the private sector.

There is no doubt that government operations are quite different from those in the private sector, and no one would suggest that the practices of the latter be lifted and applied whole cloth onto the former. Just as leading businesses have learned a great deal from some government operations over the years, especially the military but also specialized agencies like NASA and the CDC, practices from the private sector can stimulate thinking and new ideas about how the government could operate more effectively. At the heart of any such ideas is how people are managed.

Howard Risher spent decades teaching private sector managers how to run their businesses more effectively. In recent years, he has devoted his attention to a wide range of public sector organizations, running the gamut from local governments to federal agencies to the international agencies of the United Nations. He is ideally situated to help us see what can—and cannot—be borrowed from private sector experience and applied to government operations. From what Howard has told me about Bill Wilder and his years as the Human Resource Director for Charlotte, North Carolina, their combined experience is ideally suited to developing this book. The lessons they provide here for the civil service walk us step-by-step through the key factors that make the management of people, and in turn the management of government operations, more efficient and effective.

Peter Cappelli
George W. Taylor Professor of Management and
Director at the Center for Human Resources at The Wharton School

Preface

This book is the product of forty-plus years of consulting and opportunities to meet and work with some of the best management minds in every sector. It became clear some years ago that public sector organizations in the United States and globally employ talented people managed with historically common but ineffective practices that deter them from performing at their best. The potential to improve government performance is substantial.

My career has enabled me to consult with and learn a great deal about the motivations and aspirations of people working at all job levels. My interest in work and what influences performance started with summer jobs while in college. One of those jobs for two summers was building truck tires on the 4:00 p.m.-to-midnight shift. The men I worked with had years of experience, could have solved every problem, but the supervisors never asked. It was a classic us-versus-them culture—and a tremendous waste of job knowledge. Similar factory scenes have been portrayed in movies and described in novels.

Consulting has taken me into organizations from Wall Street to prisons to public schools. I have had opportunities in meetings at the United Nations and the Organisation for Economic Cooperation and Development in Paris to discuss work and its management with people from a long list of countries. Undoubtedly the most telling experience was managing a consulting practice in Washington, DC. The job took me from federal, state, and local government offices to some of the best-managed companies in the country, sometimes on the same day. Through the years I have become convinced all employees want opportunities to grow and gain personal satisfaction from what they accomplish.

My first book now two decades ago was on high performance. It was spawned by the nights building tires. It predated today's focus on human capital management. In hindsight it was not very good. But in developing the book and in the research, I learned that people are capable of performing at much higher levels than was at the time expected. The secret is in the way work is organized and managed.

It starts with management's beliefs. Until maybe a decade ago leaders saw workers as a necessary cost—and that us-versus-them approach to supervision was still prevalent. Today, leading companies manage their workers as assets that need to be fully utilized. It's a very different approach to management that is a win-win for everyone.

Government needs to change. Ineffective management is costly. Employee capabilities are too often badly underutilized. When people begin their working careers, they start with similar aspirations to be successful. Their career goals may be modest, but they want to be valued for their contributions. But my experience has convinced me that public employers too often fail to provide attractive, supportive career opportunities—and a valuable resource is wasted. Employees as well as the public are the losers.

It admittedly is not a simple problem. The practices that come together to create a positive work environment are the subject of this book and its seventeen chapters. But government has a huge gulf between its practices and those companies identified as the "best places to work." Change can start in a number of areas. It does not have to start by canceling existing civil service rules, but it has to start someplace. Reforming the mind-set that has been civil service management will take years and possibly as long as a decade.

It is unfortunate that existing civil service laws often inhibit the changes advocated in this book. The political practices common at the end of the nineteenth century that prompted the laws would be far less likely to be tolerated today with the scrutiny of government.

This book is solidly pro employee. All of the ideas discussed are consistent with the practices in the companies recognized as "best places to work." Many public employers manage employees free of civil service constraints. There is no reason to question their commitment to fairness and good government. Reform is necessary to improve government performance.

My coauthor, Bill Wilder, was human resources director for the city of Charlotte, North Carolina, when the city was widely recognized for its innovations in local government administration, including nationally recognized approaches to external and internal customer service. His team developed and implemented several new HR systems and programs designed to support the city in achieving its mission and objectives. Prior to Charlotte, Bill was director of the classification and pay program for the state of Florida.

Successful change needs a champion. It also depends on a level of trust. Unfortunately, both are too often missing in government. The stories in the media have frequently described change efforts that fail or where employees are adversely impacted. That sets back the prospects for truly positive change—and it undermines all efforts to improve government performance. No one truly benefits. Change can go in a different direction and win broad support, but someone needs to lead.

The changes in work-management practices that started in the private sector in the 1990s also gave birth to the New Public Management. That "movement" has not died, but it refocused on the role of technology, not workforce reform. Introducing new technology is straightforward. It's necessary, but the impact has proven to be limited. The potential to raise performance levels through innovative (for government) "people management" practices is far greater.

This book hopefully will trigger an interest in exploring and adopting new practices. Successful change will mean more satisfying careers and contribute to rebuilding the public's support for government.

Howard Risher, PhD

1

Creating a Rewarding and Productive Work Environment in Government Agencies

A revolution in the way work is organized and managed is contributing to the success of companies and making the work experience of their employees far more satisfying. Study after study confirms that in a supportive, positive work environment employees are capable of performing at significantly higher levels. For government, rethinking workforce-management practices will contribute to improved performance for virtually no cost. For reasons discussed in this book, public employers have tried getting on this bandwagon, but the traditional civil service thinking has impeded planned changes.

The revolution has been under way in the private sector for more than two decades. At its core it reflects a fundamental shift in management thinking. For more than a century, from the start of the Industrial Revolution and the early factories, employees were treated as a cost to be minimized. That way of thinking influenced the way work and workers were managed in every sector.

Then, starting in the 1990s, the phenomenal success of companies like Microsoft and Apple and the mushrooming importance of information technology triggered a flood of new products and new ways of doing business. Investors came to appreciate that the value of these new companies was dependent on their people and what was initially referred to as intellectual capital. In other words, companies realized employees and their knowledge are an important source of competitive advantage. Business leaders also came to realize that the cost of losing their best talent to competitors could be high. In high-performing companies, they are now managed as assets. Karl Marx must be spinning in his grave.

Through the decade of the 1990s government flirted with this new management philosophy. The phrase "New Public Management" (NPM) was adopted to refer to efforts to adapt the new business practices to government. At the federal level the Clinton administration and Vice President Gore initiated the National Performance

Review (NPR) to promote the reinvention of government "from a top-down bureaucracy to a high performance, customer-driven organization." The initial NPR reports included plans to replace long-established "people management" practices. Similar efforts were initiated at the state and local levels as well as in other countries. Over the next several years there were scattered success stories. Charlotte, North Carolina, was prominent. But government was not reinvented; with a few exceptions, federal, state, and local public employers continue to rely on decades-old practices. Unfortunately, with 9/11 and the Great Recession the focus shifted to new priorities.

Government has examples of high performance. They occur frequently in certain areas—law enforcement, public health epidemics, severe weather events, and national security are prominent. The media routinely report on many of the important incidents in those fields.

One highly publicized incident was re-created in the 1995 movie *Apollo 13*. An exploding oxygen tank threatened the lives of the crew of the spaceship, and the movie shows NASA employees working at Mission Control Center in Houston, Texas, trying to solve the problem. Their emotional commitment, teamwork, and sense of duty are palpable. Many worked long hours until the crew was rescued. The film makes a high-performance work unit come to life.

Through most of the twentieth century, workforce-management practices had very little in common with those associated with high performance. Work was organized and managed according to a now-discredited theory—the principles of scientific management. That theory was developed in the early factories of the twentieth century. It was also the basis for managing work in larger clerical operations like those in insurance companies as well as government agencies. The goal was efficiency and cost reduction.

Jobs in both the private and public sectors were analyzed and planned using methods developed by industrial engineers. Employees were seen as "cogs" in work systems. Supervisors relied on close, "over-the-shoulder" control. Organizations and work systems were stable year after year. Employee-supervisor relationships were characterized by a level of tension. Employers relied on the principles of scientific management for decades.

The principles were the foundation for managing work when civil service systems were formalized in the first half of the century. Today's larger public sector unions were formed in the 1930s, an era of labor-management strife across the country. The combination created an environment where supervisors typically have little power and change is difficult.

What may be surprising to people who have not worked in large organizations is that many workers, if they had a choice, would prefer to work in an environment that generates a strong sense of purpose and responsibility. They like to be challenged and valued for their contribution. The long hours and intensity depicted in *Apollo 13* are extreme (along with the life-or-death pressure), but the sense of commitment and the importance of their work effort gave those workers a feeling of satisfaction that more than justified the time spent. Few workers have similar opportunities, but those that do walk away at the end of the day with a feeling of accomplishment. Even when they work long hours and go home exhausted, they look forward to returning the next day. It makes their lives more fulfilling and can carry over to their time with their families and friends.

Jobs that have a similar sense of excitement and drama are rare, but employers, both private and public, can adopt policies and practices that make work far more satisfying than is typical in work situations controlled with traditional close supervision. In the right work environment people can and will be far more productive. Research some years ago found that with new work-management strategies, discussed throughout this book, workers can be *at least* 30 to 40 percent more productive. The changes represent a win-win for employers and their employees, since both should expect to benefit from the changes.

Many public employers will be impacted by heavy, near-term retirements. The loss of job knowledge could make it difficult to solve problems. The loss of talent is exacerbated by the problems agencies are experiencing in recruiting, hiring, and retaining young workers. A recent survey, discussed in the final chapter, with over nine hundred respondents working in state and local government found human capital and workforce issues to be the most pressing challenge. The federal situation is similar. This problem does not have a quick fix.

In this era of budget deficits, layoffs, and pay freezes, changes that enable agencies to improve results, control costs, and create a more positive work environment for employees should be priorities.

Businesses find it easier to introduce change. The so-called bottom line—company profitability—is a concern commonly used to justify change. The focus on performance is universal, and it governs the actions of managers and employees at all levels. Financial rewards for success reinforce the importance of good performance. Over the past twenty years there has been high interest in creating work environments where employees perform at higher levels. A search of the website Amazon .com, using the phrase "high performance," found four-thousand-plus books. Most discuss the factors that explain improved results.

One sector where differences in performance are well documented is health care. Larger, metropolitan hospitals rely on the same medical protocols and rely on similar equipment and information systems, but only a few, like the Mayo Clinic and Johns Hopkins, are known for their outstanding performance. The obvious reason is the caliber of their people and their commitment to patients.

There are significant differences between the public and private sectors. Those differences impede but do not preclude public employers from adopting changes similar to those increasingly common in the private sector. Some public employers have successfully adopted policies and practices that emulate those common in business—and realized improved performance. However, it is important to understand the differences and the different strategies that have been proven to work in public agencies.

This book discusses strategies to improve performance and at the same time improve the work environment. The evidence that a positive work environment will trigger better performance is solid; that linkage has been proven in multiple research studies in all types of organizations.

It's unfortunately necessary to question the apparent logic of the few elected officials and the critics of government and government workers who deny pay increases and otherwise support policies that diminish the "brand" of government as an employer. At every level, critics contend that public employees should perform better and cost less. It's understandable if the denial of increases is driven by the need to close a deficit, but if it's seen as politically motivated, it could be costly.

A certainty is that political decisions can undermine employee morale. It's also certain that poor morale triggers a loss of talent, makes it difficult to recruit new talent, and if it continues, lowers performance.

The criticism is to a degree warranted, of course. With some exceptions, government employment policies are stuck in the past. As a prime example, the federal government may well have the oldest essentially unchanged salary system in the world; the General Schedule pay system was adopted in 1949, and its roots can be traced back to the World War I era. The history of civil service legislation goes back years earlier, and that philosophy continues to influence "people management" even in state and local jurisdictions that do not have supportive legislation. Change at all levels has been glacier slow. Few public employers have developed anything close to a performance culture (although that is often announced as the intention). If it were not for the recession, employees would be able to rely on supportive elected officials as well as unions and professional associations to protect their interests. But the financial problems now necessitate a willingness to change, and that is the impetus for this book.

The general pattern of practices in too many jurisdictions is badly out of sync with the current thinking in the private sector. There are clear opportunities to improve government performance at little or no cost.

ARE CIVIL SERVICE SYSTEMS MEETING THE NEEDS OF GOVERNMENT?

With budget cuts and reduced staff, many agencies will find it difficult to continue delivering the level of performance the public expects if work-management practices remain unchanged. Agencies have lost a lot of experienced talent. Performance problems will be exacerbated if jobs are unfilled and civil service rules make it difficult to hire fully qualified new staff. For younger job seekers, the brand or reputation of government has been tarnished. When they are hired, far too many are dissatisfied with the work experience and resign earlier and in larger numbers than previous generations. For continuing employees there are frequent reports of poor morale that tends to diminish their commitment.

The hurdle is the mind-set that sometimes emerges among those working in a civil service environment. Maintaining the status quo and resisting change becomes a way of life. It's understandable why that got started years ago. Change in the past has often been detrimental to employees and their careers.

Patronage and discrimination were widespread until protective legislation was adopted starting in the late 1800s. Some states moved more slowly than others, but by World War II employment in the public sector across the country was governed by similar civil service regulations and practices. In some cases, the rules were embedded in state constitutions; in others, state legislation, and there are states where the rules were established by collective bargaining agreements. In both the private and public sectors employees were seen as a cost to be controlled.

Realistically, civil service rules served a purpose as long as government organizations experienced minimal change. There was little pressure for change until the final decade of the twentieth century. "Personnel" practices changed very little. Agencies survived nicely with those rules.

In the 1990s world of work, at least in the private sector, was transformed by a revolution. Starting with the 1990–1991 recession, companies initiated intensive efforts to reduce bureaucracy, eliminate layers of management, and otherwise reduce costs. Formal job evaluation practices were largely eliminated. Early in the decade the success of reengineering proved front-line employees could play a valuable role in solving problems. The mushrooming importance of knowledge jobs made employers aware of how important individual expertise is to today's organizations. Technology made it dramatically easier to communicate and monitor performance from a distance. Leaders empowered employees to make decisions. Those old hierarchical organizations disappeared.

For several years public employers flirted with those developments in the form of New Public Management. That encompassed a mix of efforts by federal, state, and local government agencies to become more efficient and results oriented. At the federal level Vice President Gore led the National Performance Review to improve government performance. These initiatives have not been forgotten, but the success stories were local and had little impact. At the federal level, despite the initial NPM momentum, neither Republicans nor Democrats were willing to support meaningful civil service reform.

Some public employers digested private sector practices and prospered. Charlotte, North Carolina, was a widely recognized success story. But aside from relying more heavily on computers and introducing measurement systems, jobs and work management across the public sector have seen surprisingly little change.

The Great Recession triggered high levels of unemployment, but now six-plus years later the media have started to report shortages of skilled workers. Assuming the economy continues to recover as projected, the increased demand for workers will drive up market pay levels for hard-to-fill knowledge jobs. Since IT systems are important to virtually every function, when public employers experience problems recruiting technology specialists, it could impede performance across government.

Tighter labor markets portend staffing problems for agencies that have already lost talent, and with retirement projections they know they will continue to experience a heavy loss of talent. Furthermore, new hires in entry-level jobs are not replacements for experienced specialists. When the selection process drags out for weeks and months, agencies may have to accept second-tier applicants. Businesses sometimes offer jobs to well-qualified candidates on the spot. And, of course, pay issues could also contribute to staffing problems.

Questions about staffing practices are compounded by reliance on tests. Tests may have been an effective practice at one time, but today it's understood that prior experience and a variety of "softer" skills are important to success in many jobs. That is also relevant to promotion policies, especially in the selection of supervisors and managers. The need for unbiased selection methods should, of course, not be forgotten. This would be an ideal time to review and possibly modify recruiting and selection practices.

There are also questions about traditional government pay and benefit programs. The primary problem is likely to be the level of pay relative to market levels. Needless to say, wage and salary levels need to be justified. Wage levels prescribed in collective bargaining agreements as well as in rigid civil service "schedules" are often out of sync with market levels. The federal General Schedule has been the focus of criticism from both federal unions and conservative critics, although they have very different points of view! Companies routinely conduct "market analyses" and use the information for annual adjustments. Those employers have shifted their focus from "internal equity"—those old formal job evaluation systems have largely disappeared—to being competitive in their labor markets. Since payroll is normally the single largest budget item, public employers need to justify pay levels. Credible market data can satisfy all critics.

Two related issues have not received much recent attention. One is pay for performance or merit pay. It became important in the era of New Public Management and was never forgotten, but for reasons discussed in chapter 11, was not widely adopted. It is likely to be important in strategies to improve performance. Experts have argued that millennials expect to be rewarded for their performance—anything below a B in school is close to failure! Of course, agencies will need to have a budget for those increases.

The second issue is the time and cost to administer a traditional government pay program. The issue is the traditional approach to job classification that starts with time-intensive job analysis. Human resource (HR) offices have had staff cuts and may no longer have the qualified specialists to administer programs as required. Where employers rely on classification standards, they are often out of date, and resources are not available—and not likely to be available in the future—to update them. Alternative program concepts will need to be considered.

Benefit programs have well-publicized and very serious funding problems. There are no easy answers. Private employers have eliminated defined-benefit pensions and now rely almost exclusively on defined-contribution plans. Medical benefits are also in a state of flux in response to the Affordable Care Act. There was a time when public employers were known to have lower pay levels and better benefits, but survey data shows that may no longer be true. There are also questions about job offers to satisfy young job seekers. Cost considerations make this an unavoidable problem for the highest levels of government.

Budget problems have triggered broad interest in eliminating or modifying civil service rules. Changes have been legislated or negotiated in several states, and proposed in others. While the changes typically have been adopted in states where Republicans are in the majority, proposals have been discussed in states dominated by Democrats, most notably New York, where both Governor Cuomo and New York City Mayor de Blasio have commented on problems related to the civil service regulations.

This is fundamental change that will impact working relationships and careers. There will, of course, be resistance. Unfortunately, there is a recent history of changes triggered by the recession that were adopted with little expressed concern for the impact on employees. The impact on trust and employee morale has been documented. This book suggests, or more accurately advocates, broad, fundamental change that will require cooperation. The changes will both improve government performance and contribute to a more positive work experience. Skeptics need only look to the companies recognized as "best places to work" and their many applicants. A thread running through the book is the importance of involving managers and employees in the planning. Public agencies should be "employers of choice."

Change is inevitable. However, this is analogous to trying to break a bad habit. People at every level need to change their thinking and their working relationships. By comparison, implementing new technology is "duck soup." Leadership is needed. The decisions should reflect a consensus, communicated broadly, and based on the need for good government and not political pandering.

The recent developments suggest additional civil service systems will be modified over the balance of the decade. Hopefully the decisions will be based on the need for good government and not political pandering. This book was developed to facilitate decision making.

THE FRAMEWORK FOR THIS BOOK

The sequence of the chapters reflects a distinction between the practices related to day-to-day "people management"—the focus of the early chapters—and those usually referred to as HR responsibilities. Both are important to creating a high-performance organization. The practices discussed in chapters 2 and 3 are important to linking the emotional commitment—"engagement"—of employees to the success of their agency. The balance of the book focuses on planning and decisions by both managers and HR that can be expected to influence performance. The goal is "to get the best out of people."

Interestingly, a number of the books on high performance are silent on the role of the HR function; it's never mentioned, even in the index. The argument throughout the book is that both are important. Workforce decisions made by managers and supervisors are frequently based on policies and systems controlled and administered by HR. Moreover, when employees are vital to successful change, HR is the logical choice to guide the process. Change initiatives are rarely successful in the absence of a champion.

One of the differences between the private and public sectors is the role of the CEO. In business, when performance problems emerge and organizational change is necessary, leaders do not hesitate to initiate whatever actions appear warranted. They are the catalyst to drive change. In government, elected officials see their role differently. They were typically not elected for their management expertise. Their focus is normally on public policy issues, and many have only limited prior experience managing workers. That is also true for many appointees; they were selected because of their public policy expertise.

The argument in this book is that HR specialists need to be ready to step into the role of catalyst to provide the leadership for change. Historically, the function has been responsible for administering HR systems and keeping personnel records, dealing with problem employees and employee problems, for recruiting and training, for compliance with employment law, and for helping executives and managers deal with employee issues. Those are largely backroom or reactive responsibilities. The typical HR office does not have much impact on organizational performance. That is changing in the private sector. Realistically, HR has to demonstrate its value and gain acceptance to assume this proactive role as a partner to line managers.

Occasionally, a writer argues that a narrowly defined policy change will have a desired impact on agency results. Moving to pay for performance is a possibility that is often mentioned. The implicit—and erroneous—assumption with that change is that the prospect of a few extra dollars is all that is needed. Actually, with the truly great companies, performance depends on an integrated mix of policies and practices that "fit" the organization and have won the commitment of employees. "Flavor-of-the-month," narrowly defined strategies may look attractive because they are simple but are likely to have limited impact. Those successful companies do a lot of things right. Their strategies are discussed in the articles on "best places to work." Employers working to develop a game plan to improve performance should expect to consider a number of possible changes. There is no universal answer. It may make sense to have a task force sort through the possibilities.

In far too many jurisdictions the changes needed to improve performance will be resisted because of a lack of trust. They have experienced or heard stories of heavy-handed or unfair attempts in the past to impose change. Change is always difficult to accept, and here employees are wary that the change will not be to their benefit. Overcoming the anxiety and getting employees on board is essential for successful change.

It is with that in mind that each chapter was written to highlight the strategies and alternatives known to both influence performance and contribute to a positive work experience. The intent is to help readers develop plans for successful change efforts.

There are no guarantees, but the advice and recommendations reflect the experience of acknowledged experts.

An overriding issue to keep in mind is that everything accomplished by government is attributable to employees at some level. As with great hospitals, it's the people who make the difference. The motivation of public service is for many similar to that in health care. That commitment is important to many employees. However, even the most committed can be demoralized by poor management. Effective management, in contrast, can inspire outstanding performance. Agencies at every level of government have employees with untapped capabilities open to challenges and opportunities to contribute. Helping government leaders develop winning strategies is the goal of this book.

2

The High-Performance Work Environment

The title of the initial 1993 report from Vice President Gore's National Performance Review was *From Red Tape to Results: Creating a Government That Works Better and Costs Less*. The intent was to reinvent government by adopting the best practices for managing performance from the private sector. It's now two decades and two recessions later, and the pressure for improved performance is, if anything, increasing.

At the state and local government levels, the problem is very similar. In 2010, a group of government and academic experts, the National Performance Management Advisory Commission, published a report summarizing the approaches, practices, and techniques available for improving the management of performance. The preface to their report summarizes the situation as follows:

> At no time in modern history have state, local, and provincial governments been under greater pressure to provide results that matter to the public, often within severe resource constraints. At the same time, government officials and managers are challenged to overcome the public's lack of trust in government at all levels.[1]

Public employers have tried a number of practices widely used in the private sector. The passage of the Government Performance and Results Act (GPRA) of 1993 required agencies (1) to develop long-term strategic plans, goals, and objectives for their programs; (2) to develop annual performance plans specifying measurable performance goals for the program activities in their budgets; and (3) to publish an annual performance report showing actual results compared to each annual performance goal. The strategic and annual performance plans had to describe the strategies and resources needed to meet their goals. The statute prompted agencies to install the tools and began to shift their focus from accountability for process to accountability for results.

GPRA was followed during the Bush administration with PART—the Program Assessment Rating Tool—which was followed by legislative proposals with similar acronyms, and last by the Obama administration, which discontinued PART and worked with Congress to enact the GPRA Modernization Act of 2010. The new law adds a requirement that federal agencies name a Chief Operating Officer and a Performance Improvement Officer. The impact on agency performance, now more than two decades, continues to be disappointing.

On paper, the government has installed management systems and methods that are very similar to those used for decades in business. But obviously something is missing.

This chapter sets the stage for planning a strategy to tap the potential of the workforce to perform at higher levels. It is not likely to be a simple or smooth transition. Change normally triggers anxiety and often resistance. Government is not like industry, where a chief executive can mandate change; in government, political differences are always a factor. In many jurisdictions civil service laws and regulations and/or union contracts will be barriers. Government leaders and the public will need to decide how important it is to raise performance levels. The potential is significant, and the evidence is compelling—the changes discussed here and in later chapters will contribute to more rewarding and positive work environments.

It is important to keep in mind that a work environment is a "bunch of stuff," everything from an agency's mission statement to the use of time clocks to the use of office cubicles to the recognition practices used by supervisors. This book could take a chapter simply listing the factors that influence how employees perform. When people have personal goals in their private lives, they can be passionate about achieving them. In the right jobs they will have a similar commitment at work and realize great satisfaction when they are successful. It makes their lives better. This book attempts to focus on those factors that are "manageable" and where the actions of leaders and managers can be instrumental in creating a high-performance culture.

ARE BUSINESS PRACTICES THE ANSWER?

Superficially, companies have an advantage. Their overarching goal of making money—the so-called bottom line—provides a shared vision and motivation to succeed. The universal image is that employees know and understand that profits are the driving force for business. Those who have worked in business know there is some truth to that. One common element of business is frequent discussions about elements of performance. Each function has developed its own performance measures, and the regulatory agencies require public companies to report data showing how well the company is performing. It may go unstated, but everyone understands that those measures are related to the company's drive for success. The prospect of generating personal wealth is a powerful motivator for executives to make the company a success. People will supposedly work very hard to become wealthy. That story has been told in any number of books and movies.

But if that is all that is needed, companies would never fail. Every entrepreneur would become a billionaire. The obvious fact is that some companies are far more successful than others. Companies do fail despite their use of the latest management systems. It's not like in the movies. There is more to building and sustaining success in business.

Many business practices can be copied by government agencies and contribute to their performance. But such initiatives, at least those at the federal level, have been disappointing. Frequent reports from the Government Accountability Office confirm that. Conventional business practices and systems have not enabled public agencies to generate significant performance gains.

There are stories of high performance in government—*Apollo 13* is an example, the heroic efforts of the firefighters and police when the World Trade Towers collapsed in Manhattan are another, and the efforts of government workers at all levels when a hurricane strikes are reported regularly. Many others are not in the media spotlight. The FBI has a world-class reputation. The National Institutes of Health (NIH) does also. Management systems may play a role, but the high performance is attributable in the case of agencies like the FBI and NIH to the workforce and to well-qualified individuals who perform at commendable levels, sometimes despite bureaucratic barriers.

There are significant differences in the management of government agencies. The lack of a single, ever-present motivator like the so-called bottom line is an obvious difference. Many others, some obvious, some not so obvious, influence the day-to-day working environment. This book attempts to place those in context.

A thread that runs through this book is that it is fully possible to organize and manage government agencies to raise performance levels—probably not to the level of the rhetoric demanded in election campaigns—but realistically to levels that will contribute to a better society. There are no immovable barriers.

THE IMPORTANCE OF PURPOSE

We all have dreams and goals as we grow up. They might be as unrealistic as becoming a movie star or a great athlete. But the goal of becoming a star athlete has kept millions of children on the practice fields until they have to go home for dinner. For many those goals carry over to their career choice. The goal of becoming a doctor or a teacher, for example, can be a source of motivation through the school years.

Many people at all levels have a desire to contribute to a better society. They want to make a difference. It may take the form of becoming a policeman; it might be eliminating racial discrimination; or it could be stopping terrorists. Every government agency has a purpose that can be important to building a workforce committed to achieving its mission.

Some years ago the phrase Public Service Motivation (PSM) was adopted to refer to the motivation for choosing a career in government or other organizations that focus on solving societal problems. The theory has been studied and the confirming evidence reported in academic journals. At this point it's safe to say, it's real and can be important in attracting qualified applicants. That is particularly important to young workers.

People like to be associated with a success. They want to feel they are contributing to the accomplishment of goals important to their employer's mission. Experience has shown that when measures of performance are reported regularly, people will work hard to improve on those measures. Reporting on progress in achieving goals people believe are important will inspire them to focus their efforts and commit to improving results. Chapter 14, on the importance of communication, discusses how an organization can create a shared focus to achieve goals.

However, as important as the PSM theory has become, there are other reasons for considering a career in government. Until the recent budget cutting, job security has been a reason to work in government. A better benefits package is reported to be another. For others it's a simple desire for a stable job with regular hours.

Furthermore, there is a distinction between the motivation to accept and continue in a job and the motivation to work hard for job success. What may have appeared to be a rewarding career at age twenty can lose its appeal quickly (since many jobs are not what is expected). Research shows that an individual's commitment to public service can change over time. If their experience is negative (as with continued pay freezes), they may decide to change careers or worse, "retire on the job," that is to say, put forth the minimum expected daily work effort. Continued positive experience can strengthen their commitment to public service.

THE IMPORTANCE OF LEADERSHIP

President John Kennedy captured the essence of PSM in the line from his 1961 inaugural speech, "And so, my fellow Americans: ask not what your country can do for you—ask what you can do for your country." It has been stated that his speech inspired thousands to seek a career in government.

Elected leaders regularly give speeches intended to motivate. Some are much better at it than others. FDR's speeches and "fireside" radio messages were important throughout World War II. Adolf Hitler's speeches triggered the support of the German people to support the war.

Leadership does not always take the form of public statements. It can be as simple as a "management-by-walking-around" approach that involves leaders wandering through the workplace, checking with employees about the status of ongoing work. It's been shown to facilitate improved morale, sense of purpose, and improved productivity. President Lincoln was known to informally inspect the Union Army troops in the Civil War.

Good leadership will be felt throughout the entire organization and appreciated by everyone, including employees who may never meet the agency head. Acceptance as a leader cannot be imposed or forced; it has to be earned. Communication is essential.

Everyone needs to understand the vision and goals of the organization. Ideally, everyone has input into how performance can be improved. Employees feel they are an important part of the whole and that every job matters. The result of good leadership is high morale, a sense of esprit de corps, and sustainable long-term success.

A story that illustrates the importance of effective leadership is the early history of a federal agency, Court Services and Offender Supervision Agency. It was created by merging the former parole, probation, and pretrial services offices of the District of Columbia, where they were seen as failures, as a new federal agency. It started in the mid-1990s with a series of stories in the media of criminals who were released from prison but had been responsible for horrific, repeat crimes. Preventing problems of that nature is supposedly the job of a parole office.

A visionary executive director was appointed to lead the new organization. His management team defined a series of lofty performance goals, including a reduction in the rate of recidivism—repeat crimes by criminals—by 50 percent over five years. The goals were aspirational, clearly "stretch goals," but there was an evident commitment to achieving them. When the parole and probation officers were part of the district government, their job was to sit behind a desk and meet with each offender once a month. The job was virtually meaningless. Their performance was evaluated by checking off boxes on a form.

But under the new executive director, they were sent into the community to meet with family, police on the local beat, ministers, teachers—everyone who interacted with an offender. The jobs of the renamed Community Supervision Officers were completely revised. They were enthusiastic about the changes. It was "the right way to do the job." Unfortunately, the executive director experienced unsupported legal problems and resigned. The new agency lost an effective leader, along with its plans to create a performance culture, and some of its momentum.

One of the realities of government is that elected officials along with the individuals appointed to senior "leadership" positions are generally far more interested in public policy issues than in day-to-day management. That's reflected in graduate programs in public administration. Many elected leaders and appointees have had little or no prior experience or training in managing others in large organizations. They may need coaching to appreciate their role in leading changes to improve performance.

When the importance of leadership is not recognized or leadership is ineffective, it also will be felt throughout an organization. When the individuals nominally referred to as leaders are not accepted by the workforce, there can be no leadership in the true sense. When they make pronouncements, employees are likely to ignore them or shake their heads in frustration. Employees are far less likely to commit to goals, and while they may remain focused on their own success, they are indifferent to mission achievement. Unfortunately, elected leaders sometimes make statements that fail to confirm their support for the workforce, and that can trigger lower morale, increased turnover, and weakened commitment to sustained success.

There is no reason to think management experience will ever be a requirement for elected leaders or for the policy experts appointed to senior positions. But effective leadership is too important to agency performance to ignore. This idea influenced the planning of the GPRA Modernization Act and the requirement that federal agencies name a Chief Operating Officer. The idea is again based on lessons learned in the business world. The impact of the new position has not been proven, but it should be an important step.

MANAGEMENT IS ESSENTIAL

Theorists and practitioners have determined over the years that government functions have placed far too much emphasis on "administration" and too little on management. Webster's brief definitions highlight the key difference. Administration is defined as "the act or activity of looking after," while management is "the act or skill of controlling and making decisions." Administration is no doubt adequate for a stable, efficient system or process like those in manufacturing. When organizations and jobs go unchanged for years, and workers are "cogs in the wheel," all that is needed is an administrator. However, dynamic organizations with scarce resources need someone who is authorized to "control" what happens, make adjustments, and reallocate resources to meet changing conditions.

The Clinton administration with its New Public Management had the right idea—adopting business-management practices. Management systems, goal setting, and more recently performance-measurement methods were the right mechanisms. Elected officials shape and define the overall direction and mission and broadly stated goals of agencies. They also decide how available resources are to be allocated. Their role is analogous to that of a board of directors. Executives then develop long- and short-range operating plans and performance goals. They meet regularly with managers to monitor progress and discuss corrective actions when necessary.

Middle managers and supervisors then have to make it happen. The role of government managers has been, however, much more narrowly defined than that of their counterparts in business. Businesses have to respond to changing market factors and competitor actions, and managers are expected to make decisions to adjust to those changes. In business, managers have more control over what employees do each day. An analogy is the difference between chess and checkers. In checkers all the pieces are the same, and their movement is governed by the same rules. In chess the pieces are different and can be moved in different ways. In a traditional government setting, managers are administrators playing checkers.

Companies have to compete successfully, with the goal of becoming and remaining one of the best. They routinely compare their results with those of competitors, so performance becomes a universal priority. Successful companies rely on management practices that reinforce the importance of performing at a high level. Their practices have been shown to be different from those of less-successful companies. All companies today have access that is software to tracks and report performance results and to the management practices described in textbooks. The differences are in the "people management" practices.

The practices associated with high-performance companies were documented in a 2005 study by the London School of Economics. The implications for government were discussed in the report, *Managing for Better Performance: Enhancing Federal Performance Management Practices*.[2] The report and key management practices are discussed in chapter 9, "Managing Agency and Executive Performance."

A key finding of the study is the strong relationship between the way an organization is managed and its success. More specifically, the firms that relied more heavily on management practices were more successful; those that did not were less successful. In business, of course, firms that are not financially successful tend to fail, so their sample of companies does not include many that were badly managed.

Those practices together regularly highlight and reinforce the importance of performance. Over time, this creates what is referred to as a "performance culture," which exists when employees at all levels regularly discuss performance issues and concerns at lunch, coffee breaks, and group meetings. Performance is an ongoing concern throughout the day. Managers play an important role in elevating the focus on performance in their daily interactions with employees. Simple practices like sharing performance data with employees contribute to the culture.

On a related point, research by Ethan Mollick, a Wharton School professor, shows that middle managers have more impact on performance than any other factor.[3] He makes the point that when an effective manager moves to a new role within their organization, it follows that in a relatively brief time the workers in the unit will start to perform at a higher level. There is a demonstrable difference in the performance of groups across an organization that can only be explained by the effectiveness of managers.

Research by Gallup confirms Mollick's conclusions. They have learned that relatively few people have the personal abilities to be effective managers, and that in selecting new managers employers frequently make the wrong choice. They see it as "one of the most important decisions companies make. . . . The only defense against this problem is a good offense."[4] Their recommendation is to commit to developing a selection process that makes it possible to eliminate those job candidates who would likely be ineffective.

Public employers have too often promoted people to supervisory roles based on their technical skills or on seniority. That may work when they are simply administrators, but as an old saying suggests, it results in the loss of a good technician and the addition of a poor supervisor. The selection and preparation of managers should be treated as an investment that will pay off for years. It's discussed in more depth in chapter 5—"Developing a Cadre of Effective Managers." The tools made available for use in managing employees and their performance are discussed in chapter 10—"Managing Employee Performance."

For reasons that are not clear, there have been surprisingly few comparable studies of the impact of executives and managers in government. An Amazon search on "executive performance management" produced 1,097 books. When the phrase "in government" was added, the list was cut to 58, and the titles suggest the focus is on organizational, not executive or manager, performance. In a somewhat cursory review of the leading public administration programs, only a handful of schools offer courses planned for government executives.

EMPOWERING EMPLOYEES

In traditional, hierarchical organizations employees were expected to follow orders and do what they were told. Employees had virtually no discretion to act on their own. Job descriptions were long and detailed. Industrial engineers commonly determined production quotas or performance standards. According to textbooks on organizations, the optimal "span of control" or the number of employees that a manager could effectively supervise—and maintain close supervision of—was five to no more than seven.

That approach to management worked well in static organizations where the work system and work products were standardized. A similar philosophy was reflected in the organization and management of work in government. It is still reflected in the use of performance standards (defined as the threshold level of performance that must be met to be appraised at a particular level of performance).

But when the U.S. economy was mired in the 1990–1991 recession, corporate leaders concluded that their firms were burdened by excessive costs, were slow to respond to competitive actions, and found it overly difficult to adapt to new ways of doing business. Companies undertook major change initiatives to make them more competitive. One widely adopted strategy was to delayer or eliminate layers of management. That reduced costs, but more importantly, it increased the number of employees each manager supervised.

The increased span of control forced managers to rethink their approach to supervision. Managers could no longer make all decisions. They simply did not have enough time. This opened the door to empowerment and meant that managers had to learn to trust their people.

In hindsight we now realize many employees in those traditional organizations were rarely challenged or rarely had reasons to use their full capabilities. Employees were seen as a cost, not an asset; their talents were underutilized and to a degree wasted. We think about and use assets in a very different way. When employees are viewed as assets, it is to the employer's advantage to invest in their development and motivate them to perform at their best.

The impetus was the recession, but it took several years for managers to learn to function effectively in the new work environment. A second factor was the success in the early 1990s of reengineering, which proved that lower-level employees could be trusted and were able to solve problems. Employers saw this as a way to reduce costs and raise performance levels.

A third factor that has yet to be broadly accepted in government is recognition that employees can function at high levels without direct supervision. It was forty years ago that Volvo in Sweden gained media attention for its use of "autonomous work teams." There were no supervisors. Employees worked on their own, knew what they needed to accomplish, and were accountable for results. The idea was tried by several U.S. firms, including Scott Paper in a new plant in Newark, Delaware. In interviews shortly after the plant opened, employees stated, "I thank God for the opportunity to work here," and "There is no way we will allow a union in here to screw this up." There are reasons to question traditional management thinking.

Significantly, the new approaches to supervision coincided with the growing importance of new occupations, primarily those in IT, where the employee's value depends on how well they use job knowledge to make decisions. The phrase "knowledge jobs" was adopted to refer to these new occupations.

The fact is, however, that the revolution in the organization and management of work did not gain momentum until the last half of the decade. Commonly used words and phrases like "engagement," "empowerment," "high performance," and "human capital" cannot be found in business publications early in the decade.

That was later than the launch of the New Public Management, with its focus on strategic planning, management systems, and dashboards. It is not clear if the timing explains why, but the thought leaders in reforming government have not incorporated the practices known to contribute to high performance into their strategies.

Today in business some workers have virtually no direct contact with their "boss." Technology means communication with others is taken for granted, and employees can report what they accomplish and receive new instructions from any location. Some managers are responsible for fifty or more employees. In global companies they may be based on a different continent. Teams can operate with members in different countries.

The old, over-the-shoulder supervisory model has been discarded and replaced by a myriad of variations. Older workers may be uncomfortable, but younger workers who have grown up in families where both parents work are likely to enjoy the autonomy. It's the managers who are more likely to have a problem with the redefinition of their roles. It is still possible, of course, to find pockets of employees who, if asked, would complain about being micromanaged.

Worker autonomy has always been true for certain government functions, particularly in agencies where employees are stationed and report from a remote location. In certain clandestine roles government workers have only fleeting contact with their organization. Empowerment in those jobs is nothing new.

A worker's ability to function and their value depend on their understanding of the organization's goals and what needs to be accomplished. Supervisors need to agree with their people on what needs to be accomplished, to track results, and to provide feedback. That makes communication essential, along with systems to track performance. In the right situation many workers are capable of performing at far higher levels—and thoroughly enjoying the opportunity to prove their value.

A central issue in every organization is employee motivation. It is not enough to hire qualified people. High performance depends on teamwork or collaboration, skill levels, and motivation. It also depends on knowing what needs to be accomplished. That is the subject of the next chapter—"Motivation and Emotional Commitment."

PUTTING IT ALL TOGETHER

Government is now confronted with a situation similar to that which prompted companies in the early 1990s to reorganize, eliminate management layers, and adopt new practices to improve results and reduce costs. There is a wealth of research and experience to use in developing a change strategy. The "levers" proven to influence performance are numerous and are discussed throughout this book.

Not surprisingly, there are no silver bullets. Organizational change is never easy, and the constraints in government make it far more complex than in business. Actually, it is useful to view government at all levels as a "conglomerate," that is to say, each agency has its own mission, culture, and mix of occupations. A banking department is not like the corrections department or the education department. Industry has only a few remaining conglomerates with diverse operating units. The largest may be General Electric. Those companies rely on different HR policies and practices unique to each subsidiary. Although it would be contrary to traditional civil service thinking, there is no reason to expect the HR policies that work well in one agency will be equally effective in another.

That would also hold true for managers who want to improve the performance of their work teams. The research by Ethan Mollick confirms individual managers are fully capable of creating high-performance teams. Actually, every organization no doubt has a few managers who do that on their own. They may not be able to change, for example, the pay system, but they control their working relationships as managers.

The constraint is likely to be the prevailing civil service rules and regulations. Those rules in many jurisdictions were adopted decades ago and can delay reorganizations. At the federal level, for example, it can take as much as two years for a job to be reclassified following a reorganization. When the number of redefined jobs is large, the paperwork can be daunting.

Whatever the scope of an initiative to revitalize and improve the way an agency or bureau operates, experience suggests it will be useful to create a Project Management Office and a team of individuals experienced in the agency's operations. The team should be able to involve individuals as needed with backgrounds in project management, finance, technology (as it used by an agency), law, labor relations, organizational change, and human resources. The scope of the project will dictate the time commitment of team members. The first phase is to gain agreement on goals and assess possible barriers and the resources that will be needed. The creation of the PMO sends the message that it's an organizational priority.

A high-performance work environment involves a complex set of factors. There are no simple answers. Each chapter in this book focuses on factors known to reinforce and augment the commitment to performance. In the end, the work environment will be far more positive.

ADDITIONAL RESOURCES

Van Gorder, Chris. *The Front-Line Leader: Building a High-Performance Organization from the Ground Up*. Jossey-Bass, 2014.

Beer, Michael. *High Commitment High Performance: How to Build A Resilient Organization for Sustained Advantage*. John Wiley, 2009.

de Waal, André. *What Makes a High Performance Organization—Five Validated Factors of Competitive Advantage that Apply Worldwide*. HPO Center BV, 2015. This book summarizes a global study of high-performance organizations, including government.

Katzenbach, Jon R., and Douglas K. Smith. *The Wisdom of Teams: Creating the High-Performance Organization*. HBR Press, 2015. This was originally published in 1993 by McKinsey & Company.

NOTES

1. National Performance Management Advisory Commission. 2010. *A Performance Management Framework for State and Local Government*.

2. Howard Risher and Charles Fay. 2007. *Managing for Better Performance: Enhancing Federal Performance Management Practices*. Washington, DC: IBM Center for Business of Government.

3. Ethan Mollick, "People and Process, Suits and Innovators: The Role of Individuals in Firm Performance," *Strategic Management Journal* 58, no. 9 (2012): 1001–15.

4. Randall Beck and Jim Harter, "Why Great Managers Are So Rare," *Gallup Business Journal*, March 25, 2014.

3

Motivation and Emotional Commitment

All employers, private and public, would benefit if their employees were emotionally committed to the success of the organization. That sense of commitment was portrayed in the movie *Apollo 13* when employees worked extremely hard to solve a difficult problem. There are jobs in the public sector where incumbents have to respond almost without thinking. Jobs in law enforcement, for example, sometimes require that. Many jobs in health care require a similar commitment. But in the majority of jobs and occupations, employee commitment or motivation is influenced by the way they are managed and the work environment. Gaining their commitment—motivating employees—is or should be a goal of management. The level of commitment is a key to achieving desired performance levels, and it's necessary for raising them.

It is not a simple problem, however, especially in government. An important difference, from Bob Lavigna's book *Engaging Government Employees* (2013), is that government employees are increasingly being "denigrated and stigmatized[1] as underworked and overpaid," which has had an adverse impact on worker morale. At the federal level the phrase "fed bashing" was coined in the Reagan years. Lavigna goes on to cite several factors in the work environment common in government that can weaken employee motivation, including:

> political leadership that changes frequently; hard-to-measure goals and impacts; complicated, rule-bound, and sometimes irrational decision making; multiple external stakeholders with power and influence; an older, more educated, and more white-collar workforce; strong civil-service rules and employee protections; heavy union influence; limited financial tools to influence and reward employee behavior; public visibility of government actions. (2013)

"Experts" have been writing about worker motivation for more than a century. In the early factories, it was assumed workers would not work hard on their own initiative.

The practitioners of scientific management as well as the industrial engineers who came later had little interest in what went on inside a worker's head; their goal in completing time-and-motion or efficiency studies was to get the arms and legs moving in an optimal way. The experts of the era believed that financial incentives were the key to solving motivation problems. That led to piece-rate bonus systems where workers were paid for the level of output. That train of thought dominated for decades. Since people need to earn money, financial incentives are still seen as important motivations for workers.

It's not clear if the critics fully realize the impact their criticism has on employee commitment. In the same way that positive recognition encourages improved performance, continued criticism hurts morale and performance.

Their criticism also damages the "brand" of government as employers. That, no doubt, influences the career choice of future workers. The contrast between President Kennedy's message and the disdain voiced by some candidates for elected office is striking. It will take years to rebuild the government brand.

The critics make recognition of employee accomplishments that much more important. Employees need to know their efforts are valued. The reactions to criticism and to recognition are no doubt universal.

In some respects, employee motivation is captured best by the old story of the blind men and the elephant. Each man touched a different part of the elephant and derived his image of the beast from that experience. Until recently, books on management tended to suffer from a similar problem. That is, they provided a narrow understanding of the problem.

THEORIES OF MOTIVATION

Several theories of motivation at work are discussed at some point in courses that are frequently part of undergraduate curricula. In any discussion of employee motivation someone is likely to argue the relevance of one of these theories.

Perhaps the simplest is Douglas McGregor's *Theory X* and *Theory Y*, which categorize workers into contrasting groups. Theory X assumes workers hate work, have no ambition, and to get them to perform at a satisfactory level, managers have to use coercion, threats of punishment, and possible rewards. The principles of scientific management reflect Theory X thinking. Theory Y, in contrast, assumes workers are largely self-motivated by their desire to learn and develop a sense of accomplishment. They are motivated by challenges and learning opportunities. The role of the manager is to provide guidance and support. McGregor published his theories in the 1960s, a time when "enlightened" management was best-practice thinking.

Another frequently discussed theory is Abraham Maslow's hierarchy of needs, usually illustrated with a pyramid. The most basic needs are physiological—food and shelter—and when those needs are met, people shift to a need for security, followed by a need for socialization. Professional and managerial jobs enable people to meet their need for self-esteem and finally for self-actualization. Maslow's focus on self-actualization is consistent with McGregor's Theory Y.

Frederick Herzberg is famous for his two-factor theory of motivation, which categorizes job factors as either hygiene—which can trigger job dissatisfaction—or motivators. His hygiene factors included pay, benefits, company policies, working conditions, job security, and interpersonal relations. He argued that they can only cause dissatisfaction. His motivators include recognition, sense of achievement, growth and promotional opportunities, responsibility (or ownership of the work), and meaningfulness of the work. They can contribute to job satisfaction. An important caveat is that his research took place in the 1950s, when the work environment was very different from today's. His "pay," for example, is strictly salary level; pay for performance, which also provides recognition, was then not a common practice.

Today, researchers would add to the list of motivators for public employees the opportunity for public service and for making a difference in the lives of individuals, which are known to be important. That is the central point in discussions of Public Service Motivation (PSM), which is the focus of the next section.

Although not commonly associated with a name, equity theory is directly related to the management of pay and rewards. It argues an employee's motivation is linked to his/her perception of equity, fairness, and justice practiced by management. In evaluating the equity or fairness of a manager's decisions, the employee compares the job input (i.e., his/her accomplishments or expertise) to the outcome (e.g., the salary increase or salary level) and decides if he/she is treated fairly relative to coworkers.

While the focus is often on the fairness of pay increases, the theory would hold when a high performer is treated the same as a poor or average performer. That is also seen as inequitable.

Worker performance is also explained by *expectancy theory*, which argues that workers are likely to repeat or continue desired behavior if they can expect it to be recognized or rewarded. When their efforts are ignored, after a time their performance will decline. That is to say, they are likely to repeat the behavior if it's recognized. That holds true for children as well as for pets. Behavior that is rewarded is more likely to be repeated.

PUBLIC SERVICE MOTIVATION

Repeated studies provide evidence that employees working in government were likely attracted by a desire to be involved in public service. The researchers also argue that money is less important to this segment of the workforce. A search on PSM found over twenty million hits.

While the evidence is compelling that public service is an important factor for many people, there are other possible reasons for seeking a government job, including job security. It is also possible that career decisions in health care and possibly other occupations can be explained by a very similar desire to serve others. The interest in pursuing certain careers is important for many people.

COMMENT ON "AT-WILL" EMPLOYMENT

A policy question that is central to reform is the switch from civil service status, as defined by federal or state statutes, to an "at-will" employment status. That means an employee can be fired at any time, for any reason (except for illegal reasons defined by federal and state statutes). At-will also means that an employer can change the terms of the employment relationship with no notice and no consequences.

Significantly in other sectors, the employment status of all employees is at will. (The exception is when employment terms are defined in collective bargaining agreements.) Workers are protected by a long list of statutes, federal and state, dating back to the 1938 Fair Labor Standards Act. It is safe to say at-will employment is no longer an issue outside of government.

At-will status is consistent with good government when it is supported by a management philosophy that values employees as assets and is committed to creating a rewarding, satisfying work environment. It violates the public trust when experienced, proven talent at any level are replaced for political reasons or are ordered to act in ways contrary to legislative goals. Despite the dark history of patronage, it continues to be true that higher-level employees and occasionally others lose their jobs due to politics.

There is no reason to think at-will employees perform better. The history suggests leaders have at times used the threat of being fired to motivate employees. That's unfounded and counterproductive. It's not surprising that employees push back and resist. Ill-conceived, politically driven actions in too many jurisdictions have violated employee trust, and that undermines prospects to improve performance.

There is solid evidence, however, that civil service regulations are frequently an impediment to change and contribute unnecessarily to higher costs. Civil service reform is needed. Across the country, the pressure to improve results and strengthen the public's support for government means reform efforts will continue to be a front-burner issue. It's fully possible to develop a collaborative game plan. That was the impetus for developing this book.

It would also be important to assess the impact of decisions by elected officials or leaders that have an adverse impact on employees and their lives to learn how that affects PSM measures. Since pay freezes were first announced, there have been reports of low morale. It would be useful to know how the freezes have affected the desire for public service as well as the performance of employees.

Finally, it would be useful to understand the motivation of employees who find themselves "locked in" to a job they dislike by either the difficulty of switching to new careers or the cost in lost benefits in leaving public service. Workers who are dissatisfied are rarely engaged or high performers.

The research discussed in the next section from a website of the American Psychological Association suggests actions like pay freezes may have undermined employee commitment to government careers. That could also be true of students thinking about government careers, which could have long-term adverse implications for staffing.

A research question to confirm this would involve assessing the career interests of students contemplating careers and then to conduct follow-up studies of individuals who accepted a government job perhaps five or more years after they started their careers. The follow-up should also include individuals who started but resigned from government jobs.

A related issue is the impact of PSM on job performance. There is a distinct difference between the motivation to accept a job and that which would trigger the commitment to perform at a high level. The research on the latter point has been inconclusive, or stated differently, researchers have not found a linkage. Actually, the PSM argument either downplays the importance of the factors found to be important in other sectors, or it contends that government employees are different from the rest of the population.

THE IMPORTANCE OF
MAINTAINING A HEALTHY WORKPLACE

A new issue has emerged that should help agencies and HR offices adopt a far more positive approach to improving performance with modest policy changes. It's the idea that a "healthy" organization contributes to a positive work environment for employees and to better organization performance. It's a win-win for those who are served by the organization as well as for employees, and it can be accomplished at a net savings.

That argument is supported by a website created by the American Psychological Association (APA): the Center for Organizational Excellence (www.center4oe). The purpose of the website is "to enhance the functioning of individuals, groups, organizations, and communities through the application of psychology to a broad range of workplace issues." The APA launched the website in 2013 to provide resources for employers to use in enhancing organizational health.

The linkage of organizational health and improved performance is supported by research. Healthy organizations are a better place to work and are more successful.

Similar studies by the consulting firm McKinsey & Company have confirmed the APA conclusions. Two McKinsey consultants published a book on organization health, *Beyond Performance: How Great Organizations Build Ultimate Competitive Advantage*.[2] The authors contend that "at least 50 percent of any organization's long-term success is driven by its health" (2011).

The APA website focuses not on an organization's success but on providing "an overarching strategy for promoting health and well-being of the workforce." While they do not ignore the positive impact on organizational performance, their purpose is different, but they do highlight the relationship between organizational health and performance.

The APA focuses on five dimensions of health (with the APA descriptions):

- *"Employee involvement"* (or, as it is sometimes called, empowerment) is an approach to supervision that relies on allowing employees to make work-related decisions, giving them increased job autonomy. "Employee involvement programs can increase job satisfaction, employee morale and commitment to the organization, as well as increase productivity, reduce turnover and absenteeism and enhance the quality of products and services." Employees like opportunities to demonstrate their abilities. They are typically the immediate point of contact with customers.

- *"Work-life balance"* includes programs and policies that acknowledge that employees have responsibilities and lives outside of work and help individuals better manage these multiple demands. Conflict between work and other life responsibilities can diminish the quality of both work and home life for employees, which in turn can affect organizational outcomes such as productivity, absenteeism, and turnover. Efforts to help employees improve work-life balance can improve morale, increase job satisfaction, and strengthen employees' commitment to the organization. Additionally, the organization may reap benefits in terms of increased productivity and reduction in absenteeism and employee turnover.

- *"Employee growth and development opportunities"* help employees expand their knowledge, skills, and abilities, and apply the competencies they have gained to new situations. "The opportunity to gain new skills and experiences can increase employee motivation and job satisfaction and help workers more effectively manage job stress. This can translate into positive gains for the organization by enhancing organizational effectiveness and improving work quality, as well as by helping the organization attract and retain top-quality employees. By providing opportunities for growth and development, organizations can improve the quality of their employees' work experience and realize the benefits of developing workers to their full potential."

- *"Health and safety initiatives"* maximize the physical and mental health of employees through the prevention, assessment, and treatment of potential health risks and problems and by *encouraging* and supporting healthy lifestyle and behavior choices. "Health and safety efforts include a wide variety of workplace practices that can help employees improve their physical and mental health, reduce health risks, and manage stress effectively. By investing in the health and safety of their employees, organizations may benefit from greater productivity and reductions in healthcare costs, absenteeism and accident/injury rates."

- *"Employee recognition"* includes actions by managers to reward employees both individually and collectively for their contributions to the organization. "Recognition can take various forms, formal and informal, monetary and non-monetary. By acknowledging employee efforts and making them feel valued and appreciated, organizations will increase employee satisfaction, morale, and self-esteem. Additionally, the organization should benefit from greater employee engagement and productivity, lower turnover and the ability to attract and retain high caliber employees."

The APA effectively adds "communication" as a sixth dimension, arguing that it "plays a key role in the success of any workplace program or policy and serves as the foundation for all five types of psychologically healthy workplace practices. Communication about workplace practices helps achieve the desired outcomes for the employee and the organization in a variety of ways."

The APA dimensions are closely aligned with traditional HR responsibilities. There is nothing on the list that is not controlled or influenced by HR. When the decision is made to push for improved health on those dimensions, HR is the logical champion and leader of the initiative.

A psychologically healthy workplace fosters employee health and well-being while enhancing organizational performance and productivity.

According to a national public opinion poll conducted by the APA, two-thirds of both men and women say work has a significant impact on their stress level, and one in four has called in sick or taken a "mental health day" as a result of work stress. The investment in addressing issues related to a healthy workplace will at the very least reduce the costs associated with stress.

THE CURRENT FOCUS ON EMPLOYEE ENGAGEMENT

All of the theories about motivation come together today in the focus on "employee engagement." There has been an explosion of interest and research on the subject. A Google search found over thirteen million items where employee engagement is either discussed or mentioned. No doubt the overwhelming majority are from the past decade.

The problem for employers is that "engagement" is a psychological construct. It was conceived to help people understand a complex issue, but it does not exist and cannot be measured directly. It's like love, anger, fear, and beauty—we know generally what it means when someone uses the words, but it's possible to find a number of definitions in books and articles. Each of us has our own understanding.

The widely used resource Wikipedia defines it as, "An 'engaged employee' is one who is fully absorbed by and enthusiastic about their work and so takes positive action to further the organization's reputation and interests." It is important because there is solid, consistent evidence that engaged employees perform better.

Beyond performance, however, engaged employees feel better about their work, and that carries over to their lives away from work. Their lives are made better because of their work experience. It's highly likely that their families benefit from that.

Gallup has apparently done the most research, with analyses of their survey data going back roughly two decades and including employee responses from more than a hundred countries where they conduct surveys. Although it is often difficult to "measure" employee performance, Gallup has analyzed data from their clients and found that engaged employees have fewer absences, fewer grievances, and lower

BETTER ENGAGEMENT? IT TRICKLES DOWN
FROM MANAGERS TO YOUR EMPLOYEES

by Ron Thomas

- "I do not care whether anyone here likes me or not."
- "Please do not come to me with this. I should be the last person that you come to with questions; go figure it out."
- "Now I just do my job and what is required. Nothing more."

This one-sided conversation was sent to me the other morning from one of my mentees who is struggling with a bad boss. She loves her job, but the manager dynamic is fragile, to say the least.

The conversation made me remember a terrific white paper that I recently read—"State of the American Manager"—produced by Gallup. This is a must-read for any organization that struggles with engagement.

One of the most glaring statistics was this: managers account for at least 70 percent of the variance in employee-engagement scores across business units.

THE DRILL SERGEANT DISGUISED AS MANAGER

Forget about all those initiatives you are putting together to try and close the engagement gap. The elephant in the room is the impact of the manager.

I don't care how great the job is, the camaraderie of the workmates or your peer groups, what kind of lunch is served, or day care offerings. If you have a drill sergeant disguised as a manager, that is what you are going to have to fix *first*.

The funny part of about this type of situation is that everyone knows who these people are. They flaunt this as their style, and in the case above, their view is that everyone should just "deal with it."

I was contacted by a vendor a few months back, and they wanted to show me their product app that was going to solve the feedback problem. It would allow anyone to give a thumbs-up or thumbs-down on someone's performance.

But the recent *New York Times* article about talent-management practices at Amazon shows how that type of worthwhile app could be skewed in a harmful way. My thought is that if I can't connect to you on a personal basis, I don't think the receiver of my thumbs, up via technology, cares much about it.

DISENGAGED MANAGERS = DISENGAGED EMPLOYEES

This in-depth study by Gallup showed a clear link between poor managing and a nation of "checked-out" employees. A great manager will camouflage any organizational flaws because they are connected to their people—and these people are more connected to them rather than to the organization.

While mission and vision are so important today, the first hurdle for any organization is the manager.

Organizations and leaders, this is how it works: leaders are engaged, managers are engaged, and employees are engaged. Those are the three pillars that this whole business rests upon. If any one of those columns becomes wobbly, the entire structure is at risk of falling in on itself.

Any fissures within the levels will wind their way down to the lowest common denominator.

TRICKLE-DOWN ECONOMICS
WORKS FOR ENGAGEMENT

This is one documented case of trickle-down theory that works. As companies review and discuss engagement, everybody has to be in the room. This is not just an HR exercise—this is a business issue, and it matters.

Imagine a worker interviewing for a job, and once the deal is signed, they offer to come to work four days but want five days of wages. That's something you would not agree to, but when you ignore engagement, that is exactly what you are doing—you are paying for productivity for the full week, but you are not getting it in return.

If you were to calculate that loss in productivity across the enterprise, you would quickly see the business case behind engagement.

So if your organization is ignoring bad managers and their cascading results, just calculate the amount of payroll that you are not getting the productivity to match. With about 60 to 70 percent of your workforce not giving their all, according to Gallup, that is a lot of currency flowing out the window.

That should be simple enough to understand.

These issues within your organization are not only costing you in productivity, but in talented people as well. The thing to remember is that these employees will make a decision—even if you are too afraid to confront it.

Ron Thomas is Managing Director, Strategy Focused Group-MENA, based in Dubai. He is also a senior faculty member and representative of the Human Capital Institute. He received the Outstanding Leadership Award for Global HR Excellence at the World Human Resources Development Congress.

turnover, and their organizations have more satisfied customers, better-quality work products, and less waste.

That makes it worthwhile to invest in assessing and monitoring the level of engagement in an organization. The results can be used in strategies to improve performance. The investment will pay off in lower operating costs and higher levels of satisfaction with people served by the organization.

Engagement is measured by adding up the responses to a series of scaled-response (i.e., 1 to 5) survey questions. Since there is no universal definition, every research/consulting firm that competes for this business has its own definition and asks questions designed to assess how employees feel about a unique set of issues. Gallup, as an example, relies on twelve survey questions—its Q^{12} survey.

Gallup's survey questions focus on the role and importance of managers in creating a work environment where employees feel engaged. In reading the questions, nine or ten, depending on how they are interpreted, are related to the manager's relationship and interactions with the employee. The questions cover the issues important to day-to-day supervision.

In reporting results Gallup categorizes employees as Engaged, Not Engaged, and Actively Disengaged. Engaged employees are enthusiastic and quick to take the initiative, and they commit discretionary effort and time to complete work assignments. In the most successful organizations Gallup has found they account for as many as 70 percent of the workers. Their data shows it's more typical in the United States to find engagement levels in the low 30 percent range. Not Engaged employees do their job and go home. The employees who are Actively Disengaged can and will undermine the work efforts of coworkers.

Other firms that study engagement focus in their surveys on similar as well as somewhat different issues—the organization's mission, the organization's values, internal communications, and so on. Each company uses a combination of survey questions to measure the level of engagement. It would be useful to check with other public employers to learn their experience with firms providing survey services.

A common goal is to initiate changes in the work experience (e.g., more frequent recognition of a job well done) that prompt employees to feel different and respond differently to the survey questions. It's unlikely that superficial or isolated changes will increase employee commitment. In combination the changes will be seen by employees as a noticeable shift in the approach to management. But two points are relevant: the changes can be planned and accomplished with no direct cost, and everyone will end up feeling better about their day-to-day experience.

A survey can be the trigger to convince management that investing in efforts to improve the work experience will pay off in improved performance. Top management needs to acknowledge that the organization needs to change and that they are committing to undertake corrective steps. Employees need to understand the goals, to know what they can expect, and to be kept aware of next steps. If at all possible, they should be involved in the planning. Focus groups would be useful to develop a better understanding of any problems and possible changes to raise engagement levels. It may be useful to create a task force to develop recommendations.

The current thinking suggests surveys should be conducted more frequently than annually. They can be focused on specific issues. They can also ask for reactions to possible changes. The goal is to realize improved responses over the time. Consider the survey to be similar to quality scores.

In a 2014 survey by Deloitte, 78 percent of the responding business leaders rated retention and engagement as "urgent" or "important." It is now widely understood that the level of employee commitment to the organization's success warrants top management attention and a readiness to invest in raising the level of engagement—as a step in improving performance.

GETTING EMPLOYEES ON BOARD

It's human nature to resist change. The past few years have made employees in both the public and private sectors increasingly skeptical. Many would find it difficult to trust any management statements.

But it will always be true that many government employees are committed to public service. Others may consider resigning, but are hesitant because they would be walking away from friends; valuable, accrued benefits; and, of course, the uncertainty of a new job and working in a different environment. Their level of engagement should be a concern of all leaders.

Employees may need to be convinced that senior leaders are sincere. With trust, employees will respond to initiatives to improve their work experience. It's important to them. Every employee along with their organization stands to benefit.

The starting point is the understanding that people want to work for successful organizations and will commit to achieving the goals of their group and organization when their efforts are recognized and valued. Progress in achieving the mission and the contributions of employees should be recognized in communications related to planned changes. All except the most recalcitrant employees will acquiesce and support change if they are convinced that management is sincere and they see the benefit for coworkers and the organization.

The lead dimension identified in studies of healthy organizations is employee involvement. No one knows better where change is needed. Experience confirms that with guidance, they can develop practical recommendations to address most organizational issues.

An early step to consider is a series of focus groups to understand manager and employee concerns and needs, and to suggest possible changes. A group might be asked to research best practices. A steering group composed of managers and employees should be responsible for consolidating ideas and developing a final set of recommendations.

With management's concurrence and support, employee teams should be asked to develop plans to implement needed changes, including needed resources. Management may have to push back and explain why something is not feasible, but in discussing ideas they should be able to reach agreement. If the cost is too high for immediate adoption, the recommendations can be modified and implemented over two or more years. Teams can then be assigned to manage the projects to modify or introduce more effective policies and practices. Feedback should be solicited at several points from stakeholders.

Employee involvement from inception will help to garner buy-in or ownership across the different groups. Individuals who play a role often became champions of new practices. Ongoing feedback from coworkers helps planners anticipate special circumstances and issues that could prove problematic. An additional benefit of engaging the workforce early is that employees develop an understanding of issues and hurdles, along with linkages to organizational goals putting them in position as trusted sources of information for coworkers. They can be expected to commit to making the changes a success.

A commitment to solicit employee feedback and fine-tune policies and practices at the end of the first year, and possibly again in future years, will help to gain support.

High performance depends on three basic factors: effective management, talented employees, and engaged, motivated employees. This chapter focuses on strategies to sustain motivation. When employees start their careers, they have a strong desire to be successful. Their experience can undermine and thwart their aspirations and their motivation. The balance of this book discusses the policies and practices that should be considered to help them achieve their goals and in doing so contribute to their organization's success. The gains are often impressive.

ADDITIONAL RESOURCES

The American Psychological Association (APA) website, the Center for Organizational Excellence (www.center4oe), provides citations for a wealth of additional resources related to organizational health.

The book authored by McKinsey consultants Colin Price and Scott Keller is *Beyond Performance: How Great Organizations Build Ultimate Competitive Advantage* (Wiley, June 2011). It was described in a book review as follows: "This is an outstanding book that should become a classic for its extensive research on leadership and organization effectiveness."

Another useful book is Patrick Lencioni's *The Advantage: Why Organizational Health Trumps Everything Else in Business* (Wiley, Collins Business, 2012). From a book review: "Consulting executive Lencioni has an answer for floundering businesses—aim for organizational health. In other words, businesses that are whole, consistent, and complete, with complementary management, operations, strategy, and culture."

Lavigna, Robert. *Engaging Government Employees.* AMACOM Books, 2013. This is a useful book for planning and implementing an action plan to understand and address employee engagement in the public sector.

Finally, the Gallup website, www.gallup.com/topic/employee_engagement.aspx, provides access to a number of reports and articles on their engagement research. Their research and consulting has been global and across all sectors. Gallup and McKinsey have formed a joint Organizational Science Initiative "to create the most comprehensive analytics ever on the subject of behavioral economics for organizations—or more simply, the role human nature plays in virtually all organizational outcomes."

NOTE

1. Robert Lavigna, *Engaging Government Employees* (New York: AMACOM Books, 2013)
2. Scott Keller and Colin Price. 2011. *Beyond Performance: How Great Organizations Build Ultimate Competitive Advantage.* New York: Wiley.

4

Building a Leadership Team

The role of executives in government is unlike any other in the business world or in any of the mix of not-for-profit organizations. Government executives at the state and local levels have counterparts in other jurisdictions, but federal executives are unique in the scope of their responsibilities. They all have to learn to work within the constraint of laws and regulations, and within the oversight of elected officials and stakeholders, some supportive and some less so.

In other sectors, executives have greater control of staff and resources, and the authority to initiate changes in operations. The control makes it easier for those executives to respond to unexpected external developments. To highlight an obvious difference, an HR executive in business is not constrained by civil service statutes. The authority to initiate change in response to problems is at the heart of an executive's role. Outside of government, executives only have to satisfy the CEO and for major changes the organization's board of directors/trustees.

The expectation that executives can and will initiate needed change differentiates the role of executives from that of managers. In a dynamic world, senior officials need the skills to lead.

Government executives have to learn to work effectively with elected officials and political appointees who may have little or no experience managing people in large organizations. One expert referred to appointees as "amateur managers." The frequency of elections also means executives know they may have to develop new working relationships every few years with leaders who possibly have very different agendas, goals, and values. In other sectors, executives know new leaders may have different personal styles, but they all accept and focus on the same core goals (e.g., adequate profitability) and measures to assess success. With each election, government executives need to be ready to respond to new priorities.

All of that contributes to the challenge of government executive roles. It makes it that much more important to emphasize the abilities needed to lead. The inherent difficulty of the jobs is a compelling argument for developing a focused strategy to develop individuals capable of leading. Larger public organizations need to decide if creating an executive service is the right answer.

When the federal Senior Executive Service (SES) was created by the Civil Service Reform Act of 1978, it became a model for an executive service. A number of national governments have an executive service. Several states also have created an executive service. However, the policies and practices that comprise the SES system have been modified a couple of times and as this is written are again being reconsidered. Despite the varied experience, a "best practice" program has not emerged. At the state level the interest in creating a separate service has waned (although the reasons have not been documented).

In business the leadership team is small—a rule of thumb is that 1 percent of the workforce are executives—and generally includes the same basic functions. The team is led, of course, by a CEO and includes the heads of finance, legal, marketing, information systems, human resources, and operations. The team also includes a few second-level executives; in finance, for example, a treasurer and a controller are common executive positions. The job titles are very similar from company to company. The overwhelming majority spend their careers in the same function and the same industry.

The organization of government's diverse agencies is similar to "conglomerate" companies like General Electric (GE)—there is a central "headquarters" staff and separate executive teams in each operating unit. GE, as an example, operates in eight different industries ranging from financial services to producing aircraft jet engines. In a conglomerate, the cultures, industry dynamics, product/service markets, time orientation, rate of change, and so on, are all very different—and that has implications for the most effective approach to management.

Where companies operate in multiple industries, they normally manage each business unit separately, with management practices typical of the unit's industry. They rely on a unified financial system, but each unit has its own marketing, operations, and HR functions. The headquarters staff has in-house experts who serve as consultants to the business units.

The dissimilarities across federal and state agencies are even greater than in a business conglomerate. An individual who is successful in managing a prison is unlikely to be equally successful in leading a hospital, or someone with a highway maintenance background successful as an executive in a public health agency. In business only a handful of executives, typically with a proven track record of leading organizational change, move among the subsidiaries of a conglomerate. A core program model clearly has value, but agencies should have a degree of discretion to adopt changes that reflect the leadership style and management philosophy that contributes to mission achievement.

It is important to highlight the unifying power of the widely used model for compensating business executives. All executives as well as middle managers and senior professionals participate in an incentive plan where payouts are linked in part to company performance. In publicly traded companies they also participate in stock

THE FEDERAL SENIOR EXECUTIVE SERVICE

The federal government created the Senior Executive Service (SES) with the Civil Service Reform Act (CSRA) of 1978. The purpose of the legislation was to "ensure that the executive management of the Government of the United States is responsive to the needs, policies, and goals of the nation and otherwise is of the highest quality." The SES includes most managerial, supervisory, and policy positions classified above General Schedule (GS) grade 15 or equivalent positions in the executive branch. The Office of Personnel Management (OPM) is responsible for government-wide policies, direction, and oversight. Today, there are roughly 7,900 "SESrs" (along with 2,400 political appointments).

To quote from the OPM website, "The Government's senior executives would be held accountable for individual and organizational performance."

The members of the SES corps lose their civil service rights and become at-will employees. However, experience with several situations over the past two or three years confirms lawyers can make it very difficult to terminate poor performers.

The federal SES has not met expectations; it's been "fine-tuned" several times over the years. Most recently in December 2015 President Obama issued an Executive Order—"Strengthening the Senior Executive Service"—with changes to be rolled out over the next two years. Frequent reports of problems after almost thirty years have made the SES a focus of critics.

A report also released in December by the U.S. Merit Systems Protection Board, "Training and Development for the Senior Executive Service: A Necessary Investment," confirmed that government has failed to provide adequate training and development for the SES corps. As reported, "For many executives, investment in their development appears to be insufficient, inappropriately targeted, or both."

Investing in the development of executives should be a commitment by every public employer concerned with agency performance.

---

option (or similar) plans. That contributes to a "we're all in this together" culture; they all benefit as team members when the company is successful. The compensation model gives executives a reason to collaborate and minimize the impact of interpersonal differences. The government of Canada has adopted a version of this model.

It's also common in business as well as in health care for executives to have similar educational backgrounds. Some prominent entrepreneurs, like Bill Gates and Steve Jobs, dropped out of college, but they are unusual. It's frequently true that the executives in leading companies all graduated from a short list of the highly rated business schools. Starting early in their careers, business executives develop a shared mind-set on what it means to be an executive.

Government executives do not typically have the benefit of the education, training, and managed experience of those promoted to executive positions in business. Health care and higher education also emphasize the importance of building an executive team. That is certainly as important in government as in other sectors. The role of appointed officials makes government different; they often lack management experience, lack organizational understanding, and have not gained the trust of affected employees. For those reasons proven executives should be prepared to lead change.

That reinforces the importance of agreeing on a strategy that insures an adequate investment in the development of executive talent. A central question for government at all levels is what policies and practices will be used to manage the cadre of executives. Unfortunately, the experience in public organizations where an executive service exists has not been adequately documented or evaluated.

An executive service may not be feasible for smaller jurisdictions or independent agencies, but that does not negate the importance of leadership and change-management skills. An alternative may be to include competencies important to change management along with more basic competencies for assessing candidates for executive positions. All public employers should consider the best strategy, given their resources (people and financial), to assure leaders are ready to lead initiatives to improve performance.

PLANNING AN EXECUTIVE
TALENT MANAGEMENT SYSTEM

The foundation supported by the Society for Human Resource Management has published two useful best-practice summaries: "The Search for Executive Talent" and "Developing Leadership Talent." While drafted for private sector employers, the practices could be readily adopted by public agencies.

The goal, of course, is to develop a cadre of well-qualified, effective executives and to have successors identified so that when a vacancy occurs, the talent is readily available to fill the position. That depends on an ongoing commitment to invest in building an effective executive team. The "building" depends on several interrelated processes that are discussed in this section.

The most prominent management expert of the twentieth century, Peter Drucker, summarized the importance of executive talent management in a 2004 *Harvard Business Review* article, "What Is an Effective Executive?" His central point was that

> Effective executives differ widely in their personalities, strengths, weaknesses, values and beliefs. All they have in common is that they get the right things done. Some are born effective. But the demand is much too great to be satisfied by extraordinary innate talent. *Effectiveness is a discipline. And, like every discipline, effectiveness can be learned and must be earned.*[1] (Italics added.)

It's important to keep in mind a core but implicit point of articles like Drucker's—effective means acting and leading the organization to achieve its goals. A marketing executive, for example, would only be effective if the company reached its sales goals. A labor relations executive is accountable for delivering labor peace and favorable contracts.

Executives are not the same as "managers" or "administrators." Neither would be expected to move an organization in new directions; neither would be expected to reorganize or reallocate resources.

Executives exhibit a different mind-set from managers that is evident in their approach to their jobs. To be successful, executives need to transition to "ownership" of their function, accept accountability for its impact on the organization as a whole, and develop a level of comfort in making decisions that affect the organization for a year or more into the future.

That distinction makes it important to understand the knowledge, skills, and abilities—the competencies—known to contribute to success as an executive. The components of the talent-management system are then planned to insure that those individuals promoted to executive roles are likely to be successful in managing agency operations.

As a caveat, large corporations often have an individual in HR who is responsible for managing executive talent management. That, of course, recognizes the importance of the executive team. As is often reported, business executives commonly benefit from special perquisites (e.g., cars, club memberships). However, companies do not create a separate service similar to the federal SES. Experience at the federal level suggests that a chasm now separates the SES from middle managers and does not serve government well. Recent research shows middle managers are more important than executives in raising employee performance levels (see chapter 5). Further, business executives, managers, and most professionals all participate in an incentive plan, and that reinforces the idea of the "management team." The performance-management system also ties executives and managers together via cascading performance goals. The attention to executives in business is not an isolated HR function.

Defining the Keys to Executive Success

As a first step in planning or assessing an executive service, it would be highly advantageous to define what is expected from an organization's executives. Each new administration should set aside time for appointees and executives to discuss the role of executives.

There should be agreement on how performance and potential for promotion will be evaluated. Goal setting is virtually universal at the executive level to evaluate performance (and discussed in chapter 9). In addition, it is common to assess executives (as well as lower-level employees) on a series of competencies. The combination is sometimes referred to as "the what [*results*] and the how [*competencies*]."

There is solid evidence that companies with strong executive leadership, as defined by key competencies, are more successful; the quality of leadership is correlated with growth and profitability. There is no reason to believe that would not be true in government as well. Research also shows that leadership is always contextual, and that the most effective leadership style (or combination of softer skills) depends in part on the context in which an organization operates.

That leads to the recommendation that agencies should form a task force to identify and define the competencies for senior positions to "fit" their operating environment. Every executive needs to possess the basic managerial skills, but it's likely, for example, that if a team of executives in a state attorney general's office were asked to identify the competencies that make an executive stand out, they would arrive at a somewhat different answer than a team leading a public health agency or those in a fish and game agency.

Once a competency profile is defined, it can be used for:

- Assessing job candidates
- Defining performance expectations
- Preparing individual development plans
- Succession planning
- Reinforcing the desired culture
- Assessing performance
- Reinforcing the desired culture

Competencies are widely used today at all job levels, but unfortunately there is no confirmed best practice. In many organizations they are nothing more than a box on an appraisal form. Lists of generic executive competencies tend to focus on basic management issues (e.g., managing change, communicating effectively, etc.) and not on leadership or performance.

Documenting Executive Positions

Executive positions (as well as all other positions) should be documented in position descriptions ("PDs" or "JDs" for job descriptions; the phrases are often used interchangeably) that focus not on activities but on expected outcomes or results. The traditional and still-common PD format begins with a summary of why a job exists and then lists a job's specific duties and responsibilities—activities—sometimes with estimates of how much time the incumbent is expected to spend on each. Government has been infamous for PDs that go on for pages. In the past, employees have been evaluated on how well they completed each task or activity, but that is especially inappropriate at the executive level.

An alternative format is to document how the organization will benefit (or be adversely impacted) by an executive's or manager's performance. The focus is on outcomes or goals along with metrics relevant to assessing results.

- A traditional statement might be: "Provides general oversight of all ABC activities, manages the day-to-day operations, and assures a smoothly functioning, efficient organization."
- An outcome statement might be: "Acts to manage operations to assure goals are achieved as measured by . . ." (It could also read, "The incumbent is accountable for achieving operational goals.")

The statements should state clearly how the incumbent's performance is expected to contribute to the organization's performance.

In addition, the job description could include the metrics relevant to assessing executive or manager performance.

The final section should be a list of the competencies associated with successful performance (and possibly weighted to reflect the position). The traditional statement of education and experience has never been valid or defensible and serves no useful purpose, especially at the executive level. It suggests erroneously that each degree level, regardless of the caliber of the degree program, or each year of experience adds equally to an individual's qualifications.

A 2016 report from the U.S. Army Management Staff College highlights an interesting and very likely common problem at all levels of government. Participants in development programs for new civilian executives were asked which of the core executive competencies their experience and prior training had *least* prepared them for. The most common response was financial, technology, and human capital management. Their comments suggested that they and the agencies where they worked assumed in training programs that other specialized functions were responsible (e.g., the HR office). That is to say, as managers, they had not been trained to manage those basic areas.

In business, executives would answer differently. The typical undergraduate and graduate programs would have covered those subjects (and others like business law). That early exposure to core management subjects gives business executives a broader perspective. Business managers would expect to assume increased responsibility as they progress to higher levels.

The study prompts an unanswered question: How do agencies define executive responsibilities? It triggers important questions about how executive and manager roles are defined and the requisite knowledge, skills, and abilities at each level. It reinforces the need to ask executives periodically if their training and development has fully prepared them for their roles.

Managing Executive Selection

The majority of government executives are promoted from the cadre of middle managers. However, the demands on public organizations are changing, technology is changing, and employee expectations are changing. It makes sense to look into the future a year or two to understand the problems a new incumbent will need to address. If the strategy calls for moving in a new direction, the change will need to be reviewed at the highest levels.

The position documentation provides a basis for defining the skills important to success. Emerging problems highlight the need for the skills needed to develop collaborative relationships with people in different functions and the capacity for change and flexibility.

The most widely used but also most unreliable method to assess candidates is the use of unstructured interviews led by untrained peer-level executives. Structured interviews ask questions about particular situations, critical incidents, or types of problems. Resumes are also unreliable. The most reliable but also costliest are work sample tests, judgment tests, and cognitive tests.

More "sophisticated" selection practices rely on methods to assess individual strengths and weaknesses. Paper-and-pencil or Web-based methods (e.g., Myers-Briggs) have been used for years. More recently, employers have started using multi-source or 360-degree surveys to collect information from employees to evaluate their managers. That is the approach used by Google discussed in the next chapter. The results can be used for selection, to develop individual development plans (IDPs), to create courses, and to share with coaches.

Studies show that the best decisions are based on the reports of search firms and other independent evaluators. The firms should have full access to all information. They can be expensive, but the "cost" of making a bad selection decision is considerably higher.

Executive Succession Planning

Succession planning is a structured process intended to identify qualified individuals as candidates to fill future executive openings. The process is most important when an executive retires, dies, or resigns and a replacement is unexpectedly needed. That can be handled informally as a distinct ad hoc event, but then the process is sometimes chaotic and decisions are far from systematic.

In contrast, succession management is best handled as an ongoing process with development plans to prepare candidates for future opportunities. The goal is to have a pool of candidates ready for promotion. It's the difference between a reactive, pieced-together list of candidates and a pool of prepared future leaders.

A sometimes-sensitive practice is the identification of high-potential employees (HIPOs) well before they are considered for promotion to an executive position. Investing in the development of HIPOs is common in well-managed companies. One might argue the practice violates equal opportunity policies.

It is important in succession management to give adequate recognition to diversity considerations. Planned development opportunities can be supportive of career progression for women and minorities.

Employers with well-developed succession practices have found it enhances their brand as an employer and helps with recruiting.

Executive Development

Executive development should be based on IDPs. The IDP format is not important. It's basically an agreement between an individual and his/her supervisor. For organizations that do not now have IDPs, there are multiple examples of formats and content on the Internet. They need to be updated regularly and set forth specific individual plans.

Estimates show that 80 percent of executive learning and development occurs through experience, 10 percent comes from advice from succeeding levels of "bosses" and from friends and mentors, and only 10 percent from classroom instruction.

Moreover, their acquired knowledge of how to function and succeed is the product of their years of experience and is not going to be overridden sitting in a classroom. That highlights the importance of providing meaningful developmental experience starting well before they move into an executive role. It also reinforces the reason for identifying HIPOs and starting their development early.

Another important aspect of the problem is what happens when a manager is instructed in new ways of thinking or operating and then goes back to a work environment where old approaches are still the accepted ways of addressing situations. Behaviors that are not reinforced or even worse, censured, are unlikely to be repeated. New ways of operating need to be understood as organization priorities.

To add a third element of the problem, an essential part of development is honest feedback. Everyone needs feedback to improve, but the supposed tool to document strengths and weaknesses is far from a reliable source. Performance ratings in far too many jurisdictions are straight out of Lake Wobegon—everybody is above average. A 2015 report from the Government Accountability Office confirms how serious the problem is for federal SESrs. As reported on the website GovExec, "85 percent of career senior executives received 'outstanding' or 'exceeds fully successful' ratings."[2] That, unfortunately, appears to be a common problem in government at all levels. (Executive performance management is discussed in chapter 9.)

But even if executives are provided with useful feedback, the evidence suggests many will not be able take advantage of development plans. The impediments to executive development are common in both public and private employers—inability to take time away from the job, inadequate funding, lack of leadership support, and unavailability of relevant training. At the federal level, despite the prominence of the Federal Executive Institute, the Merit Systems Protection Board reported executive development is "insufficient, inappropriately targeted, or both." Government leaders need to understand that downplaying executive development undermines current and future agency performance.

The lack of training opportunities for executives is a largely unrecognized problem. In contrast to the many executive education programs offered by business schools, relatively few stand out for government executives. Harvard's Kennedy School and Syracuse's Maxwell School lead a relatively short list. Many universities offer programs for government managers, but few have programs developed specifically for executives.

Other private alternatives include the Graduate School USA (which used to be a federal entity but is now independent) and organizations like the Center for Creative Leadership in North Carolina (although their programs are not planned for government). Many business schools offer executive education programs, although again, they are not planned for government.

In light of the few executive education programs, and the cost of those that do exist, the most broadly relevant and lowest-direct-cost practice is experiential learning through "stretch" job assignments. This requires a knowledge of each individual's career plans, developmental readiness, and the challenges that will confront assigned executives.

COACHING: EXCELLING AT THE NEXT LEVEL

Sandra D. Thomas, Executive Coach and Facilitator at Sherpa Coaching

Like many organizations, the federal government has accepted and embraced leadership development as a permanent part of their culture. Mentoring can help. Sometimes people need more, so they can maximize their strengths and minimize their weaknesses. They need the individual, intense focus that is gained from executive coaching.

As a Deputy Director for Workforce Development with the federal government, I created and managed several successful programs, one of which was a fifteen-year mentoring program. While these programs were successful, they were not enough. Managers who successfully completed our leadership development training would ask for more help. They needed to manage difficult conversations, hold people accountable, navigate challenging situations, and develop executive presence.

Often, when high performers are promoted into leadership and management positions, they are not ready to supervise or to lead others. They find it hard to motivate and inspire others to follow them. While traditional training provides many skills, often leaders need an additional push. The leaders need skills customized to meet their needs and help with practical application. Marshall Goldsmith writes: "Coaching can be an effective means of improving business results while also contributing to executive development. Good coaching leads to greater self-knowledge, new perspectives, improved performance and greater adaptability" (2007).

Coaching in the federal government has to be frequent, in-person, and with a set time frame. It must focus on specific business behaviors and produce observable results. Good coaching leads clients through an intense process designed to meet them where they are.

Many organizations have discovered that even high performers need an additional boost to get to their next performance peak. Coaching improves the performance of employees who are falling short of their potential. However, the greatest benefit of coaching accrues to current and future leaders. A coach can serve as a guide to positive changes in business behavior.

People are comfortable with their strengths. However, they are challenged when their weaknesses show. These weaknesses often limit a leader's potential. For example, a skilled program manager promoted into a supervisory position may feel overwhelmed when faced with reviewing an employee's performance or guiding an employee to better business behavior. Working with an executive coach, leaders develop skills and tools to reach their goals. According to the *Harvard Management Update*, "Under the right circumstances, one-on-one interaction with an objective third party can provide a focus that other forms of organizational support simply cannot" (2004).

During the first year of our internal executive coaching program, 93 percent of the participants indicated that the program enhanced professional interpersonal relationships. Ninety-five percent said that coaching addressed their individual business needs. Ninety-seven percent of participants were committed to achieving the goals they set with their coach and believed that their coach was effective and knowledgeable. The participants also reported positive changes including

- the ability to set goals, adhere to them, and communicate goals and expectations to others;

- sharing information, giving/requesting feedback, and following up when working collaboratively;
- the ability to understand and work with difficult people or situations; and
- increased social interaction with subordinates and colleagues.

Individual coaching allows a leader to focus on what they need to succeed at the next level. Coaching also provides leaders with skills needed to work effectively with groups and to motivate subordinates. Coaching teaches a leader to make the choice between managing and coaching. Often in the federal government, a leader wears multiple hats. While supervising a staff of thirty, they are also individual contributors. Coaching skills allow a leader to empower staff to be more self-motivating.

Coaching is essential for any organization. In the federal government, it allows the full use of limited resources. A coaching culture encourages better employee engagement and retention. Employees want to work for a leader who excites and motivates them. Employees want to work for an organization that invests in their growth and productivity. Whether the next level is a promotion, becoming a better leader, or unleashing creativity, coaching takes people to the next level at an accelerated speed with sustainable results.

REFERENCE

Goldsmith, M. *What Got You Here Won't Get You There*. New York: Hyperion, 2007.
"Methodology: Do You Need an Executive Coach?" *Harvard Management Update* 9, no. 12 (December 2004).

Sandra D. Thomas, Executive Coach and Facilitator at Sherpa Coaching, is the former Deputy Director of the Office of Workforce Development, National Cancer Institute, Department of Health and Human Services.

A similar alternative is assigning individuals to teams assembled to tackle difficult problems. When asked, leaders frequently cite the value of these assignments.

Another alternative that is both inexpensive and effective is coaching. Making coaches available to executives started roughly two decades ago, although coaches have played a role for decades in improving performance in many fields. Coaching necessarily starts with an assessment of an individual's strengths and weaknesses, which is followed by a day or two a month for as long as warranted. When an executive (or anyone) is open to the advice of a coach, it can be very effective.

A similar inexpensive alternative, mentoring, can also be very effective, especially when the relationship is informal and personal. Senior executives should be encouraged to mentor others. The mentoring could continue postretirement. It's a role that many find they enjoy.

Since variety enhances the impact of developmental practices, programs should include a mix of development experiences. Business CEOs see executive development as the single most important human-capital issue holding back their company's success. It's similarly important in government.

Agencies should consider creating a committee of senior, recognized leaders selected to represent the spectrum of agencies to meet periodically and focus on what should be done to improve executive development. They individually should be champions in their agencies for investing in executives and managers. Similar teams should meet in at least the larger agencies. Executive development is that important.

EXECUTIVE COMPENSATION

This is where politics clashes with market forces. In light of the criticism of how much "rank-and-file" government employees are paid, it is surprising how little attention is paid to the compensation of government leaders. Perhaps this is explained by the contrast with the way corporate executives are paid. It could also be because of the recent spate of pay freezes. The recession has clearly made elected officials hesitant to accept pay increases. But whatever the reason, a Google search confirms that the pay of government officials has had little media attention in the past few years.

However, the compensation of executives in government will affect the caliber of individuals interested in accepting these positions. These can be tough, demanding roles that limit the individual's time with family as well as their ability to provide for normal family goals like paying for their children's college education. The long hours and stress can take their toll on health. The pay will always be low relative to what highly qualified individuals could earn in other sectors. In places such as the United Kingdom, pay is expected to be adequate to attract applicants with business credentials. When the pay is too far below market, it has implications for agency performance, for the careers of managers and nonmanagers, and for the caliber of government leaders, which impacts public support.

Realistically, executive compensation is hardly relevant to the cost of government. Executive salaries are a very small percentage of total costs. Plus, when government is well managed, the public will be more likely to be supportive. When higher salaries play a role in hiring better employees, the added cost could be easily offset by improved performance.

Elected officials, of course, are making personal decisions to run for office knowing that the pay is comparatively low. Many have had previous careers that generated personal wealth or benefit from wealthy families. The 2015–2016 presidential campaign exemplifies how important personal wealth has become.

The pay of members of Congress, governors, mayors, and city and county executives is a fraction of what jobs of similar "size" or impact would pay in the private sector. The budget cuts following the Great Recession have prompted a number of leaders to accept salary reductions. Political considerations are always prominent in these decisions.

It's relevant that for public officials in jobs where professional credentials and prior experience are important and where employers compete for talent—school superintendents, police commissioners, health officials, investment directors—salaries rise to levels close to those in the private sector. The number of those leaders paid more

Table 4.1. Compensation of Elected Officials

In 2015 at the federal level the salaries of elected leaders include:

President	$400,000
Vice President	$223,500
Senate and House Leaders	$193,400
Senate and House Members	$174,000

The highest-paid governors in 2015 were Pennsylvania's at $190,823 and Tennessee's at $184,632. Several governors decline to accept or return their pay to the state—Alabama, Florida, and Tennessee—while the governors of Michigan and Illinois return all but $1. Since 2010, the average increase in the salaries of governors has been less than 1 percent a year according to the Council on State Government.

The highest-paid mayor is Eric Garcetti in Los Angeles at $232,000. Bill de Blasio in New York is paid $225,000, and Rahm Emanuel in Chicago earns $216,000. (In many cities and states the mayor and/or governor also has the use of a residence.) Those salaries are five or six times greater than the averages for voters in those cities but still significantly below the levels of corporate executives and professionals in those cities.

The salary of the chief justice of the U.S. Supreme Court is $258,100, and the associate justices are paid $246,800. The salary of a federal district judges is $174,000. In state courts there is a broad range of judicial salaries. The salaries of the highest-paid judges in each state range from $236,300 to a low of $126,269. Successful lawyers, of course, normally earn significantly higher compensation.

than $200,000 might be surprising. This is not to suggest those salaries are not justified, only that many in the public are not aware of the practices. Before increasing salaries above that level, it will be important to assemble justification.

A decade ago Governing.com posted a column, "Worth the Money? The Competition for Top Talent Is Producing a Cadre of Highly Paid Public Executives" (July 2004). Executives who demonstrate their effectiveness in leading agencies will always be in demand. Politics may hold down executive pay, but in the long run that only detracts from attracting talent to careers in government management.

College sports coaches are no doubt the highest paid in public institutions, with several football coaches now paid in excess of $5 million. The presidents/chancellors and senior administrators of public universities are perhaps the next highest, although the reports fail to capture the outside income for professors at leading medical, law, engineering, and business schools. In a few cases boards of trustees were willing to pay more than a new president wanted.

A universal consideration is that the salaries and salary increases of elected and appointed government leaders are constrained by political concerns, while the salaries of professionals are influenced, if not governed, by supply and demand (although at the most senior levels politics also play a role). To be sure, some candidates campaigning for office as well as some members of the public feel that public employees should not be paid competitive salaries. But the ceiling on executive salaries can impact the number and caliber of job candidates.

Inevitably, the salaries of professionals increase faster than the pay of elected officials. That leads to what is referred to as "salary compression." At some point the pay of the highest professional levels rises to the level of their managers'. At its worst, individuals at two or more levels are paid the same salary.

The public may not be sympathetic to government executives earning well above average salaries, but the most talented individuals always have career alternatives. Government cannot afford to lose them.

A strategy to mask at least a portion of an individual's compensation and improve performance is to introduce an incentive plan, with payouts tied to a combination of agency and individual performance. The awards provide an opportunity to earn increased income, but with less public scrutiny. It is a proven way to build team "esprit de corps." The Canadian government recently adopted a policy linking awards in part to agency performance (although it's too soon to know if it's working). Executive incentives are discussed in chapter 9.

EXECUTIVE REVIEW BOARDS

Corporations as well as hospitals and universities operate with a board of directors or board of trustees. Boards commonly establish broad policies and objectives; play a role in executive recruiting; support executive development; review the performance of the chief executive; approve annual budgets; monitor and assess the organization's performance; and advise on the salaries and compensation of senior executives. As the saying goes, "It's lonely at the top," and boards give leaders someone to use as sounding boards and provide resources on trends affecting organizations.

Federal agencies rely on Performance Review Boards (PRBs) to review initial performance ratings, performance bonuses, and annual pay increases for members of the Senior Executive Service, Senior Scientific and Technical, and Senior Level positions. They review performance plans at the beginning of the year and at the year's end, review agency and individual performance, and make recommendations to agency heads on performance ratings, pay increases, bonus awards, and so on.

But there is an important distinction between PRBs and the boards in other sectors. The boards in other sectors are composed of outsiders plus the company or hospital CEO and one or two company executives, most often the CFO. They include leaders from other companies, academics with expertise in the industry, prominent community leaders, and so on. In business, boards include representatives of investors (although community leaders also represent a constituency). The outside board members are the contacts for auditors and hire their own consultants.

The model does exist in the public sector. Local public libraries commonly have a board composed of local citizens. Public school systems, of course, are led by local residents. Public universities and community colleges have boards. Federal reserve banks have boards of regional business leaders.

This is not to suggest boards are needed by all public entities. Local government is frequently led by well-qualified, professional managers. Boards, however, serve several purposes.

One purpose is to give elected officials easy access to individuals knowledgeable about government operations. Experts exist in each area of government service, from public health to environmental protection to transportation. With a continuing connection, they would be available to agency leaders for advising and assistance in gaining support from external interest groups. Many would be available informally, but with formal ties they are more likely to be available and provide their expertise.

In that role advisory boards would assure the public that government is committed to satisfying expectations. In light of the public's increasingly negative view of government, the assurance should help.

ADDITIONAL RESOURCES

Lawrence, Paul R., and Mark A. Abramson. *Succeeding as a Political Executive: Fifty Insights from Experience.* Lanham, MD: Rowman & Littlefield, 2016.

McCauley, Cynthia D., and Ellen Van Velsor. *The Center for Creative Leadership Handbook of Leadership Development.* 2nd ed. New York: Jossey-Bass, 2004.

Zenger, John, and Joseph Folkman. *The Extraordinary Leader: Turning Good Managers into Great Leaders.* New York: McGraw-Hill, 2002.

Silsbee, Doug. *The Mindful Coach: Seven Roles for Facilitating Leader Development.* 2nd ed. New York: John Wiley, 2010.

Anderson, Bob, and William A. Adams. *Mastering Leadership: An Integrated Framework for Breakthrough Performance and Extraordinary Business Results.* New York: John Wiley, 2016.

Feser, Claudio, Fernanda Mayol, and Ramesh Srinivasan. "Decoding Leadership: What Really Matters." McKinsey Quarterly website, January 2015.

Ketelaar, Anne, Nick Manning, and Edouard Turkisch. "Performance-Based Arrangements for Senior Civil Servants: OECD and Other Country Experiences." OECD, 2007. This report summarizes the views of government HR executives in seven countries and the United States.

From the Executive Summary

"Performance management and performance-based arrangements for senior civil servants exist in most OECD member and non-member countries, and are indeed used in all countries under review in this study. Public service reforms during the past decades have focused on improving output, service delivery and efficiency through, for example, the introduction of output oriented budgeting and (increased) use of contractual mechanisms with service deliverers and agencies. These reforms have (usually but far from universally) been extended to senior civil servants, who have in many countries become subject to various forms of performance agreement, which specify targets that they are expected to achieve and which, to varying degrees, contribute to decisions about their financial or career rewards."

The OECD member and nonmember countries included in this report are Belgium, Brazil, Canada, France, Netherlands, South Africa, the United Kingdom, and the United States.

Key Findings from the Report's Executive Summary

- "Selecting the right staff in the first place is an absolute precondition for subsequent performance."
- "Senior civil servants are likely to be as motivated by promotion and by recognition from their peers and the public as by financial rewards."
- "Motivating individual senior civil servants to achieve targets is likely to have less impact on public sector performance overall than ensuring talented staff remain. Retaining good staff through adequate compensation, terms and conditions is a significant driver of performance."
- "Given the complexity of the linkages between individual and wider (government or ministry) performance targets, it is important that there is a clear 'line of sight.' Documentation and briefings should be adequate to ensure that senior civil servants can see the linkages between their targets and the higher level (and ultimately political) performance targets."
- "The most productive use of performance measurement is dialogue. For individual senior civil servants, clarity in performance expectations and regular opportunity for dialogue with the minister or Secretary General about obstacles or progress are the essential underpinnings of an effective focus on performance."

NOTES

1. Peter Drucker, "What Makes an Effective Executive?" *Harvard Business Review*, June 2004, 2–7.

2. Reported on GovExec website, "OPM: Not Every Senior Executive Is Outstanding," January 14, 2016.

5

Developing a Cadre of Effective Managers

The job of "manager" is in the spotlight. For decades the job was straightforward and narrowly defined. The day-to-day responsibility has been making certain the employees that managers supervise perform assigned tasks as expected. Responsibilities included planning staff activities, assigning new tasks, providing feedback, addressing performance problems, and trying to resolve employee concerns. Managers were in control and made all decisions. They had to "keep the machine running."

All of that began to change in the 1980s with quality management and its focus on front-line workers, followed by reengineering with small teams empowered to solve problems. A few years later knowledge jobs gained the spotlight. Today, we understand that culture and work environment can have a significant influence on a team's performance. We also know that workers can perform at significantly higher levels when they are engaged, have the skills, and are empowered to make job-related decisions. Managers are still responsible, but their value today lies in getting the best performance from their people.

Recent research confirms that managers have a greater impact on performance than any other factor, including senior executives. Managers create high-performing work teams. They are behind the growth and development of star performers. They are the keys to employee engagement. That's true in sports as well. When a truly great coach or manager moves to manage a new team in work as well as in sports, the performance of the new team improves, and performance of the old team typically declines. Their job now is to make the machine run better.

Some years ago a senior executive from Xerox, when it was still a high-performing company, told the story of how they had redesigned the operations of selected work units, adopting confirmed best practices, to raise performance levels—but the expected gains were not fully realized. They had failed to focus on the managers in charge. The best-performing units continued to perform better than others.

While the influence of managers can be highly positive, the potential negative impact has had much more research attention. There is an old saying, "People quit their bosses, not their jobs." That has been confirmed repeatedly in surveys. A 2015 Gallup survey found that roughly half of the people who responded quit "to get away from their manager."[1]

Government tends to have lower turnover rates than other industries—actually the rates have been roughly half as low when compared with industry patterns.

But that is not necessarily good. Turnover can be good if disgruntled or poor-performing employees resign. It's bad when the best employees quit. It's also bad when a disgruntled worker decides to stay because they have too much to lose or, worse, are unable to find a job that is sufficiently attractive or pays enough to justify resigning. If they feel locked in, their performance is likely to deteriorate, and their negative attitudes can carry over to other workers and lower everyone's morale. It's even worse when a poor-performing employee or "bad actor" cannot be terminated and continues in a job.

When all the costs of losing and replacing an employee are totaled, estimates from the private sector show it can easily be 150 percent of the employee's salary. It's higher for executives and managers.

Gallup and others have tracked the costs of disengaged employees (e.g., reduced quality, increased absences, lost customers, etc.). The total for the private sector is in the hundreds of millions. Comparable estimates for the public sector do not appear to exist. It's probably not possible for public employers to estimate the costs, but that does not deny they exist.

As the research shows, managers are the front line in building employee engagement as well as in undermining their commitment. The potential for improved performance as well as the cost of low morale makes this an important issue to consider.

SELECTION OF NEW MANAGERS

A problem common to both private and public employers is relying on outdated strategies for selecting new managers. Both, too often, base the selection of first-level supervisors on seniority and/or technical expertise. In effect, the promotions are a reward for performance in the prior job or for loyalty. Where selection is supposedly based on talent or potential for success, it's unusual to find the decision process has been validated. Few employers invest the time to confirm the abilities needed for success as managers.

Gallup lists five general talents important to being "great managers": they motivate their employees, assert themselves to overcome obstacles, create a culture of accountability, build trusting relationships, and make informed, unbiased decisions for the good of their team and company.[2] Their research in the business world shows that only one in ten managers have the full complement of talents.

Government is different in a key respect. New public employees commonly focus on having a successful career as a diplomat, a law enforcement officer, a social worker—any of the hundreds of job families represented in government. Relatively few have an initial goal of becoming a manager or executive. Among the most popular college majors, only criminal justice is directly relevant to the day to-day management of government operations.

There is experiential evidence that many public employees who reach the top of their career ladder are reluctant to become supervisors. They no doubt found the work they have been doing satisfying. They understand that the new job will be very different, but it is the only way to earn a higher salary. Too often new supervisors are provided minimal training, staff reductions have made the job even more difficult, and there are few rewards for being an effective manager. If they have worked under ineffective managers, they may not understand what is necessary for success.

In contrast, the most popular college major is business. Students majoring in business are far more likely to have a career goal of becoming a successful manager and executive. They have role models. MBA students sitting in class aspire to reach executive-level positions. They learn early what is needed to be successful and focus on developing their managerial competence. They invest energy in moving as quickly as possible to management positions. The rewards for success can be substantial.

On a related point, agency missions, cultures, and day-to-day operations vary dramatically. The skills and approach to be an effective supervisor in, for example, emergency management are not the same as in a library or in facilities management. The differences make it questionable to argue that the same supervisory/managerial style and competencies would be universally effective across government at any level.

In a corporate conglomerate, with multiple business units serving different markets and offering different products/services, each unit has the same core functions—marketing, accounting, and so on. While the cultural differences are significant, each business unit is dominated by the goal of achieving organizational performance goals. Actually each business function today has a distinct set of key performance indicators (e.g., HR metrics has become a leading-edge issue) that are largely the same across companies and industry sectors. And all functions are focused on the common need for profitability.

The differences suggest it would be useful for each agency to take the time to define the role of managers, what they are expected to do day-to-day, and to identify the competencies associated with effective supervision. That was what Google recently did, generating extensive media attention. Surprisingly, perhaps, Google and government both previously relied on a similar strategy for selecting new managers—in the past candidates were evaluated and selected based on technical expertise. Google now handles the selection of managers very differently.

GOOGLE'S ANSWER TO DEVELOP "BETTER BOSSES"

One of the earliest reports was a 2011 *New York Times* column, "Google's Quest for Better Bosses."[3] For years the company had a simple approach to supervision, as stated in the column: "Leave people alone. Let the engineers do their stuff. If they become stuck, they'll ask their bosses, whose deep technical expertise propelled them into management in the first place."

As the company grew, senior executives began to question if that was the right philosophy. They undertook a multiyear research project—Project Oxygen—that involved an intensive analysis of employee survey data, performance reviews, and focus groups.

The project led to a comprehensive program, built around eight key management attributes, Google's Rules for Managers, in order of importance:

1. Be a good coach: provide constructive feedback, with positive and negative, and meet one-on-one often.
2. Empower your team and don't micromanage.
3. Express interest in team-member success and personal well-being.
4. Don't be a sissy: be productive and results oriented.
5. Be a good communicator, and listen to your team. Communication is two-way.
6. Help your employees with career development.
7. Have a clear vision and strategy for the team.
8. Have key technical skills so you can advise the team.

The analysis was the basis for defining how Google managers are expected to manage their people. To highlight a key point, the company learned technical expertise was last on their list. The attributes have been incorporated into the selection process for new managers, training programs, and the performance-management system. It's been several years since the changes were adopted, and the company can point to statistically significant improvements in managerial effectiveness and performance.

The model for the managerial role is significant because it's based on internal information, collected directly from Google employees.

Many employers would have turned to books or articles from "experts" and adopted a generic management model. Those answers, however, often end up on a shelf and fail to gain acceptance.

Laszlo Bock, Google's head of "people operations," the company's HR office, has since published a best-selling book, *Work Rules! Insights from Inside Google That Will Transform How You Live and Lead.*[4] Mr. Bock was interviewed on TV, and the book was reviewed in the *New York Times, Fortune,* the *Wall Street Journal,* and a number of other publications.

The media coverage of the book is solid evidence that business now recognizes the importance of the human resource function. That point is worth repeating because it's all too obvious that government has not. When asked what makes Google special, Bock responded with, "It's our people." Many critics of government would not agree.

It's easy to argue, "Well, government is not like Google." However, the idea that employees in government are somehow different or would not thrive under supervision based on the Google philosophy lacks credibility. Thinking about this with an open mind, employees should be involved in discussions of effective supervisory practices. That makes sense for every employer. It does not have to be a multiyear,

WANT BETTER MIDDLE MANAGERS? THEN REDEFINE WHAT IT IS TO BE A GOOD ONE

by Thomas O. Davenport

In her recent *Wall Street Journal* article, Rachel Feintzeig quotes an AT&T executive on the importance of middle managers. "Who runs this company?" the executive asks. "We do, right here," is his answer.

He's exactly right. But when Stephen Harding and I wrote our book on the importance of middle managers—*Manager Redefined: The Competitive Advantage in the Middle of Your Organization*—we went farther. We said that managers are centers of insight and influence, underappreciated in many organizations, but endowed nonetheless with the potential to make dramatic contributions to enterprise success.

In most organizations, this potential remains untapped.

THE PROBLEM WITH MIDDLE MANAGERS

The simple truth is that many organizations have created middle-manager jobs that just can't be done well. The result is systemic manager frustration.

Data from Towers Watson's 2012 Global Workforce Study indicate that, worldwide, only 44 percent of managers describe themselves as highly engaged, compared with 59 percent of the executives to whom they report. The problems begin when companies promote their most technically expert contributors into manager roles. They believe (wrongly in most cases) that the most skilled expert will prove to be the best leader of other technical performers.

Because the new manager is a top producer, she finds herself acting as a player-coach, torn between leading and performing the same tasks done by those she leads. Also, because many organizations strive to become ever flatter, the new manager—already expected both to make widgets and to lead widget-makers—often takes on more employees to supervise.

The result is a manager who has neither the time nor the skill to create the productive workplace that employees demand. Little wonder managers say they are disengaged.

HOW TO MAKE THEM MORE SUCCESSFUL

What can organizations do to enhance manager morale and, more fundamentally, make them more successful?

The answer is simple but difficult: take the job apart and rebuild it. Identify what elements of the role make a real difference to corporate strategy and emphasize those. Revisit the competency model and refine what it really takes to be a good manager.

Rather than shifting administrative burdens from HR to managers, do the reverse—provide them with the support they need to engage their employees and ensure high productivity, and let HR worry about administration.

Certainly train them more and better, but first make sure that hiring and promotion processes put the right people into manager jobs that are structured to focus on what matters to the organization.

Thomas O. Davenport is a senior consultant with Towers Watson, a global human resources consulting firm, based in San Francisco. Davenport concentrates chiefly on helping clients improve the people-focused elements of business strategy implementation. He's also the author of two books: Manager Redefined: The Competitive Advantage in the Middle of Your Organization *and* Human Capital: What It Is and Why People Invest It.

statistical study. Nothing in the Google approach or their findings is incompatible with government.

Actually, the differences across government agencies make relying on a single model questionable. Separate studies in each agency could easily result in different profiles of the criteria defining how managers should interact with staff. Employee buy-in and acceptance of the criteria is far more important than any possible value in trying to impose generic, government-wide competencies. One-size-fits-all answers are rarely the best. The conclusions will no doubt always be very similar, but a question might be, "Why not allow that to emerge from separate agency analyses?"

Given the common characteristics of agencies that serve the same purpose (e.g., corrections, health, education, and others are very similar from state to state), it might make sense to undertake, for example, a multistate study, with the expectation that the conclusions will be used in each jurisdiction.

Bock is quoted in a *Wall Street Journal* article as saying, "Honestly, work just sucks for too many people." He goes on to argue that's not inevitable. With "better bosses," everybody wins, including the public.

GENERAL ELECTRIC REINFORCES THE IMPORTANCE OF COACHING

A separate development is GE's new approach for managing performance, "GE's Real-Time Performance Development,"[5] posted on the *Harvard Business Review* website. For the company now infamous for espousing the forced distribution or "rank-and-yank" approach to rating employee performance, this is a dramatic change.

The authors say: "At its core, the approach depends on continuous dialogue and shared accountability. Rather than a formal, once-a-year review, managers and their direct reports hold regular, informal 'touchpoints' where they set or update priorities that are based on customer needs. Development is forward looking and ongoing; managers coach rather than critique; suggestions can come from anyone in an employee's network."

The touchpoint discussions focus on progress in achieving goals, changing priorities, problems that need to be addressed, and resources that are needed. It's an ongoing dialogue that is future focused. They also discuss behaviors, or strengths, that should be continued and areas and ways to improve. The approach is consistent with a continuous improvement philosophy.

The new approach is discussed later, in the chapter on employee performance management (chapter 10). The point here is that the new approach emphasizes what is best understood as coaching. That is consistent with the first of the Google rules.

The goal is to coach employees to improve their performance going forward as well as developing their knowledge, skills, and abilities. It's intended as an ongoing process. That is a far more positive role for managers than the traditional year-end evaluation. It's similar to a coach in sports or a teacher, which is a role many enjoy playing. Managers coming out of a professional/technical field may need to develop new skills, but the transition will be to everyone's benefit.

PREPARING MANAGERS TO MANAGE

Technology is not going to solve government's performance problems. And practices like Six Sigma have a limited impact. There is a reason why the business media carry frequent articles on high performance, employee engagement, and the "best places to work." High performance is only possible when the workforce is engaged. Managers are the key. The potential gains from an empowered, engaged workforce far exceed the returns from technology or small gains in efficiency.

There is a sharp contrast between the old, over-the-shoulder supervisory role common throughout the last century and the approach that gains the best performance from today's knowledge workers. The gains come from creating a work experience that gives workers a sense of value and accomplishment.

Manager training has been evolving to reflect what we have learned about organizations and employee performance, but this is not at its core a training problem. It's been estimated that 70 percent of what we learn is on the job. Here the focus is on changing expectations, redefining the manager-employee relationship, changing both the message and the tone of daily interactions, and adopting new coaching behaviors. If the new approach and behaviors are not reinforced, they're likely to be dropped. Training is important, but this requires a broader change strategy.

Often the most difficult change is simply letting go—empowering workers to make job-related decisions. This will lead to innovation and new ideas, but it will also trigger occasional mistakes, so there is a risk, however small. Managers and employees both need to establish a high level of trust. That reinforces the importance of maintaining a dialogue to stay abreast of progress and problems. To emphasize the point, it's coaching, not control.

It may seem to be an overstatement, but there is an aspect of the Golden Rule. Managers and supervisors should consider how they would prefer to be supervised.

The change strategy also needs to involve employees as the other half of the relationship. They need to understand what to expect and what is expected of them. Effective supervision is best understood as a working relationship.

There will always be a need for managers to understand the basics like budget planning, but that's not the purpose of this book. A wealth of books and websites discuss those subjects. Virtually every university offers courses and workshops on public administration. Courses are also offered as part of Certified Public Manager programs.

All of this is unlikely to happen—actually, it would be impossible—without top management concurrence. Change is close to impossible without the solid, repeated support from leaders. They need to voice their commitment and make the changes a priority. They will need to explain why it's necessary and what they hope to achieve. They need to paint a picture of the future. That message has to cascade and be accepted at each level of management. When it comes from leaders, resistance is less likely.

The necessary changes to create a high-performance environment will also have to be accepted by the lowest-level employees. The Google "Better Bosses" project provides a model for understanding how they want to be managed. Simply asking employees what would make their jobs more satisfying and enable them to raise their performance levels is a conversation that should be received enthusiastically.

They should also be asked to play a role in evaluating and identifying ways to improve existing work processes. That will help to insure that they embrace and champion any changes. Employees can be asked periodically, perhaps annually, to comment on their work experience and the need for continued refinement. That will help to sustain their cooperation and commitment.

The conclusions from the information gathering should be provided to a task force of recognized, high-performing managers. They are well qualified to redefine the role of managers.

Additional groups can be asked to reconsider the selection process for new managers, necessary training programs, a career ladder for managers, and the performance-management system used with managers. Finally, the managers who exemplify the new approach to management should be recognized and rewarded. The best can be asked to coach others. Those who fail to change their behavior should be moved to nonsupervisory positions. Moving them out of supervisory roles will send an important message.

An often-unrecognized benefit of the changes is that both managers and employees should realize higher levels of job satisfaction, enjoy their work experience more, and develop better working relationships. No one enjoys working in a job where they know they are ineffective. Early successes will help everyone to be more open to the changes.

The changes will take a least a year, but moving more slowly than necessary may send the message that it's not a priority.

ADDITIONAL RESOURCES

McCorkle, Suzanne, and Stephanie Witt. *People Skills for Public Managers.* Taylor & Francis Inc., 2014.
Sampson, Stephen J., and John D. Blakeman. *Social Intelligence Skills for Government Supervisors/Managers.* HRD Books, 2006. These authors have similar books on Law

Enforcement Officers, Correctional Officers, and managers and supervisors in those agencies and in the Sheriff's Department.

Cohen, Steven, and William Eimicke. *The Effective Public Manager: Achieving Success in Government Organizations*. Wiley, 2013.

Durant, Robert F. *Why Public Service Matters: Public Managers, Public Policy, and Democracy*. Palgrave Macmillan, 2014.

DiTullio, Lisa. *The Government Manager's Guide to Leading Teams*. Management Concepts, 2014.

A number of books and websites discuss the skills and competencies needed to be an effective manager. An example is *Skills for New Managers* by Morey Stettner (Brief Case Books, 2000).

The Certified Public Manager (CPM) is a professional designation established for the purpose of improving performance and advancing best-practice standards for public sector managers. The CPM is a comprehensive management-development program based upon a selected set of competencies. The CPM is awarded upon completion of a CPM program accredited by the National Certified Public Manager Consortium. CPM graduates come from public, private, and nonprofit career fields. The programs are offered by a designated university in each state and vary somewhat from state to state.

NOTES

1. http://fortune.com/2015/04/02/quit-reasons/.

2. Gallup, op. cit.

3. "Google's Quest to Build a Better Boss," *New York Times*, March 12, 2011.

4. Laszlo Bock, *Work Rules! Insights from Inside Google That Will Transform How You Live and Lead* (New York: Grand Central Publishing, 2015).

5. https://hbr.org/2015/08/ges-real-time-performance-development.

6

Competing for Talent
Recruiting, Selection, and Onboarding

In early 2016 the national unemployment rate fell below 5.0 percent. It has not been that low since 2007. Economists argue that is the full employment level. In most large cities the rate is even lower. Critics contend that the official level understates the true picture, but nevertheless when unemployment is low, employers find it more difficult to recruit and retain qualified employees, and the competition for talent pushes salaries higher.

Projections show state and local governments will add more than 750,000 employees by 2024. Federal employment will fall slightly over the years. These are net changes; the added workers will offset the projected high retirement levels, deaths, and voluntary turnover. The anticipated job openings over the decade are much higher. Public employers will, for example, have openings for 230,000 social workers and 260,000 police officers. HR will be busy.

Budget problems will continue to deter adding new employees in many jurisdictions. But across the country, public employers with job openings will need to compete for talent. A 2015 survey by the Center for State and Local Government Excellence shows that 73 percent of the respondents hired employees, while only 11 percent maintained a hiring freeze.

Employees are not going to quit, regardless of how dissatisfied they may be, if no jobs are available. Older workers have been reluctant to retire in the uncertainty of the recession. However, retirement is inevitable. As Neil Reichenberg, executive Director of the International Public Management Association for Human Resources, stated, "You can delay retirement, but you can't delay aging." As the economy improves, many employees will look at their future prospects differently. Agencies have to be ready for what could be a significant loss of talent. (Chapter 8 focuses on strategies for managing an aging workforce.)

The fields where employment will grow fastest are those in health care and social services related to the country's aging population. Several of the occupations are prominent in state and local government. At the same time several occupations historically prominent in government will experience slower-than-average growth, including law enforcement, office support, librarians, and court services.

If agencies are to improve performance—or in agencies with heavy attrition, maintain performance levels—they will need to overcome the loss of talent and add staff and capabilities in fields important to the future. The demographics make this an unavoidable problem.

But it's more than numbers. Government in some states is managing its workforce in a time warp dictated by statutes now decades old. In contrast, in the private sector work-management practices have changed more in the past twenty years than in the prior century. In leading companies, the changes have contributed to a much more satisfying and productive work experience. They are seen as "best places to work" and "employers of choice." Civil service laws unfortunately impede similar changes in human capital management. Civil service reform has strong opponents, but it is clearly possible to protect worker rights and at the same time provide public employers the flexibility to compete for qualified talent.

As attrition increases, vacancies will need to be filled, especially in the management ranks. The recession and budget deficits have enabled public employers to ignore the demographics, but that cannot continue for long. (The demographics are discussed in chapter 8.) It would be decidedly advantageous to initiate a comprehensive review of employment practices before the increasing vacancies trigger agency problems.

The review should include the following steps: (a) anticipated workforce attrition for at least two years; (2) the supply of qualified job candidates in local labor markets; (3) the usual sources of applicants; (4) the "brand" of government as an employer; (5) historical times to fill vacancies; (6) the satisfaction of agency leaders and managers with the hiring process; (7) feedback from applicants and recent hires; (8) the performance of new hires; and (9) turnover rates for new hires in the first two years of employment. Metrics to assess performance have been developed for several steps. The review could also include a comparative analysis of market pay levels to determine if pay is an issue. It would be best completed by a task force of representatives of the major agencies. It should not be surprising to conclude from the review that hiring practices need to be overhauled.

WORKFORCE PLANNING

A basic step is anticipating retirements. It's straightforward to monitor employee ages; every manager should do that periodically to avoid the problems of an unexpected early retirement by a key employee and the loss of essential job knowledge.

The HR office should complete its own demographic analyses by age, occupation, and function at perhaps six-month intervals to know what to expect.

A number of public employers already offer some form of retirement counseling to employees who are approaching the age when they will be eligible. Offering counseling will help an employer track employees thinking about retiring. It's an inexpensive but usually greatly appreciated benefit.

The discussion of executive succession planning in chapter 4 is relevant also. Extending the practice to lower levels is an investment to avoid having vacancies stand open for extended periods.

In the same way, it's useful to monitor voluntary resignations to identify patterns by occupation, age, gender, and so on. It would also be useful to track trends of grievances, absences, and other indicators of dissatisfied employees—and poor supervisors.

In more "normal" economic times the pattern of turnover from the recent past can be used to predict the future. Since the recession, employee dissatisfaction has had several years to fester; morale is low. Employees may have stayed because there were few job openings in any sector. That will change if the economy continues to recover. Unfortunately, millennials who may not be encumbered with mortgages and large family expenses are likely to be among the first to resign.

Still, if someone on the staff is reasonably good with multivariate statistical analyses, and the demographic data are readily available, an analysis of voluntary resignations over the past two or three years should help to anticipate near-term turnover.

The "looking back" analyses should be combined with projections of future staffing needed to support new technology or equipment, and new organizational mandates. The needed staff should be specified in the plans prepared by managers across each organization.

For organizations that were forced to lay off staff or that have experienced heavy turnover or retirements, the workforce planning should also look at overtime hours and dollars. Overtime is frequently not managed closely, especially when employees have been denied pay increases. Unusually heavy workloads and overtime hours can be demoralizing if they continue for extended periods.

However staffing needs are anticipated, once the openings are posted and recruiting begins, if vacancies take more than a few weeks to fill, it would be advantageous to have available temporary or part-time people to fill in as needed. Asking coworkers to "fill in" when someone resigns can get tiring and exacerbate dissatisfaction.

WHEN THE "BRAND" OF GOVERNMENT IS A PROBLEM

Recruiting starts even before a job is advertised. Individuals planning their career or looking for a new job develop an impression about the type of employer they want to work for from media reports as well as from family members, friends, and as students from teachers. Job seekers today do their homework. Research has confirmed public employers broadly benefit from the attraction of Public Service Motivation, but then other employers also benefit society and offer attractive careers.

The PSM argument is best understood as an aspect of what is known as employer "branding." As the world of work has become increasingly transparent and people have learned how to research employers on the Internet, employers have become increasingly sensitive to how their jobs are perceived by prospective applicants. The business model of the websites Glassdoor.com and JobAdvisor.com is based on making "inside" information on an employer's work-management practices available to job seekers. It's very likely the availability of employer information will continue to increase.

Employer branding is similar to product marketing, with the goal of enhancing the image or reputation in the labor market. Marketers have for decades used marketing strategies to build brand awareness, loyalty, and trust to win the hearts and minds of consumers. Now HR practitioners are being increasingly called upon to use similar marketing skills to win the hearts and minds of employees and prospective applicants.

This is particularly important for public employers because (1) information is more readily available, often on public websites; (2) some elected officials and candidates for office have an unfortunate practice of making critical comments that are repeated by the press; (3) although not stated as criticism, when government work practices are better than those common in the private sector, the story is sometimes highlighted by the media; and (4) unions and other employee supporters respond to critics in a way that also highlights government practices. Unfortunately, information about the "warts" (e.g., the pay freezes) usually gets more attention than the rewards of public service.

Based on an employee's career plans and personal motivators, their prior work experience, and their sources of information about employers, job seekers will consider the alternatives convenient to them and decide to apply based on factors such as an employer's culture, its approach to workplace flexibility, or the perceived career opportunities it offers.

The emphasis on branding is largely responsible for the prominence of and media attention to the projects to recognize the "best places to work." There are now lists of the "best places" for virtually every industry, every major city, and a number of countries. At the federal level, the Partnership for the Public Service annually names the best agencies to work for. To this point no website recognizes the best state or local agencies.

Government leaders may not be comfortable "selling" the organization as a place of employment. However, if applicants are too few in number or not adequately qualified to fill vacancies, the answer is to develop a strategy to enhance the brand. It should be obvious that refraining from critical and counterproductive comments about employees is important.

Employees play a central role in defining an organization's brand as an employer. The 2013 Edelman Trust Barometer—Edelman is a global communications marketing firm (edelman.com)—found that the views of employees are a more trusted source of company information than the CEO. Employees are by far the trusted authority on a company's culture, integrity, working conditions, and related issues.

Edelman's research shows that "for those companies in which employees say their company is engaged in societal issues, we see a tremendous increase in employee engagement and business performance. For example, in companies engaged in societal issues, employees said they were more likely to

- "do the best job to serve the customer" (90 percent versus 78 percent for companies not engaged in societal issues),
- "recommend products and services to others" (87 percent versus 66 percent),
- "be motivated to perform" (84 percent versus 62 percent) and
- "recommend the company as an employer" (82 percent versus 57 percent).

It is reasonable to extend their findings to employees working in government and its engagement in societal issues. It is likely to be true that when government employees are satisfied with their work experience, they will also be solidly enthusiastic promoters of the organization as an employer.

It would be highly advantageous to emphasize policies and practices that contribute to a positive work experience. That is a thread running through this book. It is also a goal in committing to be an "employer of choice." That is the announced intent of Tennessee's state government and is discussed in a case study at the end of chapter 16.

It would also improve the brand to rethink the organization's website and the information applicants see when they research job opportunities and subsequently submit applications. That is the subject of the next section, on recruiting. Portraying an organization as important to society and as a good place to work is not costly.

When managed properly, the employer brand has significant benefit in helping to attract, retain, and engage the type of employees that organizations require to deliver success. The brand concept is at its core a communication problem and because of its importance is discussed again in chapter 14.

Possibly the best evidence of the importance of branding was the announcement by NASA of the number of applications for its next class of astronauts—18,000 applications for a class of 14. That is more than double the number in NASA's early years.

ELEMENTS OF A SUCCESSFUL RECRUITING STRATEGY

Successful recruiting, whether hiring from the outside or promoting from within the organization, requires several strategies operating in concert. The recruiting process is undergoing dramatic change. Unfortunately, some public agencies have not changed their recruiting practices in any meaningful way in years. Finding job postings in obscure countries is sometimes easier than in a couple of states.

This is in no way intended to be a "magic pill," but following are several core practices that will increase the likelihood for success:

- Managers, supervisors, and human resource staffs need a solid understanding of the organization's mission and core values. If these do not exist in written form, they should be developed and clearly communicated, since both are critical to the organization's ability to hire employees to provide public services. The mission and core values need to be strongly supported by elected officials.
- A generally competitive pay and benefits program needs to be in place that will allow the organization to compete for talent. Employees should understand the compensation philosophy and be able to expect that compensation will be managed consistently with the philosophy. To remain competitive, it is essential that comparative market analyses are conducted on a regular basis.
- The organization should have a strong affirmative action philosophy and policy that includes, but is not limited to, a strong commitment to diversity and inclusion.
- The organization should be proactive in the hiring, retention, and upward mobility of individuals with disabilities. Some organizations have taken specific actions to address this potential labor pool, including the states of Vermont, Washington, New Mexico, Florida, and Kansas.
- Talent-management practices should (1) anticipate employee attrition, including retirements; (2) assess individual capabilities and skill gaps; (3) support and encourage employees in developing their skills; (4) recognize and reward employee accomplishments; and employ other strategies that will allow the organization to hire/promote in a timely manner.
- A thorough understanding is needed of the labor markets for all positions in the organization, whether local, statewide, regional, national, or international. It is also important to identify the key competing organizations, public as well as private.
- In those organizations that have a "civil service" system, it is essential that the member agencies and bureaus understand how the system works and be proactive in identifying methods to work within the system, yet speed up the hiring process as much as possible.
- Where possible, current employees should be involved in developing recruitment strategies and invited to participate in the actual recruitment efforts. Recruiters understand the technical and legal side of recruiting, but people doing the work can often communicate more effectively with potential applicants. They will add credibility to the process. Companies are now adding videos of employees talking about their work experience in the "career" section of their websites.
- Where possible and practical, internship programs should be developed that may produce interns who want to work for the organization on a full-time basis. For example, internships can work well for engineers, attorneys, and research associates.

- Relationships with colleges and universities, as well as community colleges and technical schools, should be developed to keep them aware of vacancies and anticipated openings for new graduates. This also provides access to interested students. Also, for organizations with public safety employees, relationships should be established with military installations to communicate with personnel with requisite skills who expect to leave military service.
- A complete "game plan" should be developed for conducting specific recruitments. This increases awareness of what steps are planned and usually reduces the likelihood of missing critical steps. The plan for recruiting a key position, such as chief of police, is provided as an example at the end of the chapter.

An open question for recruiters is the strategy for posting vacancies. Several websites are widely used by government employers, including the International City/County Management Association and the League of Cities. The Leagues of Cities or Municipalities located in each state also post jobs. There are also Associations of County Commissioners in various states. At the federal level, the website USAJOBS.gov lists job openings.

In addition, there are numerous websites for specific occupational areas. The International Public Management Association for Human Resources has job listings for HR positions. The International Association of Chiefs of Police has job listings for upper-level law enforcement positions. Many states have state police chief associations with vacancy listings. North Carolina is an example. A number of other professional groups covering private sector and public employers also list vacancies.

Many jobs, however, are not listed on obvious websites or are common to many industries (e.g., technology jobs). Public employers have to be willing to post on commercial websites like Monster.com and Indeed.com. The cost is nominal compared to the "cost" of a job standing open for several months. Those websites generally will attract a broader mix of applicants, including many workers who may not have considered government in the past.

Regardless of where jobs are posted, it is important to evaluate the experience periodically. Is a source producing a sufficient number of qualified applicants? Are they being hired? Are they proving to be solid performers? Can they be retained for a reasonable period? Are they innovative?

It's also important to learn if managers are satisfied with the flow of applicants. Does the hiring process make good use of their time? It's also useful to invite applicant comments on the job posting as well as the recruiting and hiring process. If the answers are not positive, it may be time to reconsider how recruiting is handled.

Defining performance goals and metrics to track efforts to improve recruiting would be a proven strategy for HR. The data could include measures like diversity hiring.

Some employers still treat job postings the same way they used a bulletin board years ago. "Tacking up" a government job description is hardly an effective way to post vacancies. Public employers should consider innovative practices. Eleven practices that have recently emerged are summarized in "Emerging Practices to Improve Recruiting" (see pp. 65–66).

EMERGING PRACTICES TO IMPROVE RECRUITING

In early 2016 two prominent experts posted "best practice" ideas to attract applicants in the emerging tight labor market. Although their intended audience was presumably the private sector, the following are important to government agencies working to enhance recruiting.

- *A focus on employer branding will continue to grow.* Job seekers "will want to know as much as possible about the job, company, culture and corporate values." Employers should be prepared to have honest conversations about jobs and HR policies.
- *Anonymous resume screening and blind interviewing will be adopted.* With the pressure for increased diversity, selection is more objective when the personal characteristics of applicants are unknown. Internet questionnaires and telephone interviews help to avoid biases.
- *Increasing speed of hire will help to increase the quality of new hires.* The best-qualified applicants do not have to wait. Many are able to secure job offers and drop off applicant lists within ten days.
- *Referrals can be treated as an increasingly important source of new hires.* Employers identified as "best places to work" are able to rely heavily on referrals. Their employees are eager to "sell" the opportunities, and their referrals have high quality and high retention rates. Plus, the cost per hire can be dramatically lower.
- *HR should work to improve the candidate experience.* Employers are working to simplify the process to apply and to do a better job of staying in touch with applicants. The best practice now is to maintain contact with regular update messages. Those invited for interviews are given tours of work areas, presentations, and luncheons.
- *All recruiting applications and communications must be deliverable on a mobile platform.* Smartphones are widely used by job seekers to identify job opportunities. They are the primary way to apply, and many will reply far faster to messages and job offers if they can use their phones. They also make it possible to conduct video interviews.
- *Calculate the costs resulting from a bad candidate experience.* When applicants are dissatisfied with the way they are treated, they tell their friends and post negative comments on websites like Glassdoor.com. The result is fewer applications, especially if the experience is reported to college career centers.
- *Take a forward-looking approach to recruiting.* Initiating a study of those employees approaching retirement will make it possible to anticipate job openings. New analytical methods can also help to predict turnover.
- *Focus on recruiting innovators.* In reviewing applications, look for those where the individual demonstrates their aptitude for innovation. They tend to be more productive and are comfortable with change.
- *Improve the selling capability of your job descriptions.* Government job descriptions tend to be boring and reinforce the notion of bureaucracy. Allowing job incumbents to reword them will make them easier to read. Adding statements about the mission and performance goals makes the jobs sound more important.

- *Video becomes prominent in recruiting messages.* Videos of employees at work and discussing their work experience have been found to attract considerable positive attention. The technology makes it possible to move away from tedious, boring job descriptions. Videos can also be used in extending highly personal and inviting job offers.

Practices were selected from two websites:

http://www.shrm.org/hrdisciplines/staffingmanagement/articles/pages/5-recruiting-trends-2016.aspx and https://drjohnsullivan.com/articles/recruiting-trends-for-2016-and-their-supporting-best-practices.

ARE CIVIL SERVICE COMMISSIONS STILL NEEDED?

Friday, February 12, 2016, saw the end of an era in Wisconsin. That is the date the governor signed a bill rewriting "the state's 110-year-old civil service system by eliminating job applicant exams, centralizing hiring decisions within the governor's administration and tossing so-called bumping rights, which protect more senior employees from losing their jobs during layoffs" (reported by the Associated Press). That, of course, was preceded in 2011 by legislation that severely restricted the power of public sector unions in Wisconsin to bargain collectively.

Wisconsin is not alone. Arizona, Colorado, and Tennessee enacted reform legislation a couple of years earlier. Kansas was reported to be finalizing a legislative proposal. Early in the prior decade Georgia, Florida, and Texas also passed reform legislation. Others have adopted less comprehensive changes.

The talent-management goal is twofold: to enable agencies to hire and retain the best qualified applicants, and to manage careers to make the best use of individual capabilities. Despite the emphasis on "merit" in the early civil service legislation, few would argue that either goal by today's standards is well served. If anything, traditional civil service practices are a barrier to talent management.

The general idea of civil service legislation and a Civil Service Commission is at the heart of government's staffing problems. In large, diversified organizations no practical purpose is served by centralizing the hiring process. Nor does it make any sense to require a standardized approach to recruiting or selection. That also applies to standardized job descriptions, job classification and performance standards, or uniform pay levels across a state.

Government agencies have to compete for talent in many labor markets and in many locations. While the attention is often on the higher competition in urban areas, it can also be difficult to recruit qualified candidates to isolated, rural areas.

There will be times when an agency finds it difficult to recruit qualified candidates for a specific job. The high-skill, high-demand jobs where government competes with industry are an ongoing problem. Recruiting police is also an occasional problem. Agencies need to have the discretion to adopt new practices, including offering higher starting salaries when necessary.

The problems are exacerbated when hiring practices are dictated by statute. Competing for talent requires flexibility and an ability to change tactics in response to market developments.

There will always be concerns with patronage and discrimination. There can be no assurance that a newly elected governor or mayor will not push for changes that violate management principles or standards of fairness. Laws can always be changed; policies can always be ignored. When elections bring in new leaders, they should have the authority to appoint key people with the credentials to carry out the mandate espoused in the election campaigns. With the current emphasis on transparency and the many observers of government, there is little chance the heinous practices of the nineteenth century will reoccur.

When the federal government created the Office of Personnel Management and dissolved the Civil Service Commission in 1979, Congress also created the Merit Systems Protection Board (MSPB) to oversee HR practices and to ensure adequate protection for federal employees against abuses by agency management. The role of Inspector Generals at the federal level could also be adapted to "police" personnel actions. There are also, of course, federal and state employment laws today to protect employees from unfair practices. There are alternatives to the commission model.

An often overlooked problem that is common in organizations with strict civil service regulations is that managers are not truly "managing" their people. When they have no control over how the workforce is deployed, they cannot be held accountable for the unit's performance. Furthermore, if there is pressure to improve performance, they may not have the skills or the working relationships to make that happen.

Hiring managers should be involved in defining job requirements and in recruiting. They should also be able to involve coworkers. They know better than anyone the jobs, working conditions, sources for recruiting, labor markets, and so on. Working in partnership with HR specialists is a proven strategy in every other sector. When managers are involved, it is far more reasonable to hold them accountable for results.

That partnership is particularly important when recruiting for senior management positions and agency heads, where the job requirements are situationally defined. The "fit" with other leaders and managers is critical. To illustrate the care that should be taken, at the end of the chapter is an overview of the steps that might be followed to recruit a new chief of police.

There are a number of metrics to monitor hiring decisions. A unit like the federal MSPB or an office similar to the Inspector Generals can make certain the decision process is unbiased and satisfies requirements for diversity or other goals. It would also be advantageous for a central HR office to evaluate the effectiveness of the recruiting process—and to post the data as a way to avoid criticism and complaints.

Staffing is or should be a core concern for anyone concerned with good government. Ability to recruit and retain well-qualified new hires can have a profound impact on agency performance. Companies recognized as "best places to work" outperform other companies for a reason. It's at least in part attributable to the caliber of their people and the way they are managed. When highly qualified people are managed effectively, they can perform at significantly higher levels. Successful companies strive to be "employers of choice" for a reason. The strategy can work in the same way for government organizations.

It is highly unlikely that public employers operating with a civil service commission will be able to adopt the policies and practices of "employers of choice."

THE NEW EMPHASIS ON "ONBOARDING"

Since the earliest businesses, every new employee has passed through a transition from applicant to employee. For years this was referred to as "new employee orientation," but over the past decade or so that phrase has been replaced with "onboarding."

There are important differences between the old and the new. Orientation is a brief event, sometimes limited to the time it takes to sign necessary forms before the new employee is put to work. Onboarding is a process than can extend over weeks or months.

Reasons for this include the belief that new employees should be informed as much as possible regarding the culture of the organization and relevant performance expectations. A well-planned onboarding process helps avoid early resignations attributable to a lack of information employees should have had close to their start date. The process can also help to create productive working relationships with coworkers.

The actual onboarding steps will depend on the size of the organization, the level and status of the job, the number of employees in the same work area or building, the work shift, and any equipment relevant to the job. If the employee relocated and is new to the area, the process can include after-work steps to help the employee and family get settled. Here is a series of common steps:

- Provide current employees with information on the new person being hired; encourage them to spend time with him/her.
- Ensure the work location is as comfortable as possible and fully equipped.
- Send new employees essential information such as dress code and parking provisions.
- Have specialists from HR meet with the new employee to discuss subjects like training, benefit provisions, and options that will affect their family and work life.
- Ensure they understand how their job fits with broader work processes.
- Give the employee a tour of the work area and introduce the person to other staff, including managers as appropriate.
- Have the new employee participate in an orientation program.

CONNECTIONS, ONBOARDING, AND THE NEED TO BELONG

by Talya N. Bauer, Professor of Management and
Affiliated Professor of Psychology at Portland State University

I believe that relationships that connect us as human beings matter. In fact, belongingness theory says just that. Few would actively disagree with the statement that relationships matter. However, when it comes to onboarding, many organizations expect that a new employee's need to belong and to connect with colleagues will simply "work itself out" with time. It might—but then again, it might not.

I first became exposed to the three levers (confidence, clarity, and connection) of successful onboarding over twenty years ago as a doctoral student at Purdue University while studying research scientists working toward doctoral degrees in the "hard" sciences. Our early work indicated that these three levers are important keys to engagement, effectiveness, and retention of newcomers, and this has been confirmed by subsequent research. These levers are three of the five C's of onboarding (which are compliance, confidence, clarity, connection, and culture). Helping new employees feel more confident, have greater role clarity, and feel more connected all matter. *But when individuals feel more accepted and connected to those around them, it is easier for them to ask clarifying questions and gain confidence.* Thus, when I am working with organizations to help them maximize their onboarding program success, I recommend that after they have dealt with the basics of strong onboarding, they focus on specific ways to help new employees feel welcome and to jump-start the process of their connections even before they arrive on the first day on the job.

The manager holds a special key to the connection process. Sushil Nifadkar of Georgia State University and I studied new software engineers in India, which resulted in a paper in the *Journal of Applied Psychology* titled "Breach of Belongingness." We found that being unable to establish meaningful connections with coworkers led new engineers to seek less information. However, if the new engineer and his or her manager were able to connect, the newcomer could overcome this hurdle even in the face of conflict with coworkers. In other words, the relationship the new employee has with his or her manager really mattered, as it helped the new employee feel like they belonged somewhere in the organization. This relationship enabled them to freely seek information from the supervisor and hence succeed in the organization.

So hopefully I've convinced you that when it comes to onboarding success, relationships matter. Relying on new employees to "sink or swim" when it comes to connecting with coworkers and managers is a risky strategy. Organizations can help new employees maximize success by engaging in onboarding best practices that I have developed based on research on new employee success. I hope you find them useful.

Talya N. Bauer is Professor of Management and Affiliated Professor of Psychology at Portland State University. She is an award-winning researcher and teacher who is a recognized leader in understanding the socialization and onboarding of new employees. She specializes in relationships at work and how they influence individual and organizational effectiveness and well-being during the employment life cycle.

Table 6.1. Onboarding New Employees

Best-Practice Checklist for Fostering Connection

☐ *Make the first day special for new employees.* Meet with them, make sure someone takes them to lunch, and that the atmosphere is welcoming. This simple connection matters for success over the long run.
☐ *Recognize that the manager plays a special role.* Make a special effort to connect with the new employee on their first day of the job, even if it's just to say hello and welcome.
☐ *Check in with new employees to make sure they have what they need on their first day* as well as a week later when new questions may have arisen.
☐ Remember new employees are anxious to make a good impression. *Tell them how happy you are to have them join your team.* Doing this early on has a much bigger positive impact than waiting until later.
☐ New employees need to learn specific rules and procedures. *The most effective way to do this is to get them comfortable with the other best practices so they are receptive and able to focus on learning.*
☐ *Be consistent with onboarding practices for new employees.* Some issues about your organization may be "old news" to you, but it's all new to them. Have a written onboarding plan in place and enact it every time.
☐ *Make sure your values and culture are projected in how you treat and greet new employees.* Stories tell who you are.
☐ *Establish time-based milestones to check in with new employees to see how things are going.* For example, 30-, 60-, 90-, and 180-day milestones are good markers to consider.

- If not done in the interviews, provide information on expectations and work processes.
- Conduct job-related training.
- Where possible and practical, provide a mentor.
- Tour the surrounding work areas.

The goal is to make a new employee as productive as possible, as quickly as possible.

One of the recognized experts in this new area is Talya Bauer. She suggests that the process should focus on the three C's—confidence, clarity, and connectness. She emphasizes the importance of building relationships (see p. 69 and Table 6.1).

Onboarding is best when it reflects a philosophy that sends the message "You are now part of 'our family.' We want you to be successful and to feel your contribution is valued. We know the first few days and weeks are somewhat stressful and want to make you confident you made a good choice in working here."

ADDITIONAL RESOURCES

Blake, Jeff H., Heidi Sutherlin, and Nancy Pile. *Hire for Higher Performance: The Best Hiring Practices to Boost Business Results, Increase Employee Engagement, and Advance Your Own Career.* Amazon Digital Services LLC, 2016.

Heneman III, Herbert, Timothy Judge, and John Kammeyer-Mueller. *Staffing Organizations.* 8th ed. McGraw-Hill Education, 2014.

Barrett, Katherine, and Richard Greene. "Can Government Hiring Get out of the Stone Age?" Governing.com. February 2016.

http://www.eeoc.gov/employees/index.cfm. This website provides a basic understanding of federal employment laws and the EEOC approach to enforcement.

http://www.siop.org/Workplace/employmenttesting/overview.aspx. The website of the Society for Industrial and Organizational Psychology provides a great deal of current thinking on the use of tests in employee selection.

http://media.eremedia.com/uploads/2015/09/03122304/ERE-Benchmarking-Metrics-v2 .pdf?submissionGuid=f6695510-269d-4442-94c4-80aa31f89887. This website provides a long list of the metrics developed to monitor performance in recruiting and staffing.

MODEL RECRUITMENT PROCESS
FOR A CHIEF OF POLICE

The following is an example of a comprehensive recruitment process. The position to be filled is Chief of Police for a municipal unit of government. This is an example only. Also, this example is written as if the work is being conducted by a consultant. The approach could be modified to be used by internal staff. Organizations have to decide what works best for them; however, it is noted that the steps included in this example have been used by many organizations and consultants with substantial success. It is also noted that this "model" can be modified and used for other key positions.

Outline of the Recruiting Process

The recruitment process includes, but is not necessarily limited to, the following steps to achieve the goal of attracting a qualified applicant pool for the position and to identify the best-qualified candidate.

Phase 1—Background Review

- Meeting held with the City Manager and other key staff to review and agree upon the action plan for the search.
- Review of the job descriptions for senior positions in the department, its organizational chart, and operating procedures. A tour should be conducted of the Police Department.
- Meeting with Police Department command staff.

Phase 2—Development of the Employment Profile

The profile will include basic information about the city of _____ and the Police Department. The primary information is (1) anticipated law enforcement issues confronting the city and the department for the next three to five years; (2) the role of the Chief of Police; (3) major departmental objectives; (4) desired professional experience; and (5) personal characteristics.

The steps in developing the profile are shown below. Meetings will be held with the following to obtain their input for the profile:

- Mayor and council members (small group or individual meetings)
- City Manager
- One or more community representative focus groups. Representatives to be appointed by council and/or City Manager.
- Current or former Chief of Police
- Other command staff of the Police Department
- Focus group of noncommand-level and civilian employees in the Police Department
- Key city department heads (group meeting)
- Other law enforcement officials in the general area
- Others as deemed necessary
- An option for citizens not participating in focus group meetings is to make available an electronic input process on the city's website.
- Draft an employment profile to be developed and approved by the City Manager.
- The profile is to be printed and used in the recruitment and selection process. It is recommended that copies be provided to those persons who participated in the input process and to all employees in the Police Department. The profile will also be accessible through the city's website.

Phase 3—Advertising and Networking Process

- Consultant to prepare ads for review and approval of the city and post ads on various websites and in publications approved by the city.
- Recommended advertising sites include:
    (The sites are to be determined by the competitive geographical area identified for the position and where it is felt advertising efforts will be successful. For illustration purposes, assume the search is nationwide in scope.)
    o National law enforcement professional organizations
    o Chief of Police Associations in [State] and other designated states
    o [State] League of Municipalities
    o [State] Association of County Commissioners
    o City's website
    o Other sources as may be identified by the city
- Consultant will network with other law enforcement jurisdictions and organizations to identify possible candidates.

Phase 4—Application/Resume Screening Process

- Consultant to conduct an initial review of all applications/resumes received, with the objective of identifying the top twelve to fourteen candidates. Consultant may contact these candidates by telephone to obtain additional information.
- The preliminary list of candidates, with applications/resumes, and a brief written candidate profile, will be reviewed with the City Manager and other key staff as determined, with the objective of identifying a smaller number of the best-qualified candidates whose credentials meet those identified in the employment profile, and who will continue in the process.
- Upon approval by the city of candidates to proceed, the consultant will develop and transmit an in-depth questionnaire relevant to key components of the position to each candidate in order to obtain additional information. Upon receipt of the completed questionnaires, the consultant will conduct a preliminary (telephone) interview of each candidate. The City Manager will be encouraged to participate in the telephone interview.
- The consultant will conduct a preliminary Internet search of information relevant to these candidates.
- The completed questionnaires, telephone interview results, and other information will be reviewed with the City Manager for approval of those candidates who will undergo the next step, which will include an assessment center, in-depth interviews, and other exercises if so determined. The City Manager may wish to talk with each of the finalists by telephone prior to conducting the formal interview/assessment and final selection process.

Phase 5—Interview/Assessment and Final Selection Process

- City to approve dates of the interview/assessment process and members of the interview panel. The consultant to work with the city in identifying a panel of assessors, which is recommended to include outside law enforcement officials and city administrators, in addition to others that may be identified.
- The consultant to develop interview/assessment exercises, including interview questions and dimensions to be rated, subject to approval by the City Manager. It is recommended that at a minimum, there be an in-depth interview of each finalist by a panel to determine the candidate's technical qualifications and their ability to work within the organization and community ("fit" and "chemistry"). It is also recommended that the city consider having each candidate complete a written exercise and make an oral presentation to a hypothetical group (internal panel) on a topic relevant to the city and the Police Department.
- Conduct the assessment center with each candidate.
- Identify one or more finalists to continue in the selection process.
- It is recommended that an in-depth background investigation of one or more finalists be conducted by a licensed private investigator. It is also recommended that a polygraph examination be conducted by a licensed polygraph examiner of

the same candidates. The consultant will assist the city in identifying a private investigation firm and polygraph examiner, both of whom will be independent contractors to the city.

- The city may also wish to have one or more personality profiles completed by finalists continuing in the process.
- Follow-up interviews to be conducted as determined by the city.
- On-site background checks of outside finalist(s) to be conducted by city staff. The consultant to participate if determined by the city.
- Decision by the city regarding the successful candidate and job offer. The consultant to assist the city in developing the job offer.
- After acceptance of job offer by the successful candidate, decision to be communicated to all concerned parties.
- Consultant to provide suggested "coaching tips" for the city to use with the new chief.
- Consultant to provide feedback to finalists not selected for the position.
- Unsuccessful applicants to be notified.

Note: Meetings should be held with the City Manager to provide search process updates and facilitate the completion of the search process. Written reports provided where appropriate.

7

Investing in Workforce Capabilities

At one level, training departments have changed little since they were first created in the years after World War II. Formal, "classroom" training is still the dominant method. At another level, learning and the role of training specialists are undergoing a more rapid transformation than any other HR area. The urgency for revitalizing workforce development in the public sector is aligned with the rapid change in workforce demographics. With the impending retirement of large numbers of baby boomers, it is imperative that executives pay attention to this inevitable change in the development needs of the future face of the workforce.

One strategic move in the training industry is to move past the "check the box" view of workforce development to create a learning-centric environment within the organization. Removing event-based language such as "training" and replacing it with learning and development workshops instills a new message in how to view employee growth opportunities. This type of approach creates a lifelong learning mindset and promotes learning and development as the norm rather than as an event.

Technology is central to this transformation. The use of technology can facilitate important changes in learning. Central to these changes is the ability of workers to share their work-related problems and experiences with others through platforms such as chat rooms and discussion boards, by working and learning collaboratively to find solutions to problems.

Not too many years ago e-learning approaches were new, but recently a "legend" in the field of learning, Dr. Clark Quinn, referred to them as "knowledge dumps tarted up with trivial interactions." The use of technology now should focus on the best way to facilitate the acquisition of needed employee capabilities.

The latest development is the emergence of internal collaboration platforms referred to as Enterprise Social Networks (ESNs) that support and encourage collaboration and knowledge sharing among employees. The ESNs are important because:

- learning for these employees is now integral to doing their jobs;
- they enable peers to share their thoughts and to learn from each other;
- work-related "knowledge" is readily available and not a separate resource; and
- "learning" is no longer a process controlled by HR or limited to a learning-management system.

The development of ESNs represents a significant change that could diminish HR's role or change HR's role to one of support and coordination for workers, thus, HR remains in a transactional state of existence. ESNs enable workers to learn from coworkers and to do so across the country. This potential threat to HR's value is minimized when HR takes a strategic approach to fostering workforce development. This requires a proactive approach to leading learning versus administering training, a subtle but critical change.

ESNs have enormous potential to overcome what has been "the dirty secret" of training—the forgetting curve. When employee development is relegated to a training event, the transfer and application of learning is minimized. The numbers from studies over the years vary, but it's unavoidable that much of what people "learn" in training is forgotten very quickly. To highlight how costly the problem is, the estimates are that people forget 50 percent of what they learn in one hour, 70 percent by the next day, and 90 percent-plus within a week. There are strategies to enhance retention, but employers are wasting a significant portion of the money spent on training. It has been described as "pumping gas into a car that has a hole in the tank."

The studies behind those numbers, however, were conducted in traditional training sessions. With ESN technology, new knowledge and skills are immediately used, and the value of the knowledge and skills is reinforced. Moreover, it's far from passive; individuals have an immediate need and are actively seeking the knowledge. Workers realize the value of what they learn in their satisfaction in solving a problem and their improved performance.

Another relevant approach to learning is experiential learning. This type of learning provides workers with immediate application and transfer of knowledge and skills through the use of case studies, on-the-job scenarios, and skill practice. Experiential learning provides real-time value for workers as they learn together in a collaborative setting while sharing best practices and problem-solving solutions.

THE CENTRAL IMPORTANCE OF
CREATING A LEARNING ORGANIZATION

In 1990, an MIT professor, Peter Senge, published a landmark book, *The Fifth Discipline: The Art and Practice of the Learning Organization*, that described organizations as dynamic systems in a state of continuous adaptation and improvement to survive and prosper in a continuously changing world. His book and argument spawned global interest in the idea of a learning organization where management and employees are continuously working to create, acquire, and disseminate knowledge.

STATEMENT BY THE TENNESSEE
STATE CHIEF LEARNING OFFICER

Implementing initiatives that provide continuous learning opportunities is no longer a luxury, but a necessity. As Chief Learning Officer for Tennessee, I have the privilege of collaborating with leaders to focus on how we can create a learning community within state government. An organization that focuses on creating a learning community differs from a more traditional organization by adapting to a changing culture, attracting and retaining a talented and committed workforce, embracing diversity and innovation, and promoting emphasis on learning and growth. Perhaps most telling is that learning organizations do not stifle creativity but create a culture that invites it. Learning organizations assume that learning is an ongoing process, not simply one-time events. Learning becomes part of an overall strategy founded on the concept of continuous improvement. Learning becomes part of the very culture of the organization, a way of life for all employees. Learning is not just for a select few, but learning opportunities are created for all members of the organization, holding to the belief that enormous human potential lies locked and undeveloped in the organization.

A strategy for creating a learning community is essential for state government. To meet the challenges of a rapidly retiring workforce, a shrinking labor pool, and the loss of critical institutional knowledge, we collaborate with executive state leadership, embracing the department commissioner's vision for learning and development for state employees.

Dan LaFontaine coined the famous movie trailer phrase, "In a world where . . ." Now, imagine a world where public service organizations offer learning and development programs that are not seen as check-the-box, "been there, done that" events. Rather, learning communities are established, and continuous improvement is central to the cultural mind-set.

Learning is ongoing, and one never truly stops developing in the knowledge and skills needed to become more efficient and effective. And if learning and development can extend beyond the workplace and reach out to the community at large, then such programs truly model the very idea of a public servant. Enjoy the many opportunities the state offers for growth and development!

Note: This was extracted from a statement by Tennessee's Chief Learning Officer that serves as the introduction to the state's training resources.

That was the precursor for what today is a knowledge organization in which employees generate, transform, manage, use, and transfer knowledge to achieve organizational goals. Knowledge workers have been described as those "who have to think for a living," and increasingly the phrase encompasses all workers empowered to address day-to-day problems.

All of that is in direct contrast to the climate in a bureaucracy where workers only have to know how to perform their job but have no need to understand how their performance contributes to the mission of the organization or even if the organization is succeeding. In a bureaucracy the focus is on efficiency in a stable world.

Employees are "cogs" in work systems controlled by management. A major failing of a bureaucracy is its inability to change and adapt to its environment and respond to new problems.

All of that sounds highly conceptual and theoretical but is central to creating a high-performing organization where employees have knowledge and skills and are empowered to tackle problems. A high-performing organization is broadly synonymous with a learning organization. Employee capabilities are central to high performance. But it's more than increasing their knowledge and skills. To raise performance levels, they need to know they are expected to try new approaches and will not be disciplined for failed initiatives if their reasoning is sound.

To quote a frequently cited story about GE's former CEO, Jack Welch, when an employee made a costly mistake and assumed he would be fired, Welch is reported to have responded, "Hell no, I just invested $5 million in your development."

A key philosophical issue is the shared commitment to managing and leading employees as assets that warrant ongoing investment to increase their value and not as costs to be minimized.

Where learning is a core value and an organizational priority, HR and the training and development (T&D) staff have an opportunity to define a broader, more proactive role to support employee growth and career advancement. Rebranding training and development would be critical to change the mind-set, and thereby the culture, of how a workforce approaches learning and growing on the job. The T&D team can play a role in several ways:

- Work with managers and subject matter experts (SMEs) to identify current and emerging job-related competencies and develop competency profiles for job families and career stages.
- Collaborate in developing a performance-management system that facilitates the assessment of individual competence, and strengths and weaknesses relative to the job profiles.
- Create the building blocks of the learning organization: a supportive learning environment, concrete learning processes and practices, and leadership behavior that provides reinforcement.

THE GOAL IS IMPROVED PERFORMANCE

One of the themes highlighted in the *ASTD Handbook* on training (see Additional Resources at the end of the chapter) is a shift "from learning to a focus on improved performance." The point is that training is best managed as a "means to an end," and the end goal is improved performance.

For over half a century the impact of training has been evaluated using the Kirkpatrick model. The measurement scale is defined at four levels, with the third level defined as applying learning to influence job behavior and the fourth achieving targeted results. The model was enhanced recently to emphasize the importance of monitoring and reinforcing the application of new knowledge and skills on the job. The revised model also makes it important at the fourth level that training impacts the employee's performance.

At the fourth level the value of training is conceptually based on a return-on-investment comparison of the cost of the training with the benefit in dollars to the organization.

The new focus starts with defining the results an employee is expected to produce, based on performance metrics, and then relying on the best-performing employees as SMEs to understand the best approach to perform at a high level. The SMEs are in the best position to understand the context in which work is done. The training is then planned to reinforce the behavior associated with desired results. The learning process should mirror the way high performers do the job and include practice of key tasks.

A focus on performance makes it important to assess the results within the context of the work environment. Employees, of course, do not work in isolation. Their performance is influenced by several factors in addition to their knowledge and skill. Those factors include the culture and work-group norms, the technology, the work process/system design, the supervisory style and effectiveness of the immediate supervisor, and recent actions by top management (e.g., a pay freeze).

The factors beyond training need to be considered in planning and evaluating the need for training. It's not that all the issues can or should be addressed as an all-inclusive project, but it may be that training will prove to be wasted if employee performance is controlled by other factors. The SMEs are in the best position to identify the issues that could undermine the value of training.

THE FLEXIBILITY OF BLENDED LEARNING

New but yet-to-be-evaluated technology applications are mushrooming. Technology obviously will be playing a prominent, no doubt increasing, role in the future of training. It disseminates information quickly, consistently, and inexpensively to large audiences. It also has the flexibility for individuals to pursue learning in their own time and place. But it has limitations; it limits interaction and has little promise to motivate behavior or attitude change. Traditional classroom training, mentoring, and coaching—person to person—will always be important in certain situations. That should not be forgotten.

The key is planning the right combination or "blend" of classroom and technology-based learning. The leading edge for planning training sessions is to rely on a version of Benjamin Bloom's "taxonomy of educational objectives" to break down a session into its component educational objectives and decide how best to achieve the objectives. The objectives state what those involved in the training should be able to do at the end of the program.

Bloom's taxonomy builds from the simplest to the most difficult and includes knowledge, comprehension, application, analysis, synthesis, and evaluation. Variations have been proposed, but this is a good framework for this discussion.

Everyone remembers the tests of "knowledge" in school where good grades depended on recalling facts from memory. When that is the objective, the training can rely on self-directed, self-paced, technology-based modules. Countless people can open the program and only have to listen. The goal is best understood as the dissemination of information. Unfortunately, many "training" programs fall into this category. This is what is referred to as "check-off-the-box" training.

At the next level, "comprehension," program participants are expected to demonstrate their understanding by explaining the subject to others. In school those open-ended questions were intended to test comprehension, although a student with a good memory who could dump memorized material was able to get a good grade. It's difficult to confirm true comprehension. When training programs end with a well-considered test, comprehension can be confirmed.

The objective of "applying" is to have learners use what they learn "to do something." Typically, training programs at this level involve interaction and discussion among participants. They also need time and appropriate situations to practice. Training that involves a virtual classroom can be effective for many subjects, like developing skills to use a new computer program.

"Analysis" involves breaking a problem or complex task into component parts to learn how they interrelate and relate to a purpose. Success at this level enables someone to use their knowledge to solve other, similar problems. For teenagers learning to drive it involves the understanding of how to react to different traffic situations. Both virtual and actual classrooms can play a role. Practice is essential, along with exposure to somewhat different situations.

A level that is sometimes dropped in articles is "synthesis," which refers to the ability to use knowledge and skills to produce variations or modified ideas or mental models. It's the extension of understanding from one domain to others. Words like *create*, *devise*, and *invent* are used in discussions where an individual is using his or her past learning experiences to address new problems.

At the "evaluation" level, learners develop the ability to make sound, reasoned decisions based on what they know. In an organization, only people with experience are normally trusted to make decisions. (Those with a lower level of knowledge may develop information to be used by decision makers.) Decision makers have to be able to understand and interpret information and apply their knowledge to make decisions. This level of learning has to be taught in a collaborative setting.

True expertise is needed for what has been suggested as an added level, "creating," where knowledge is used to formulate new theories, or in a field like medicine, to plan new treatments. Few training projects would have the goal of creating something new.

The point is that technology is well suited to certain training objectives but that interaction either with an instructor or with other participants is essential to achieve higher-order objectives. In planning training programs, it is important to consider what level of knowledge is needed. In many situations technology can be used effectively to provide important background information. Of course, the questions are not limited to whether technology should play a role. Technology makes it possible to provide training for employees in multiple locations and avoid travel costs. Blended training does complicate the planning, but it can assure leaders that the training will be delivered cost-effectively. A possible problem is that until the program developer gains appropriate experience and skill with blended programs, the planning will take longer, and early efforts are not likely to be successful.

Technology will unquestionably play an increasing role in the future of training and development. New applications will undoubtedly continue to be developed. Actually, the potential for employees to learn from each other or from those distant and even unaffiliated (e.g., professors) by relying on the broadest variations of ESNs is unlimited. At the same time there is a continuing role for instructor-led programs and for participants to be able to discuss the material and learn from collaboration. The problem will continue to be how to best combine the two alternatives into successful programs.

The most meaningful test of program effectiveness is evidence that the experience leads to improved job-related knowledge and skills, and over time, improved performance.

ASSESSING TRAINING NEEDS

Employee training has long reflected the idea of a curriculum in education. Every "student" has to take predefined courses. Some subjects, to be sure, are important to all (or certain job families) of employees. The introduction of new policies falls into that category. Announcing a reorganization would also be relevant to broad groups. Except for those whose day-to-day jobs will be altered by the changes, their need falls under the first level of Bloom's taxonomy—knowledge. The changes announced are necessary and represent a nominal cost.

Employees whose jobs are directly affected and will have to apply new knowledge in their work lives will need a higher level of training.

The curriculum approach also suffers from another flaw. It assumes all employees have the same training needs and that a "talking head" instructor can be a universal source of knowledge. More importantly, making the change simply as an announcement ignores the possibility that people can learn from each other.

Many organizations have treated the onboarding of new employees as well as the training of new supervisors or the introduction of new HR policies as one-way communication, the most basic form of training. It is learning at the "knowledge" level. If that is the thinking behind, for example, onboarding practices, it may explain a number of organizational problems.

Training intended to support the development of new capabilities or ways of working is best managed as an investment. It is an expense that is warranted only when it's instrumental in avoiding or solving problems. As with any investment, the expected payoff—the return—has to offset the cost of the training. Successful training starts with an assessment to understand the nature of problems and the employees who would benefit.

Training-needs assessment is also needed to obtain top management's agreement to make the investment and the local manager's concurrence with the time and cost of proposed training. The training has to enable the manager to generate improved results. The assessment should include an estimate of the costs and the time that will need to be invested. It's necessary to convince management that the training will benefit the organization.

Training for new hires or recently promoted employees should start with job analysis and a job description. If the job description is current, it could possibly be updated and augmented with interviews or surveys of incumbents. At the executive level, it's common in larger companies to rely on assessment centers.

For lower-level employees the performance-management system should be planned to produce data relevant to individual training needs.

Training intended to develop new individual capabilities needs to be supported with time to practice. The new knowledge or skills will need to be refined and possibly assessed again. Employees should also have the benefit of coaches. A good analogy is a training camp for football teams or spring training in baseball.

If the goal is to improve performance, the goal should be to support employees in improving their skills. A culture that values learning is important. The goal also makes it important to focus on the skills known to be important to performing at a high level. That is a subject best addressed by senior, recognized high performers serving as subject matter experts.

DEFINING THE ROLE OF SUBJECT MATTER EXPERTS

High-performing job incumbents are well qualified to serve as SMEs in defining training needs. They bring to the problem an understanding of the knowledge and skills needed to perform at high levels as well as the other factors affecting employee performance. A small team of incumbents from the same job family can complete their work in two or three meetings.

They can be asked to develop a profile of occupation-specific competencies to be used in appraising performance and in defining individual strengths and weaknesses.

To provide continuity, similar groups should be asked annually to consider how changing agency goals and new technology have changed training needs. Their experience will enable them to prepare their assessments based on current performance concerns.

They have the unique advantage of discussing the issues with coworkers prior to their more formal role of assessing emerging training needs. When they return to their work units, they will be credible sources reporting what transpired. In that regard they can become a trusted communication channel.

MANAGERS PLAY A CENTRAL ROLE

Yes, the statement is correct: "employees need to be responsible for their own development." It's become close to a mantra. A Google search produced thirty-two million hits.

It's certainly accurate. Every teacher can attest to the problems disinterested students pose. Lack of motivation can be a problem in every situation where people are expected to learn.

But all the evidence suggests people want to have jobs where they can grow and develop. That thread runs through virtually every discussion of motivation. Growth means career progress, recognition, and increased satisfaction. It also means employees will be receptive to added responsibilities.

Managers are a key. Empowerment is fundamental to growth. Encouragement to take on new problems is important. Honest feedback and coaching are valuable. Trust is essential.

Their assessment of employee strengths and weaknesses is the basis for individual development plans, which set the stage for continued employee development.

Individual managers can create a learning environment, but top management leadership is needed for a learning organization. When leaders make it a priority, every manager is likely to get on board. Many will need coaching to change their management style. The best should be recognized and rewarded to reinforce top management's commitment. But they can expect to realize increased satisfaction from the improved performance and the increased engagement of their people.

NEW POSITION?—LEARNING EXPERIENCE MANAGER

The need for a chief strategist is critical if an organization is seeking to transform itself and the workforce. The commitment to learning and learning strategies begins at the top of an organization and is cascaded down throughout the organization. When this happens, learning and development move beyond the "training" approach and become a key in the strategy to accomplish organizational goals and strengthen the skills and abilities of the workforce.

The consulting firm DDI posted a couple of blogs in early 2016 on the need to rethink the traditional foundation of leadership training and development. The first was titled "Kim Kardashian, Twitter and Leadership." The second was "Why You Need a Learning Experience Manager." Their focus is on leadership development, but their argument is relevant to the broad training and development field.

It's widely understood that in tough times training budgets are among the first to be cut. The problem, of course, is that many training programs have minimal or uncertain business value. It would be instructive to learn how many employers in all sectors cut their training budgets in the year or two following the 2008–2009 recession. It would be even more telling to learn how many have restored the funds to prerecession levels.

It is, of course, completely reasonable for organizational leaders to initiate cuts in any budget that is not clearly contributing to better performance. In the public sector, it would be impossible to show that expenditures for training and development are offset by financial gains or savings. But it is also not enough to ask program participants if they "liked the experience."

In other areas "quality control" has been widely accepted for years. Financial functions have auditors. Marketing research people measure the impact of ads. Proofreaders are common in publishing. Quality control managers are virtually universal in manufacturing. Court systems provide for appeals. Recently (as discussed in chapters 10 and 11) companies have formed calibration committees of managers to review performance ratings and pay increases to minimize bias and increase the perception of fairness.

Here it might be advantageous to separate the specialists who plan and deliver learning programs from those who evaluate them. The new role would report to the Chief Learning Officer and focus on identifying training needs and evaluating the impact of training. The title might be "Learning Experience Manager." The function could also be responsible for evaluating developments in the use of technology. That dichotomy is similar to the distinction between budget planning and auditing. It's similar to the common divide between production planning and quality control.

Experienced trainers naturally tend to think they are effective and to be more comfortable with traditional methods. The DDI blogs make the point that the field is "more limited by our imagination than the technology itself." This is a time of breakthroughs in the use of technology. The authors cite the use of Google searches—3.5 billion per day—as evidence of the quest for knowledge and understanding. That, they argue, confirms technology's power "to engage others, share knowledge, and impact behavior."

They see the role of a Learning Experience Manager as providing "more options to learners for consuming the same information."

The problem is also reflected in the way teachers at all levels from first grade to graduate school continue to rely heavily on traditional classroom instruction. Public schools have vocal critics, but here testing is solidly accepted. The evaluation of training is not nearly as rigorous.

FROM TRAINING TO INDIVIDUAL
PERFORMANCE TO RESULTS

All training is expected to benefit the organization. It would have been common years ago to plan around the level of proficiency and skill level needed to perform at an acceptable level in a current job. There was no interest in supporting personal growth. The development needed to grow and qualify for the next career stage was limited to a few candidates. When employees were seen as a cost, this made sense.

Training then was an added cost. HR did the training, and once an employee knew how to "do the job" and where to go for lunch and bathroom breaks, training ended and the employee started to work. It was only when new equipment or new procedures were introduced that an employee could expect additional training. Supervisors checked on performance occasionally, but they were not accountable for developing employee capabilities. In that environment, when a recession occurs, hiring generally stops and training is no longer needed. Organizations that operate with that philosophy still exist—but they have trouble attracting top talent.

Today organizations that want to grow and prosper understand that they are more likely to be successful when employees at every level are committed and engaged. Everyone is expected to contribute. The strategies and action plans to create that work environment have been a common theme in the chapters of this book. Research has confirmed that people want to grow and develop, and that an employer's support for development makes an employee more valuable and strengthens their commitment to the organization. It also enhances the employer's brand for future applicants.

Knowledge and skills are essential to good performance. Learning is important to every job, but even world-class training does not guarantee good performance. Well-qualified people with the best degrees are not always high performers. Individual performance depends on a number of factors in addition to knowledge and skills. In the typical situation it's the manager who creates a high-performance culture.

Organizations succeed when employees work together. That starts with leadership and proven work-management practices. Well-managed organizations perform at significantly higher levels.

It starts with training. Leaders that fail to support employee skill development both inhibit the organization's performance and impede employee careers.

ADDITIONAL RESOURCES

Biech, Elaine, ed. *ASTD Handbook: The Definitive Reference for Training and Development.* Alexandria, VA: ASTD Press, 2014. The book contains ninety-six "chapters" by leaders in the field of training and development.

Knowles, Malcolm S., Elwood F. Holton III, and Richard A. Swanson. *The Adult Learner: The Definitive Classic in Adult Education and Human Resource Development.* 8th ed. New York: Routledge, 2015.

Stolovitch, Harold D., and Erica J. Keeps. *Training Ain't Performance.* Alexandria, VA: ASTD Press, 2006. This book and the one that follows are entertaining and practical guides for every trainer.

Stolovitch, Harold D., and Erica J. Keeps. *Telling Ain't Training.* Updated, expanded, enhanced 2nd ed. Alexandria, VA: ASTD Press, 2011.

Garvin, David A., Amy C. Edmondson, and Francesca Gino. "Is Yours a Learning Organization?" *Harvard Business Review*, March 2008.

8

Strategies for Managing Older Workers

The aging government workforce has been an issue for writers for well over a decade. Repeated reports have shown government employers have more workers over age forty-five than nongovernment employers. Older workers have been the fastest-growing segment of the workforce. For the next decade and longer, large numbers will be reaching retirement age and leaving the workforce. This cohort has been referred to as a "the silver tsunami." The wave will hit the beach of government sooner than almost any other sector.

In a relatively short period, agencies will lose accumulated job knowledge that will prove very difficult to replace. The impact will be concentrated at the executive and manager levels, where baby boomers still dominate. Currently, two workers exit the workforce for every one worker who enters. Although the demand for bright, talented generation X employees—those ages thirty-five to fifty—will increase, the supply of experienced workers will decrease in the coming years. Instead of early-retirement incentives, it could be that incentives to continue working will be needed.

The demographic facts are different in every jurisdiction. Notwithstanding the media focus on millennial-generation workers, for many public employers the projected loss of older workers and their job knowledge will make this a more important near-term problem.

THE DEMOGRAPHIC FACTS

The issue is the relative size of the generations. After World War II roughly 75 million baby boomers were born by 1964; generation X runs to 1981 and includes only 55 million people, and they were followed by an added 66 million millennials born by 1998. The numbers in the age groups change with deaths and immigration but not enough to fill the openings as baby boomers retire.

According to the Bureau of Labor Statistics, in 2014 the U.S. workforce was roughly 144 million, including almost 8.7 million working in elementary and secondary schools and 6.7 million working in "public administration." (According to the Census Bureau, government hospitals employ an additional 1.3 million.)

When the public sector employees—schools and public administration—are subtracted from the total workforce, the data show 44 percent of the nongovernment workforce are older than age 45, compared with 51 percent and 52 percent of the workforce in education and public administration, for a government total of 7.9 million over age 45. The latter includes workers in "justice, public order, and safety activities," which accounts for 42 percent of the public administration workforce and includes a higher proportion of younger workers. When those workers are backed out of the total, the number of workers over age 45 in schools and other public administration jobs exceeds 6.5 million.

Those are national totals, and as always, individual jurisdictions will be above and below the averages; in some jurisdictions the workforce is dominated by older workers. In nongovernment sectors only15 percent of the workforce is older than 55; the comparable percentage working in government is 26 percent.

THE REALITY OF AN OLDER WORKFORCE

The numbers by themselves are interesting but relevant only when considered in the context of their impact on government. The numbers represent a problem for the public sector for several reasons.

- As background, workers in other sectors change employers far more frequently. Experts argue that millennials will be frequent job hoppers, but that's been true of other generations as well. A recent study shows workers born from 1957 to 1964 held an average of 11.7 jobs from ages 18 to 48. The pattern for men and women is very similar. While job changing slows down with age, it never stops. Of the jobs that workers began when they were 18 to 24 years of age, 93 percent ended in fewer than 5 years. Among jobs started by 40- to 48-year-olds, 32 percent ended in the first year and 69 percent ended in less than 5 years. As a generalization, until the 2008–2009 recession, the overwhelming majority of workers in the private sector could find a comparable job if necessary in a relatively brief time.
- Anecdotal data for workers in the public sector suggest a very different pattern. Turnover until the past few years has been low, the work was stable and secure, and workers tended to stay for much longer periods. With each year of experience, it is less likely they will voluntarily decide to resign.

- If older workers become disgruntled for any reason and decide to switch to the private sector, they sometimes experience difficulty finding a new job at a comparable salary and conclude they cannot afford to quit. They then feel "locked in" by what they would lose by resigning. That can exacerbate their dissatisfaction and trigger diminished work engagement.
- Actually, many older workers in good health would prefer to continue working rather than retire. It's been reported that "about three quarters of individuals approaching retirement . . . would like to keep working in some capacity, yet only about a quarter of them actually do. . . . Older workers want to keep working first and foremost because it keeps them engaged with other people, and also to feel as though they're contributing" (Cappelli 2014). A study years ago showed that men in professional occupations who continue working live longer. (The study predated the transition of women into professional careers.)
- The low turnover and recently the recession have meant relatively few younger workers have been added to the payrolls. In other sectors they bring with them a higher level of comfort and more recent exposure to new ideas, along with expertise in using new technology and social media. The skills of older workers can become stale, and many become increasingly resistant to change.
- New hires also start at lower salaries than the workers they replace. Plus, new-hire benefit costs are lower. The long service of public employees is central to the pension-funding problem.
- Public employers tend to provide better postretirement benefits. In the private sector, postretirement cost-of-living pension adjustments and retiree medical coverage are very rare. Public employers are also far more likely to provide for early retirement with benefits more generous than actuarial equivalent. Now that defined-benefit plans are not common in the private sector, public employers spend substantially more for retirement benefits. The higher costs can make it difficult to maintain a competitive wage and salary program.
- Private employers today rarely have unions. That gives them more flexibility to change the benefits package and if necessary to reduce costs by raising the level of employee contributions. In government, older workers have greater power to defeat proposals to reduce benefits through the influence of unions and support of elected officials. That makes it very difficult for public employers to follow the trends in the private sector.
- There have also been reports that agencies are experiencing heavy turnover among young workers and veterans in the first few years of employment. That has been attributed to dissatisfaction with the work experience. They may also be frustrated by seniority-based practices. Low government salaries can be an added factor when nearby jurisdictions offer higher pay or companies have jobs requiring similar skills.

STEPS TO INCREASE THE
ENGAGEMENT OF OLDER WORKERS

The numbers summarizing government's older workforce are a given. Retirement at some point is inevitable for everyone. Employers have years invested in their experienced workers, but as they approach their earliest retirement date, if they do not feel valued, their level of commitment will begin to decline.

Rather than planning simply to replace older workers—traditional thinking—public employers should develop a strategy to take continued advantage of the knowledge older workers have developed. Each employee's decision to retire depends on circumstances that include their sense of how they are valued and their ongoing work experience. Looking to the future, the demographic facts suggest public employers will need to retain older employees as long as they remain productive.

While the focus here is on older workers, it is important to keep in mind the needs and expectations of all workers. It's very possible the workforce includes employees born anytime between the late 1940s and the early 1990s—roughly a forty-five-year period. That encompasses three generations of workers, each with its own values and career plans. Broader recommendations to create a high-performance work environment have been discussed throughout this book.

Steps that should be considered include:

- Commit to creating a culture of knowledge sharing. A key is the executive team making a visible effort to regularly meet with internal experts on key practices to understand newer methods and work practices. They should agree to attend community-of-practice sessions and group discussions of new technology. They should also agree to attend discussions of feedback from clients/customers. Workers should be encouraged to lead discussions in their areas of expertise.
- Engage older (possibly those over age fifty) employees in discussions of how their work experience can be enhanced. Two important themes are how their job-related knowledge can be better utilized and any policies or practices that undermine their ability to perform at their best. That should facilitate a discussion of serious problems. The goal is to send the message that they are valued.
- A common weakness in government people-management practices is employee dissatisfaction with recognition and reward practices. In contrast to the private sector, where there are frequent reasons to celebrate competitive "wins" or accomplishments, public agencies and the critics tend to focus more often on situations involving poor performance. People at all ages want to be valued and recognized for their accomplishments. Unfortunately, older workers are in some organizations taken for granted; the employer's focus is on younger workers. Those years of service awards are nice, but it would be more powerful to recognize true achievements. Where surveys show that is a problem, it would be useful to expand the reasons to recognize employees.

- Job descriptions should be updated to remove any statements that suggest employee age. The emphasis should be on requisite knowledge, skills, and abilities, and not on experience or education requirements.
- Offer older workers opportunities to use a portion of their work hours (e.g., a day or two a month) to develop ideas to improve the results of their unit. Require them to develop proposals for their planned projects with estimates of the time, needed resources, and the expected results.
- To assure continued access to the expertise of older workers, a similar alternative is to permit them to retire, start pension benefits, and then return to work with a part-time schedule that fits their unit's operation. The part-time role can be a way to transition to retirement but also to keep their knowledge available for a longer period. State laws governing pensions vary, but the demographic facts suggest greater flexibility will be needed.
- A Deferred Retirement Option Plan (DROP plan) is a related alternative that is especially attractive to employees with credited service at the pension plan maximum. DROP plans allow the employee to continue working for a few years. In the planning stage the plan provisions should be assessed by an actuary for costs, but the DROP plan defers the benefit payments until the end of a specified period.
- Review the performance-management system to confirm that the focus is on results and competencies specific to a job family and career stage. Rely on groups of experienced, high performers to identify and define job competencies. All workers should agree that their performance has been rated on criteria intuitively relevant to their job. There should be no reason for claims of age discrimination.
- Analyze recent personnel actions—ratings, promotions, pay increases, bonus awards, layoffs, and disciplinary actions—for evidence of discrimination. Complete a similar analysis at least annually. The analysis should also look for consistency with policies.
- Provide training for managers and supervisors in dealing with the issues related to an aging workforce. The sessions can also be used to communicate the organization's policies and workforce facts. The sessions can give managers an opportunity to share experience and seek advice. A proven strategy, especially for younger managers, is to confer with and seek the input of older workers in planning.
- Define formal mentoring and coaching roles that give older workers a reason to share their knowledge with younger workers. Communicate the initiative as recognition of the expertise demonstrated by highly regarded older workers and the learning opportunities for younger workers.
- Create groups that include both older and young employees to discuss and collaborate in addressing problems and future operating plans. Mixed groups can also be assigned to tackle special projects. Working together provides opportunities for knowledge transfer as well as occasions for older workers to demonstrate their expertise. Emphasize the value of day-to-day collaboration.

- A wellness program would benefit all employees, but it could be especially valuable to older workers. Providing for health screenings, health risk appraisals, smoking cessation programs, physical activity and weight loss programs or counseling, a personal health coach, and stress-management training would help to hold down medical costs. There are legal issues (e.g., protected health care information), but those can be avoided.
- Offer caregiver support for workers struggling with caregiving responsibilities for younger dependents, older loved ones, or both. Caregiving responsibilities are cited as one of the primary reasons why mature workers need work schedule and work location flexibility. Studies show the majority of older workers have to deal with those issues at some point in their careers.
- If an older worker has a disability, it would be advantageous to consider modifications to his or her job duties and/or working environment to enable them to remain productive. It is highly probable that this will become increasingly important as workers grow older.
- Create a group of retired employees with recognized expertise and treat them as consultants who are available to tackle problems. They should be paid on a basis that recognizes their value and the market for comparable expertise. They can also be used to fill in for employees on leave or vacation. Another possible role would be serving as instructors.

WORKFORCE PLANNING TO HIGHLIGHT THE PROJECTED LOSS OF TALENT

Workforce planning is not new. At one level it's a simple, numbers exercise. A basic purpose is to understand the dynamics of the workforce, documenting the movement of workers up and through the organization. That should be done by agency, occupation, and job classification. It's also useful to document career patterns, along with the experience of new hires. The movement of individuals to fill openings can be planned level by level and serve to plan recruiting efforts.

The usual purpose is to develop a staffing plan with anticipated openings and a list of internal candidates. That's unrelated to improved performance, but here the analyses are a key to understanding the cadre of older workers. Knowing their ages and work histories is the first step in identifying those that would be costly to lose.

To refine the understanding of the workforce, if someone on the staff has a good, basic understanding of predictive statistics, it would be useful to develop two models that predict resignations and retirements. The models would use recent resignations and retirements (expressed as 1/0) by occupation as "dependent" variables and readily available "independent variables" such as salary, age, gender, minority status, education level, years of service, and time to "normal" retirement age, with data going back possibly three years.

If performance ratings are credible, they can be added to the analysis. It's important to know who is leaving but also if their personal characteristics are useful in predicting which employees are likely to leave, thus making it possible to initiate changes to avoid the loss of the talent. Knowing the characteristics of workers most likely to leave also makes it possible to identify those most likely to stay.

Looking narrowly at historical patterns, however, ignores any anticipated changes in the organization, plans to introduce new technology, planned mergers, and so on. Perhaps most important, it ignores the emergence of new knowledge and skills not represented in the workforce. Focusing narrowly on internal plans also ignores the prospects for recruiting people with key skills in the labor market. Both are important to workforce planning.

A good starting point is to share the projections with leaders familiar with near-term plans for the organization. Discussions should be held agency by agency and department by department. Each agency represents a somewhat different problem. The goal is to understand talent needs and specific skills needed for the future.

It takes time, however, to hire, deploy, and train talent. If there is not enough time to develop needed skills, experienced workers will have to be hired, brought in as temporary employees, or the work outsourced. The level of the analysis will be dependent on the willingness to invest time. That needs to be balanced with the cost of losing key talent or having jobs go unfilled.

Concurrently it would be useful to assess the availability of the skills in the labor market, and to decide if it's feasible to hire the talent. The analysis should consider market pay levels, since that will be a factor in deciding if it's realistic to recruit needed talent.

At a different level, the results of the workforce planning exercise can serve as a guide for employees to consider and plan for future job opportunities. Workers in all age groups and occupations want to grow, tackle new challenges, and learn new skills. The argument for defining career paths has been focused on young workers, but a more comprehensive model that defines the knowledge, skills, and abilities needed in jobs—competency profiles—across the organization can also be used by older workers to consider job alternatives.

One of the decided advantages of government is that it is (or should be) fully possible for employees to restart their careers in a new agency or to find opportunities where their skills are a better fit or simply to get away from a bad supervisor. Defining competency profiles for occupations and job levels requires an investment, but it will pay off in increased engagement at all levels and can demonstrate to older workers that their needs are met best by continued employment.

ADDITIONAL RESOURCES

Hitch, Chris, Ph.D., and Brad Kirkman, Ph.D. "Engaging Older Workers Strategically." An executive briefing published by the SHRM Foundation, 2014.

Cappelli, Peter. "Engaging Your Older Workers." HBR.org, November 2014.

Walker, David. "Older Workers: Some Best Practices and Strategies for Engaging and Retaining Older Workers." U.S. Government Accountability Office, 2007.

Rothwell, William J., Harvey Sterns, Diane Spokus, and Joel Reaser. *Working Longer: New Strategies for Managing, Training, and Retaining Older Employees.* AMA Innovations in Adult Learning. AMACOM Books, 2008.

The New Flexible Retirement, a survey report from the Transamerica Center for Retirement Studies in collaboration with Aegon Center for Longevity and Retirement, January 2016.

9

Managing Agency and Executive Performance

It was more than twenty years ago that the National Performance Review and Vice President Gore raised the prominence of performance management in government. In 1993, Congress passed the Government Performance and Results Act that required agencies to define strategic goals, measure performance, and report to Congress, The Office of Management and Budget (OMB), and the public. Since then, additional laws have been enacted relevant to the management of performance, but the history makes it clear that effective performance management cannot be mandated. There are no silver bullets.

The progress by state and local public employers has been mixed. Compared with federal agencies, the smaller size and geographic proximity mean leaders are not as distant from where the work is done. Specialized offices to track performance—Compstat in the New York City Police Department and Citistat in Baltimore are frequently cited—were created as far back as the mid-1990s and have been replicated in a number of jurisdictions.

Agencies at all levels have invested repeatedly in new versions of the systems to manage goals and metrics. Everyone appears to agree it's the right answer. Focusing on achieving performance goals effectively is the universal practice for managing performance in business and has been for half a century. But government's experience with management systems, goal setting, and performance measurement has been disappointing.

A recent column by David Ammons ("Getting Real about Performance Management," ICMA website, 2015) discusses the reality that is at the heart of the problem. In a nutshell, his point is that the metrics have been used for reporting but not used in day-to-day management.

The obvious fact is that whenever performance does not satisfy expectations, something needs to change. To quote from the column,

Performance management doctrine declares the rules governing the optimum practice of performance management. Among the key rules are these: goals must be clear; performance measures must be relevant, actionable, and used for management purposes, not just for reporting; and executives must engage in responsible oversight while granting important decision authority to program managers and supervisors.

In other words, an organization can adopt systems to track metrics and tell its managers how to collect and monitor performance data, but Ammons's research shows the data are not being used to initiate the changes needed to improve performance. Ammons argues that is not performance management—since performance is not being managed!

The problem is compounded, according at Ammons, by the reluctance of government leaders to delegate the authority to front-line managers and employees to initiate changes in work systems. They are in the best position to understand the nature of problems and develop solutions. It contributes to a sense of pride and accomplishment, and ownership of making the changes a success.

Business leaders have shifted dramatically away from a top-down control management style over the past decade or so. Ammons's point is that the public sector has not accepted the change of management philosophy—and that will continue to be a barrier to improved performance.

THE STARTING POINT—GOALS AND MEASURES

Defining goals with measures to monitor progress is the starting point. In all endeavors where people need to agree on what they want to accomplish, one of the very first steps is to agree on their goals, and the measures tell them when they have succeeded. In everything related to performance—school, sports, health—there is probably no more widely used practice. The practice was first highlighted by Peter Drucker in his 1954 landmark book, *The Practice of Management.*

But Ammons is correct: goals and metrics are only tools. An element that is too often missing in government is the shared commitment to continuous improvement. The competitive environment in business provides a reason to push for higher and better. So-called stretch goals are common. People like the challenge of working to achieve difficult goals. They like the feeling that they contributed to winning. In business, of course, there are also financial incentives to succeed.

Central to the problem in government is a lack of focus on people-management issues. This starts at the top. The individuals who run for public office as well as those appointed to senior positions generally are interested in public policy issues. It is uncommon to find elected officials who have significant experience managing a large workforce. Many had prior careers and degrees in fields very different from organization management. And, of course, there is often political opposition to proposed changes.

GOAL POWER: USE IT, OR IT'S USELESS

by Shelley H. Metzenbaum

Goal power.

John F. Kennedy understood the power of a goal when he announced in 1961 the goal of landing a man on the moon in a decade and returning him safely back home, a goal reached eight years later. The world health community understood it when it set the goal of eradicating polio in 1988, a goal it has nearly met and continues to manage aggressively. Bill Gates understood it when he wrote in his 2013 annual letter that "you can achieve amazing progress if you set a clear goal and find a measure that will drive progress toward that goal in a feedback loop" and then treated the United Nations' Millennial Development Goals as more than just words on paper, but also objectives to which he might contribute intelligence and resources.

People across the federal government are also learning to tap the power of well-framed, ambitious goals in a few priority areas. This was reinforced earlier this month when the Office of Management and Budget Director, Shaun Donovan, announced the fourth round of federal agency near-term priority goals, goals to be met within the next two fiscal years, now posted on Performance.gov along with progress updates on previous priority goals.

Wait a minute, you might wonder, how can a goal improve results, lower costs, or make programs more fair, understandable, and accountable? A strong body of experience and research finds that if a stretch goal is understandable and ambitious, while reasonable relative to available resources, it tends to motivate effort, stimulate discovery, and communicate priorities. Even without threat of penalty or promise of reward, a well-framed goal tends to unleash people's instincts to do well and contribute to something bigger than themselves. Stretch goals inspire, inviting and challenging people to focus their efforts. Combined with frequent data-rich discussions that identify where progress is being made, where problems exist, why, and what actions to try next to accelerate progress on the goal, they encourage people to test better ways to make progress with available resources. If not too numerous, clearly defined priority goals serve as a convenient shorthand for inexpensively and concisely communicating to people in and beyond an organization where to concentrate effort, intelligence, and other needed resources. When organizational leadership changes, new leaders can use goals to convey quickly where to stay the course and where priorities have changed. Also, specific goals are handy for inviting knowledge from those outside government, enlisting assistance that accelerates progress on a goal and encouraging consideration of the appropriateness of a goal relative to other priorities.

Progress has been made on many federal priority goals. Patent review and veteran disability claims processing take less time, and backlogs have dropped. Energy intensity in Defense Department facilities is also falling, while the department's renewable energy production and procurement are rising. The percentage of twenty-five to thirty-four-year-olds with college degrees is going up, while general aviation accidents and adult cigarette smoking are going down. Plus, several intriguing FeedbackUSA pilots have been initiated as part of the customer service cross-agency priority goal—asking "customers" to tap buttons indicating satisfaction level on passport, Social Security, and other interactions with the federal government to provide easy, fast feedback that is already revealing areas needing attention.

Progress has also been made on the process. This year, agency priority goals were announced at the beginning of the first fiscal year for which the goals are set, four months earlier than usual. Donovan announced the goals, indicating not only their importance, but also suggesting their use in deciding on funding to propose in the upcoming budget.

Two particularly interesting process developments are the creation of the new Leadership Delivery Network and the White House Leadership Development Fellows. The first will bring twenty-five goal leaders together every other month to learn from and brainstorm with each other and outside experts on how to drive progress in these priority areas. The second takes on the very intractable challenge of managing progress on cross-agency priority goals requiring action from multiple agencies. Sixteen fellows from different agencies with a range of skill sets and perspectives have been chosen through a rigorous selection process to support implementation of cross-agency priority goals and initiatives, starting in November.

Of course, not every goal is progressing as expected and, in truth, it is still too hard to see performance trends on most priority goals over multiple years. Is that because some goal leaders and perhaps agency heads still view goal setting and performance measurement as annoying requirements? Do they not appreciate how powerful goals can be when they are actually used to improve performance and inform the public? I hope not, but I fear that in some cases that is still the case.

The bottom line is goals are useless unless used. The most useful goals inspire broadly and motivate specifically, not just those in government but those outside of it, as John F. Kennedy, the world health community, and those who set the U.N. Millennial Development Goals understood. Have you looked at the government's new priority goals? Do they make sense and excite you? If they don't, have you provided feedback through Performance.gov or other means?

Goal power. Use it or it's useless. That goes for those in government, but also for us, as citizens, who want high-performing government.

Shelley Metzenbaum joined the Volcker Alliance as its founding President in May 2013 and now serves as a Senior Advisor. She served as Associate Director for Performance and Personnel Management at the White House Office of Management and Budget from 2009 to 2013. Dr. Metzenbaum is recognized as an international expert in the field of public sector performance management and measurement.

This column was originally published as a blog with hot links on VolckerAlliance.org and GovExec.com on October 29, 2015.

That is in direct contrast to the experience of business leaders who rose to that level by succeeding at lower levels. They lead a team committed to the company's success. At each career stage the success of executives and managers depends on achieving the results expected of their units. The best are promoted. The rewards increase at each level.

The problem in government is compounded by the interests of the faculty in the typical college political science or public administration department. The degree programs often have more courses on human rights than on human resources. In contrast, the faculty in business schools in each department are focused on improving the functioning of businesses. Government would benefit if universities were more focused on educating future managers.

Improved performance can only happen if there is an agreement to change. There is, of course, the often-mentioned discomfort people have with accepting change. Civil service systems along with unions can be an impediment to change, although that varies from state to state. Perhaps this explains the somewhat-narrow focus on technology and management systems. New technology is easier to accept than behavior change.

There is an important but subtle distinction between "managing" and "administering." Administrators focus on maintaining performance levels, keeping stakeholders satisfied, and staying within budget. They run something—keep it going—and satisfy expectations. Supervisors can be good administrators; results-focused executives would not be satisfied working as administrators.

In contrast, managers manage. Managing is similar to the role of a military commander relocating troops in the middle of a battle. Effective management has to include the authority to initiate change.

A core practice in high-performance companies is regularly scheduled, commonly monthly meetings, where progress in achieving goals is discussed along with emerging problems. The purpose of the meetings is to reach agreement on changes needed to achieve the goals.

It's also important that everyone involved in operational planning focus on defining individual goals that will contribute to the broader goals at the next-higher level of management. Illustrations of cascading, interlinked goals are common in textbooks on management. Every executive and manager should be able to articulate what they expect to accomplish to contribute to the success of their organization. They should also be able to state what would be outstanding performance and the threshold of unacceptable performance. They know what they are capable of achieving.

Looking back, government recognized the need to develop an executive cadre in the Civil Service Reform Act of 1978 when organizations were largely stable and middle managers were expected only to keep things going. The adoption of separate HR policies for executives, however, introduced a chasm in the expectations separating executives and middle managers. The latter continued to be covered by the federal civil service system. The development of middle managers should be a higher priority.

THE MODEL FOR EXECUTIVE
PERFORMANCE MANAGEMENT

The process governing the management of executive and manager performance has been refined over half a century. It's virtually universal in every sector, including many government jurisdictions. It's discussed in a chapter in a book from a leading authority on management, Dr. David Ulrich, *The Leadership Capital Index: Realizing the Market Value of Leadership* (2015). Ulrich has been recognized as a "thought leader" by a number of business and professional groups.

He summarizes it with Figure 9.1:

- Overall commitment to performance accountability management. The process adopted to manage performance is similar at all levels of management and in every sector. It's cyclical, starts at the beginning of the year, involves regular discussions throughout the year, and is repeated again the following year.
- Positive accountability conversation. Experience shows many of the widely espoused practices—forced distribution, KPIs, behavioral anchored rating

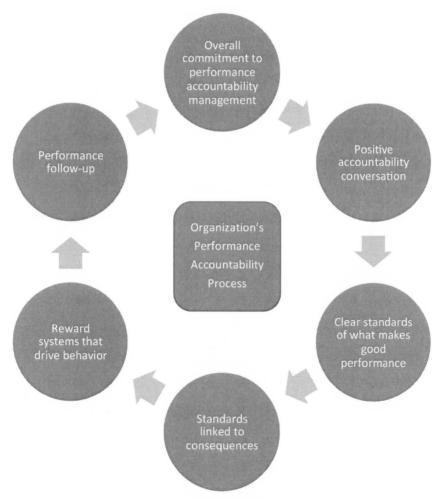

Figure 9.1. Framework for Organization's Performance Accountability Process.

scales, and so on—are not the keys to improved performance. The "key to effective performance accountability was less the specific performance appraisal practice and more the ability to have a candid, thorough, positive, and specific performance conversation with employees. These affirmative conversations are not just a calendared event; they work best as an ongoing process when leaders interact regularly with employees." The goal is to create "a positive relationship between leader and employee."

- Clear standards of what makes good performance. "Performance accountability requires that this conversation include a clear set of expectations about what the employee should deliver and how to differentiate high- from low-performing employees. Employees need to know what is expected of them so that they know if and when they have done a good job. Employee accountability goes up when expectations are within the control of the employee." When employees actively participate in defining what is expected, they are much more likely to be committed to those standards. In addition, if situations change, they are quick to adapt them to new conditions without waiting to be told.
- Standards linked to consequences. "Accountability requires consequences. Differentiated performance requires differentiated consequences. Consequences can be positive or negative, financial or nonfinancial. *To build accountability, performance needs to be directly tied to consequences.*" (Emphasis added.)
- Reward systems that drive behavior. "People generally do what they are rewarded for doing. The criteria [used to determine] incentives send clear signals about what matters most." In other sectors incentives are tied directly to achieving expected results. Financial incentives are close to universal for executives and managers, but nonfinancial, informal rewards are used daily by all managers. (See the discussion that follows.)

  Ulrich lists the following behaviors adapted from another expert, Dr. Steven Kerr, and suggests that a way to diagnose reward practices is to determine if they would be encouraged or discouraged.

  √ Coming up with or trying new ideas
  √ Exceeding authority to get a job done
  √ Presenting a boss with unpopular views
  √ Setting easy goals then achieving them
  √ Violating the chain of command if necessary

- Performance follow-up. "Performance accountability begins and ends with positive accountable conversations." A key issue is the importance of leaders following up to review and discuss progress, possible reasons to modify expectations, and planned actions.

Ulrich's discussion is relevant because he highlights the importance of accountability and consequences. He makes the point that accountability is not meaningful unless it is linked to consequences. Both are always a factor in the private sector and at all levels, including entry-level jobs. It's taken for granted. It's basic to working in business.

When accountability is linked to consequences, employees have a strong reason to analyze work processes and identify possible ways to improve the process. That makes a learning opportunity.

Accountability is often mentioned when performance problems occur in government, but it's not unusual to learn that nothing happened. Further, accountability in the private sector is associated with outstanding as well as unacceptable performance. Executives benefit from success and are hurt financially when they fail to achieve goals. That is reflected in the planning of financial incentives. Too often in government concerns about accountability surface only when performance problems occur. In business the public emphasis is on rewarding good performance; problems are handled discreetly.

In business, leaders make performance improvement a priority. Internal communications emphasize repeatedly the need to improve over prior levels. Observers of government have commented that leaders in public organizations have not made the same level of commitment. Managers and employees need to understand that high levels of performance are a priority.

CREATE A PROGRAM EXECUTIVE OFFICE

The starting point for a broad-based initiative to improve performance could be the creation of an office that provides leadership and makes expertise available to agencies to address performance issues. The office—the program executive office (PEO)—would be similar to the quality-management offices that exist in many health care organizations. Similar management teams are sometimes formed to guide major IT and acquisition projects. The PEO would be staffed by specialists who provide internal coaching and consulting, training, coordination, and perhaps most important, performance planning and monitoring.

A specific purpose in creating the office is to strengthen each agency's use of goal setting along with the metrics to track progress in achieving goals.

The office should be led by someone who has had prior hands-on experience with performance planning and goal setting and with the implementation of performance-management systems. The role is similar to that of a Chief Operating Officer in business. They will at times need to "beat the drums" and generate internal support from people who would, under other circumstances, be reluctant to get involved. At times the office will need the support of legal advisors, financial/budget specialists, a liaison contact with the legislature, and public affairs. The office head should report to the highest possible level to send the message that this is a priority.

Federal agencies now have a similar office headed by Performance Improvement Officers, but there is not much evidence that they have had a significant impact on agency performance.

The intent is to shift the culture from one that resists change to one that encourages managers and employees to work continuously to improve the work-management paradigm. Agency success in improving performance should be rewarded as a way to recognize the shift in culture.

The basic functions are similar to that of a quality office:

- To develop a reporting system and dashboard to track agency metrics and progress in achieving agency and individual performance goals;
- To consult with managers and employees of an agency to assess opportunities to improve performance;
- To monitor and provide assistance to address performance problems;
- To keep track of new performance-related IT products that become available and assist agencies in determining IT requirements and in evaluating and testing new systems;
- To monitor and evaluate HR policies and practices intended to support performance;
- To maintain a working knowledge of leading-edge thinking for improving agency results;
- When new systems or practices are installed, to assist in developing a roll-out strategy;
- To draft internal regulations and if needed assist in drafting legislation to facilitate needed change;
- To develop a communications strategy to keep elected leaders and the public aware of progress in improving agency performance; and
- To develop a strategy for collaborating with unions and stakeholders.

As with quality management, this involves a continuous cycle of planning, evaluating, and improving work-management processes to improve performance.

In smaller jurisdictions, the alternative to a PEO—since the thread that ties these functions together is better workforce management—is managing the initiative out of the headquarter's HR office. However, that is likely to stamp it as an HR project and unfortunately reduces the prospects that managers and employees will truly get on board. More importantly, it rides on having an HR staff with adequate change management expertise.

STEPS TO INCREASE THE FOCUS ON PERFORMANCE

Public agencies will never be run like a business, but a number of management practices are common in highly successful companies that could be adopted in government. In combination the practices are instrumental in creating a culture where solid performance is a priority.

The starting point is a 2005 study conducted by a team at the London School of Economics (LSE) that was funded by McKinsey & Company. The goal was to learn if the way a company is managed contributes to its success. Their focus was on the impact of a series of eighteen day-to-day, middle-management practices (although three are relevant only in manufacturing). Members of the research team conducted interviews in more than seven hundred medium-size manufacturing companies in four countries (the United States, the United Kingdom, France, and Germany). Each company was scored on their use of the practices. The research findings confirm that the way an organization is managed is important to its success. (The focus on similar companies made it feasible to compare and isolate the impact of the management practices.)

They found a strong relationship between the way an organization is managed and its success. More specifically, those firms that scored high on their use of the management practices were more successful; those that scored low were less successful. In business, of course, poorly managed firms often fail, so their sample of companies does not include many companies that were badly managed.

The management practices can be grouped into four areas: "shop floor" management, performance monitoring, use of performance measures, and the management of human capital. The shop-floor management issues are, except in rare situations, not relevant to government. The others are all potentially applicable in any organization, public or private. The fifteen practices are listed below.

In France and to a lesser degree in Germany, there are tough labor regulations, specifically making dismissal costly and difficult. The research team learned that restrictive labor regulations impede an organization's adoption of better management practices.

They also collected data on the average hours spent by managers, use of sick leave, and a self-reported measure of managers' "work/life balance." None of these questions and their responses were found to be associated with company success.

Significantly, all of the fifteen management practices affect an organization's management of its people and could readily be adopted by any organization, including public agencies. The following is the list of management practices that are associated with high performance.

Performance Monitoring

- Performance is tracked continually and communicated, both formally and informally, to staff.
- Performance is reviewed in meetings led by senior leaders at least monthly, with follow-up actions to ensure continued improvement. Results are communicated to staff.
- Regular performance conversations focus on changes in business climate, possible need to revise goals, analyzing problems, and addressing root causes. Meetings are used for feedback and coaching.

Performance Targets

- Performance plans balance financial and nonfinancial performance targets.
- Company goals focus on shareholder value (this could be mission-related goals), cascade with increased specificity to lower levels of management, and are reflected in individual goals.

- Long-term targets are translated into specific short-term "staircase" targets planned to achieve the long-term goals.
- Targets are genuinely demanding—"stretch goals"—and grounded in solid performance facts.
- Performance measures are well defined, strongly communicated, and reinforced at all reviews.
- Failure to achieve targets drives retraining for the manager in areas of weakness or a job change to where skills are more applicable.

Human Capital Management

- Managers are evaluated and held accountable on the strength of the talent pool they develop. Training and development opportunities are provided for top performers.
- Ambitious stretch performance goals with clear performance accountability and rewards are established.
- Company does whatever it takes to retain top talent. Managers are responsible for working to keep the proven performers.
- Company tries to provide a unique "value proposition" to attract talented people. Company HR practices are planned to achieve this goal.
- Company actively works to identify, develop, and promote top performers. Managers are assessed on the basis of career plans for individuals.
- Company moves poor performers out of the company or to less critical roles as soon as weakness is identified.

The study and a follow-up survey of the use of fifteen practices in state and local governments as well as in universities are discussed in a 2007 report published by the IBM Center for the Business of Government, "Managing for Better Performance: Enhancing Federal Performance Management Practices," by Howard Risher and Charles Fay. The report can be downloaded at www.businessofgovernment.org.

It's no doubt true that no employer would "score" high on all fifteen (or eighteen) practices. However, each in some way is related to effective performance management. Each reinforces the message that performance is a shared priority. In any combination their impact should trigger improved performance.

It is significant that the LSE study was silent on two central issues—the use of individual performance goals and the use of financial incentives to reward executives and managers. Both are universal in all industries and countries (with a developed economy) and therefore unlikely to be determinants of high performance. The use of performance goals was, of course, discussed previously.

REWARDING EXECUTIVE PERFORMANCE

Financial incentives are effectively universal for executives and middle managers in business, health care, and the majority of not-for-profit organizations. There is solid evidence that incentives trigger better performance. The evidence suggests that the dollar amounts do not have to be large; the incentive rides on an employee's control of the payouts based on his or her performance.

The belief that outstanding performers should be recognized and rewarded is deeply entrenched in U.S. culture and supported by psychological theory. When productive behaviors are not recognized and reinforced, they are less likely to be repeated.

In business, executives are rewarded for performance in three ways—salary increases, cash incentive awards, and stock options. The "big" rewards reported by the media are from stock options, but the gains are never certain, especially in an unpredictable stock market, until the shares are sold. It's safe to say that outside of government, all executives and managers work under pay-for-performance policies.

Salary increases for executives and managers are based on an assessment of the "what and the how," where the "what" are results and the "how" are competencies. Numerous published sources discuss executive competencies. But incentives linked to results are far more potent motivators.

In other sectors incentives are part of the employment contract and documented in job offers. For planning and communication, the amounts are expressed as a percentage of salary, referred to as a target or guideline award. The target awards typically range from 50 percent at the CEO level to possibly 10 percent at the lowest level of supervision. Participant payouts are usually based on performance relative to a combination of company and individual performance goals. When the executive and company perform as expected—that is to say, meet their goals—they can expect the target amount. Actual awards are higher than the target amounts for exceeding goals or lower if the goals are not achieved.

Linking payouts to specific company and individual goals sends a message about priorities and reinforces individual accountability.

Each goal is weighted (as a percentage of 100 percent). Payouts typically start at a threshold 80 to 90 percent of the goals and increase by formula to possibly 120 percent of the target amount. There is an incentive to exceed the goals. To illustrate the calculations, if the target award is 10 percent and the base salary is $100,000, at the threshold performance level the award might be $5,000 and at the maximum it might be $15,000. In that example, the actual payout could vary by as much as $10,000 depending on the individual's performance. It's the swing in prospective payout that triggers the incentive.

For this discussion, incentives are differentiated from bonuses. Incentives are tied by what is best understood as a formula to metrics that track performance—that is, results and incentive dollars are linked. Plan participants can estimate their payout at any point in the year based on projected performance.

Bonuses, in contrast, are typically based on what can only be described as subjective decisions. Recipients can never be certain what, if anything, they can expect until the year ends.

The distinction is captured by the "donkey and carrot" idiom. When the carrot was tied so it dangled in front of the donkey's face, the beast kept walking, trying to catch the carrot. When he could no longer see the carrot, he stopped. That is central to the reason companies generally limit their use of "bonus" awards to small amounts, used by supervisors as "spot awards" to recognize small achievements.

Another important distinction is that incentives are an integral component of the compensation package. The combination of base salary and the target award is aligned with market levels. For example, if surveys show the average competitive "cash compensation" is $120,000, and the planned target is 20 percent (to keep it simple), the base salary would be determined by dividing $120,000 by 1.20 or $100,000. If the job incumbent earns the full target award ($20,000), the total cash compensation would be competitive.

That is very different from the understanding often expressed by critics of government. Bonuses are frequently seen as an "extra" on top of a competitive salary. Presumably only the best performers earn a bonus award, but that, of course, depends on the fairness of the decision process. Since the awards are not linked to metrics, there is no basis for understanding the rationale. Incentives, in contrast, are readily explained and understood.

A final point is that executive compensation in business, hospitals, and universities is controlled by members of the board of directors or trustees, individuals working to promote the success of the organization but not employed by the organization. They in a very real sense are independent and rely on their own experts. Public agencies certainly could create outside committees composed of individuals knowledgeable about an agency's mission and performance to govern executive pay decisions.

MANAGING FOR HIGH PERFORMANCE

Ammons focused on a core issue. Public agencies have invested in management systems, but technology alone does not raise performance levels. The information generated by technology feeds the day-to-day decisions to take advantage of opportunities and respond to problems. High performance can be realized only when managers and employees are empowered to initiate changes based on metrics and performance data.

The management philosophy reflected in a continuous improvement strategy is the foundation for raising performance levels.

It's not a simple problem, nor is it "brain surgery." The practices discussed in this chapter and throughout this book come together to create and sustain a culture where there is mutual trust and performance is a priority. Risk taking and possible failure has to be accepted as a possibility when people are empowered to adopt new ideas. Leaders need to communicate—and reinforce with their actions—their expectation that staff members will respond to unanticipated problems without prior approval.

There are many stories of government employees performing at extraordinary levels. In some agencies, exemplary performance is expected. The National Institutes of Health, for example, have a world-class reputation. But that level of performance is unlikely to become the new norm unless it is encouraged by leaders. The message from leaders has to cascade throughout the organization. It's too often forgotten that everyone wins when agencies perform at a high level. Success breeds success.

ADDITIONAL RESOURCES

Ulrich, David. *The Leadership Capital Index: Realizing the Market Value of Leadership.* Berrett-Koehler Publishers, 2015.

Whitehurst, Jim. *The Open Organization: Igniting Passion and Performance.* Harvard Business Review Press, 2015.

Ingram, Pat, ed. *In Pursuit of Performance: Management Systems in State and Local Government.* Johns Hopkins University Press, 2007.

Ammons, David N., Ellen G. Liston, and Jordan A. Jones. "Performance Management Purpose, Executive Engagement, and Reported Benefits among Leading Local Governments." *State and Local Government Review* 45, no. 3 (2013): 172–79.

Overview of the Federal Performance Framework (2015), https://www.whitehouse.gov/sites/default/files/omb/assets/a11_current_year/s200.pdf.

Metzenbaum, Shelley. *Performance Accountability: The Five Building Blocks and Six Essential Practices.* IBM Center for the Business of Government, 2006.

Risher, Howard, and Charles Fay. *Managing for Better Performance: Enhancing Federal Performance Management Practices.* IBM Center for the Business of Government, 2007.

10

Managing Employee Performance

Sustained, improved performance depends on both managers and the people they supervise. It's not about working harder; it's about working smarter. That is to say, employees become more focused on achieving important goals. Individual managers can, of course, make that happen for their team, but an organization can only do it if it adopts a new performance system and makes it an organizational priority.

Performance management has always been one of those "can't live with, can't live without" practices. Companies frequently have problems similar to those in government.

Many articles in business journals have confirmed that the practice is broadly disliked, but in the end it is a rare company that has actually dropped the practice for two reasons: (1) everyone learning a new skill benefits from feedback and (2) employers need to be able to defend adverse personnel actions attributed to poor performance. A performance system is basic to creating a culture with a shared commitment to good performance.

This chapter is about the management of performance; that is, the day-to-day process to support employees as they perform their responsibilities. Performance management has acquired a negative connotation. The chapter begins with recent reports of the ways two prominent companies have shifted their practices to emphasize an approach to managing performance that enables them to unleash and take full advantage of employee capabilities.

Few public employers have made employee performance a priority. Improved performance is not possible if it's not expected and encouraged. Just as with a great quarterback or a star pitcher in baseball, people who achieve superior performance have benefited from feedback and coaching throughout their careers. In high-performing teams as well as work organizations, the commitment to greatness is a reflection of leaders and their management philosophy. Successful teams expect all "players" to contribute.

The history going back almost a century is still part of the problem today. When performance appraisals were first introduced, the intent was to limit the authority of managers in the early factories. Until that point they had total autonomy to hire and fire. History shows that many were discriminatory and arbitrary in their actions. Unfair, punitive managers were a reason employees joined together to form unions. The new personnel offices were the police to impose workplace fairness. The early appraisal policies had a limited purpose—*to confirm that employees satisfied performance expectations, did what they were told, and stayed out of trouble.*

That reality did not change significantly for decades. Managers resented the year-end requirement, spent as little time on it as possible, and cooperated very reluctantly with what was seen as "another HR requirement." In the decade or two after World War II, psychologists focused on creating a more defensible appraisal form and rating scale but failed to solve the problems. Performance ratings had no real consequences, so managers took the easy way out and acquiesced to inflated ratings. Employees only had to meet minimal expectations.

Over all the years the only important change was the introduction in the 1950s of the concept of management by objectives (MBO) by business guru Peter Drucker. Today in business, variations of MBO are close to universal for performance planning and evaluation for business executives, managers, and many professionals and are also widely used in other sectors. The achievement of goals reinforces individual accountability and at year end is linked to salary increases and incentives.

But the appraisal process is still barely tolerated. Many successful companies acknowledge two practical problems: far too many employees are rated at high levels, and a small percentage are rated as unacceptable. For managers, inflated ratings help sustain positive working relationships. Both reflect a manager's discomfort with providing honest feedback. No one working in Lake Woebegon believes they are average. The trend is related to the well-documented gradual rise in academic grades in school.

A third common problem is rarely acknowledged—many managers have only a few occasions when they can observe employees performing their jobs. That is one of the reasons for the increase in multi-rater or 360-degree feedback. But with many knowledge jobs it's not possible to "observe" what an employee does; the only recourse is to base ratings on results. That does not, of course, obviate the value of feedback.

GENERAL ELECTRIC'S CONTINUING LEADERSHIP

It is not clear why, but General Electric (GE) has been repeatedly at the forefront of change in the management of performance. Almost two decades ago GE and its then-CEO Jack Welch were credited for introducing a widely adopted but now heavily criticized policy, the forced distribution—"rank and yank"—policy.

Under that policy the top 20 percent were rewarded generously with bonuses and stock options while the bottom 10 percent were rated as unacceptable, which resulted in termination. A number of leading companies like Microsoft and Ford adopted a similar policy. The interest in the policy emphasizes how important performance is in the business world. As companies learned, however, it had a devastating impact on employee morale. The negative consequences have prompted most of the companies that adopted the policy, including GE, to end it. The practice is indefensible.

GE is also credited with introducing what has been considered to be the "best practice" for assessing performance—the so-called what and the how, where the "what" are the expected results and the "how" are the competencies and behaviors associated with job success. The approach combines the traditional look back at what was accomplished—the "what"—and a look ahead at development needs—the "how"—to improve an employee's prospects for future success. It's not a universal practice, but it's used widely.

More important is GE's latest change as discussed in the 2015 *Harvard Business Review* article "GE's Real-Time Performance Development." It's significant in part because the article's authors are line managers, not HR specialists. An overriding but often ignored issue is that the day-to-day management of performance is the responsibility of managers and supervisors. It is not an HR problem. To use a sports analogy, HR plays a role in coaching on the sidelines and at game time brings in the towels and the Gatorade when there are problems. (The importance of the new argument for middle managers was discussed in chapter 5.)

The new GE approach was described by the authors as follows:

> At its core, the approach depends on continuous dialogue and shared accountability. Rather than a formal, once-a-year review, managers and their direct reports hold regular, informal "touchpoints" where they set or update priorities that are based on customer needs. Development is forward looking and ongoing; managers coach rather than critique; suggestions can come from anyone in an employee's network.

The sports analogy is again useful. GE managers are transitioning from control to coaching, offering advice and support after each play—the "touchpoint" conversations.

To highlight a key point from the article, GE managers *"used it [the new approach] to drive a fivefold productivity increase in the past 12 months."* Performance gains of that magnitude would be unheard of under the old approach to supervision and impossible from any other strategy.

GE's IT people developed a simple smartphone app to support the new approach. It accepts voice and text inputs, attached documents, and handwritten notes. That helps both managers and employees to keep track of progress and record accomplishments, and it facilitates the touchpoint discussions.

Managers at GE still have the traditional year-end review discussion with employees, and they rate their people on the same three-level scale. But it needs to be emphasized that there should now be no year-end rating surprises. Employees should know throughout the year how they are performing and what to expect.

GE continues to base compensation, promotion, and development decisions on the ratings by managers. Ratings are necessary to support those decisions. Aside from legal reasons, they need to be credible and seen as fair.

An often-overlooked aspect of the *Harvard Business Review* article is the commitment to collaboration and empowerment. Again the authors describe what unfolded:

> We jumped into the pilot by building a collaboration room where teams could engage and develop new ways of working. We gave them a shared goal on productivity and full autonomy and decision-making authority to figure out how to get there. Instead of each group working separately to optimize its portion of the process, as might have happened in the past, the new performance-development approach helped them work together to optimize the overall results.

And finally, "We're finding that the new performance-development system is promoting trust between managers and employees—the foundation of high-performing teams. The shift from 'command and control' to '*empower and inspire*' is dramatic, and, as evidenced by our fivefold increase in productivity, it is yielding significant benefits for our employees and customers."

The phrase "empower and inspire" should make the change attractive to every employer. The new approach makes the focus and conversations much more positive.

HIGHLIGHTING THE NEW
WORK-MANAGEMENT PHILOSOPHY

Considerable attention has been paid to executives in government but decidedly less to middle managers and supervisors. However, recent research shows managers have a greater impact on performance than any other factor. When a truly good manager moves from one work group to another, it is almost always true that the performance of the new group improves and that of the old group deteriorates. The analogy of a good coach in sports is relevant.

Not too long ago managers were expected to assign tasks, maintain discipline, and confirm that each task was completed on time. It was common to promote the most senior or most technically proficient as new supervisors. The old approach to supervision has been described as "over the shoulder," or in other words, managers were expected to monitor employee work efforts closely.

All of that has changed or should change with the emerging understanding of knowledge workers. Their value depends on what they know and their ability to apply that knowledge. That can only happen when they are empowered and encouraged to improve performance. If nothing is done differently, there can be no improvement. Where the goal is to raise performance levels, the manager is the catalyst for getting the best work from their people.

Google exemplifies the new work-management philosophy. The conclusions from Project Oxygen, discussed in chapter 5, helped the company to define the role and expectations of managers. The study and their conclusions were discussed in a number of articles and also in the best-selling 2015 book by Google's Laszlo Bock, *Work Rules! Insights from Inside Google That Will Transform How You Live and Lead.*

Central to Google's management philosophy are beliefs expressed by Bock in a March 2015 article in *Fortune*: "*You either believe people are fundamentally good or you don't.* If you do believe they're good, then as an entrepreneur, a team member, a team leader, a manager, or a CEO, you should act in a way consistent with your beliefs. If people are good, then they should be free. Too many organizations and managers operate as if, absent some enlightened diktat, people are too benighted to make sound decisions and innovate." (Italics added.)

Bock does not define what he means by "good," but the context suggests several words: committed, capable, and trustworthy. Equally important is how he would define "not good," along with the implications for how those employees should be managed. Clearly they are not committed and cannot be trusted.

He argues that the way to make work better is through transparency, goal setting, frequent performance feedback and coaching, and a less-hierarchical work structure that empowers employees to solve problems for themselves while encouraging them to critique their bosses just as often as they critique themselves and each other.

In the book he lists ten principles "to transform your team and your workplace." Several would be a stretch for government, but he starts with two that are directly relevant:

1. "Give your work meaning." "Work consumes at least one-third of your life and half your waking hours. It can and ought to be more than a means to an end. In too many environments, a job is just a paycheck. Even a small connection to the people who benefit from your work not only improves productivity but also makes people happier. And everyone wants his work to have purpose. Connect it to an idea or a value that transcends the day to day and that also honestly reflects what you are doing."
2. "Trust your people." "Be transparent and honest with your people, and give them a voice in how things work. And the only way for that to happen is if you give up a little bit of your authority, giving them space to grow into it. This may sound daunting, but in reality it's not too risky. And if you are part of a team, make this plea to your boss: Give me a chance. Help me understand what your goals are, and let me figure out how to achieve them. Small steps like these create the trail to an ethos of ownership."

Google trusts its employees to make sound decisions in the best interests of the company. Bock's response to what makes Google special and so successful is, "It's our people." Employees are similarly responsible for government's achievements, although that is too often not acknowledged.

Government is not going to emulate the Google work environment. But agencies can redefine the role and expectations of managers, and they can adopt policies that reflect Google's core people-management philosophy. It would be highly advantageous to have leaders at the highest agency levels make this an organizational priority. Both managers and employees would benefit.

The new GE approach and the Google approach emphasize expecting managers to get the best from their people. Unfortunately, the highest levels in government frequently do not share that commitment. But the Google approach—asking employees what they think of the current approach to performance planning and management—would be a good first step.

This represents a significant organizational change for virtually every public and private organization. It would be best to start as Google did, with a project to identify and define the supervisory style that would be most effective. Focus groups would be the place to hold those discussions. Agency leaders should make it very clear that the change is a priority.

To reinforce the need for change it would be advantageous to emphasize the preferences of young workers. A great many books and articles have been written about the expectations of young, millennial workers. They are the future, and they need to find the public sector work environment and job prospects attractive.

FINE-TUNING THE PERFORMANCE-MANAGEMENT PROCESS

A performance-management system is best understood as a tool to be used by managers and supervisors. The purpose is to guide managers in the steps associated with the management of performance and to facilitate interactions between a manager and his or her people. As with the new GE approach, it is also a place to record relevant performance information, including the manager's assessments. As with the tools of a carpenter or an auto mechanic, it is the skills of the user that make the difference.

Eliminating the performance system or even eliminating ratings is not going to satisfy employees or managers. The best-performing employees want to be recognized. The organization needs to identify the poor performers. Unless an existing system is totally dysfunctional, investing the time for fine-tuning to address concerns is less costly, less disruptive, and easier for everyone to accept. The fine-tuning should involve both managers and employees. They want the assurance their concerns have been heard.

But when there is a consensus that a system is "broken," it would be advantageous to create a task force to evaluate the alternatives and make recommendations to develop a replacement.

If ratings are to be linked to pay increases and/or career prospects, the year-end ratings have to come down. Ratings have to be seen as fair and credible, and no group can have a perceived advantage.

WHY PUBLIC SECTOR PERFORMANCE MANAGEMENT MUST CHANGE

By Liam Ackland, President—North America, Acendre

Much of today's press has focused upon the shifting landscape of performance management within some of the world's largest corporations, such as General Electric, Microsoft, Adobe, and Accenture. Over the last year, these organizations have announced that they are abandoning the annual performance review. The announcements have met with much fanfare, for good reason: many of these companies are long considered models of employee management.

It's hard to dispute that organizational needs must evolve with the changing workforce, as boomers retire and millennials represent the majority in more and more companies. A less-regimented system with increased feedback fits this new reality. "The world isn't really on an annual cycle anymore for anything," said Susan Peters, GE's head of human resources. "I think some of it, to be really honest, is millennial-based. It's the way millennials are used to working and getting feedback, which is more frequent, faster, mobile-enabled, so there were multiple drivers" in making GE's change.

Continual feedback—with regular communications between supervisors and their staff—is quickly emerging as the norm. Even for firms abandoning annual performance reviews, the need for increased interaction is acknowledged.

THE PUBLIC SECTOR: RIPE FOR A PERFORMANCE-MANAGEMENT OVERHAUL

While not receiving as much publicity as the private sector, public sector performance-management demands are evolving as well. The changes are somewhat similar to private industry, but arrive with their own unique set of challenges. Probably most notable: the need to adhere to numerous regulations and government mandates. Federal regulations are often tied not only to hiring, but also reviews, employee classifications, promotions, and compensation.

And the government is dealing with arguably even greater problems here than the private sector. Its annual satisfaction surveys reveal disheartening numbers, with worker satisfaction at just 64 percent and leadership scores even worse. Staff morale is also low. Because countless research findings demonstrate that organizations with happier, more engaged employees outperform their counterparts, the survey proves especially troublesome.

The federal government may have a bigger hill to climb overall. But it can score significant wins in a short period of time. Surprisingly, much of the government today is still tethered to paper processes, for example, with little or no automation. This results in an abundance of issues, including redundancy, wasted resources, and an inability to gain decision-making insights from analytics and reports.

Data can drive change. But in a pen-to-pencil universe, there is a dearth of data.

Compounding the issue, highly regulated public organizations still face challenges seen in the private sector. Federal agencies, health care groups, and higher-education institutions are competing for the same talent as commercial industries. Both go head-to-head in efforts to recruit millennials, retain top staffers, and develop all employees in the workplace, so they can succeed. The out-of-favor annual review presents no more appeal to government workers. So it still makes sense to boost the frequency of communication between managers and employees, enhance engagement, and rely less on an annual conversation and grading system.

However, regulations may still require a yearly review, which means U.S. agencies aren't getting rid of them anytime soon. Thus, the conversation should steer toward how to improve them.

Problems with federal performance management—including cumbersome and resource-draining paper dependencies, leadership gaps and employee morale, engagement and retention challenges—are well documented. Many of these issues stem from a scarcity of innovation, making evolution to an automated, paperless world virtually unattainable from a cost, time, and implementation perspective.

Fortunately, technology helps organizations adapt. Modern systems are replacing public sector legacies such as pen-to-paper or fillable forms systems, enabling agencies to take a significant step forward. The benefits of this modern technology are persuasive for traditionally slow-moving federal agencies:

- Faster implementation
- Greater incremental change for broader acceptance
- Solutions that are more configurable and adaptable to agencies' unique processes
- Better decisions through insightful analytics
- Interoperability to ensure smooth integration with other HR systems
- More cost-effective deployment with minimal resource requirements

BEYOND PERFORMANCE MANAGEMENT

The evolution of performance management really extends beyond individuals. For example, with performance data in place, organizations will have a better understanding of their workforce. In the highly competitive public health care sector, it's important to know whether existing talent can fill roles as people leave. Often, organizations employ team members who can step into a new role, whether the move involves a promotion or a little extra training. This is critical in the federal government, with a looming retirement crisis.

Having a strong sense of your talent base—including professional goals, professional potential, and interest in acquiring additional skill sets—makes it easier to recruit from within. Performance-management software streamlines this process, automating talent assessment and recognizing opportunities for professional development.

In addition to identifying strong candidates to fill particular openings within your enterprise, you can examine which sought skill sets already exist within candidates—and which require development—before they can transition to a new role. High-potential junior professionals, for instance, might benefit from leadership training to prepare them for supervisory roles. Other staffers could take classes to hone a specific, hard-to-recruit skill set.

THE NEW WORLD

Across the globe, organizations are realizing their most valuable asset—their people—compels a different way of being managed. While leadership is phasing out the annual review in some areas, it will likely remain in many parts of the public sector for the foreseeable future. But old methods of managing performance do not have to stay in place. Not when current technologies allow agencies to upgrade the standard review, while simultaneously embracing the new world of increased and enhanced employee engagement, interaction, leadership development, and performance improvement.

Liam Ackland is President—North America, Acendre. Ackland oversees Acendre's North American operations, which focuses on delivering cloud-based talent-management solutions to government. Acendre's solutions are deployed in more than two hundred organizations around the globe, including almost one hundred government agencies, helping these organizations recruit, engage, retain, and develop their employees to improve workforce performance.

A performance system is defined by the criteria adopted for evaluating performance and the technology used in its administration. The system's value is determined by the people who live with it. It makes sense periodically to ask the managers and employees who use the system to assess it and recommend changes. It is important that they believe it's meeting their needs. The best performers in both groups, managers and employees, will readily offer feedback. They know what's working and what's broken. Inviting their feedback can become an annual step to improve the work environment.

The technology is the easy part. The market for performance systems is highly competitive, with a number of vendors. The only problem is that the best system today might be outdated in months. The best technology, however, has little impact on how the process is perceived or on the manager's coaching skills.

The fine-tuning is in the choice and specification of the performance criteria. For executives and managers, the focus in every other sector is on performance relative to individual performance goals. Basing an evaluation on what they were expected to accomplish is intuitively the right approach. Every employee should be able to state what he or she is expected to accomplish. They should also know what would be seen as outstanding performance and also the threshold or minimum acceptable level. Relying on goals or other planned results is consistent with the "what and the how" and is important at every level.

The system should be planned to highlight the issues managers need to discuss with members of their staff. That is a key. It should be planned to facilitate those discussions and help managers focus on job-specific issues. A fundamental problem with older performance systems is that the criteria were always generic and often abstract. Performance dimensions like "initiative" or "teamwork" were typical, despite not being applicable to all jobs—and not having a common understanding across managers.

To refer to history again, the use of the same criteria for obviously different jobs dates to the early concern with unionization. Then a mechanic would be evaluated using the same criteria as a painter. The idea was to treat everyone the same. But, of course, there was no real interest in raising performance levels. That requires feedback on job-specific issues.

To use a sports analogy, when a soccer/football coach meets with a goalie to discuss performance, the issues will always be different than if he/she were meeting with a winger or a halfback. For the same reason, the ideal performance criteria to assess the performance, for example, of an accountant are not the same as those relevant to an engineer.

A similar analogy is teaching. Teachers would never use the same test for history and math. Different jobs require different skills and have different expected results.

The analogy also applies to the career stage. The math taught in middle school is the foundation for math taught in high school. Tests have to be specific to the grade level. In the same way it makes no sense to use the same criteria for a new hire and a seasoned veteran.

As an example, a new graduate working as a Parole Officer has to master writing and presentation skills to be successful in court. But at a higher career stage, those skills are superseded by others. For example, high-performing Parole Officers have to be able to play two roles—law enforcement and social worker—and their effectiveness depends in part on being able to switch instantaneously between roles as appropriate to deal with an offender.

The textbook purpose for performance management is to assess how well an employee is performing his or her job. There is no reason to compare one employee with another and certainly no reason to compare employees in different job families. It serves no purpose, and if it impacts employee careers, it is indefensible. The focus should be on what an employee was expected to accomplish along with an assessment of their strengths and weaknesses in light of their training and experience.

High-performing job incumbents and their managers are well qualified to identify the relevant performance criteria with minimal guidance. The best performers know what's important to the performance of people in their field. A small group, for example, of accountants can normally do that for accountants in two or three meetings. It's very likely that they will be able to find previously defined competencies on professional accounting websites. As jobs change, the criteria should be revisited.

One of the solid success stories in the federal government is the pay and performance system implemented by one of the intelligence agencies, the National Geospatial-Intelligence Agency (NGA). They relied on a number of committees, each focused on an occupation to develop job-specific criteria. NGA has won awards as a best employer.

Each employer needs to consider how much time they are willing to invest in developing and keeping a performance system up to date. Fine-tuning is essential to stay abreast of change.

THE FOCUS FOR EXECUTIVES
AND MANAGERS—RESULTS AND COMPETENCIES

The management of executive performance sets the stage for how effective it will be at lower levels. If it's not a priority for executives, it's very unlikely to be a priority at lower levels.

Efforts to improve government management have to start with executives and managers. To be sure, there are differences between a business executive and a government executive—compensation is the most obvious—but both are the front line for planning and management of their organizations. Both should be held accountable for the performance of the operations they lead.

The purpose of executive-performance management is well stated in revised federal regulations for the Senior Executive Service (SES), released in 2015:

> In order to improve the overall performance of Government, agencies must establish performance management systems that hold senior executives accountable (within their assigned areas of responsibility and control) for their individual performance and for organizational performance by—
>
> - Encouraging excellence in senior executive performance;
> - Aligning executive performance plans with the results-oriented [organizational] goals required by [legislation];
> - Setting and communicating individual and organizational goals and expectations that clearly fall within the executive's area of responsibility and control;
> - Reporting on the success of meeting organizational goals (including any factors that may have impacted success);
> - Systematically appraising senior executive performance using measures that balance organizational results with customer and employee perspectives, and other perspectives as appropriate; and
> - Using performance appraisals as a basis for pay, awards, development, retention, removal, and other personnel decisions.

Each state and local jurisdiction should consider whether the purpose as stated for the SES is consistent with the local management agenda. If the statement is broadly endorsed by local leaders, then the problem is how to best plan and operationalize local policies and practices to achieve the purpose. As a starting point, it would be useful to determine where current practices fall short.

In business the foundation for planning, managing, and evaluating executive performance has not changed in decades. The only change is the introduction of software to monitor progress and facilitate decision making. As stated previously, the core practice is based on individual performance goals that align with and contribute to achieving organizational goals.

A key difference when compared with business is that elected and appointed officials frequently do not have extensive experience managing organizations or holding employees accountable. Their focus and expertise is public policy, not day-to-day management. Many have not had management training. They would benefit from guidance in defining performance standards, holding progress meetings throughout the year, and in evaluating year-end results. The differences in experience and focus result in inconsistencies that weaken the process. That's why coaches can be so valuable.

In the business world, individual performance goals are universal, extending down into the professional ranks. When employees reach the executive level, they have lived with the process for years. At each level supervisors rely on goals to manage their people. At each level they know they are accountable and will be rewarded for achieving their goals.

It's not simply that goal-setting skills are important, however; it's the process of goal-based management. In well-managed companies, managers have regular meetings, at least monthly, in which they discuss progress, developments, and so on. They agree on adjustments needed to improve performance. The process is ongoing and future-oriented, focusing on progress and steps to succeed. The new GE approach exemplifies the process.

The new book *Leadership Capital Index* by David Ulrich, *Business Week*'s number-one management guru, provides a valuable framework for looking at the executive process. Ulrich prescribes the management process to hold executives accountable for performance. His chapter titled "Performance Accountability Process" is a good overview of the best practice and is summarized in chapter 9.

The performance-management process is essentially the same at all levels. It starts with agreeing on what the employee is expected to accomplish and concludes with evaluating how well he or she satisfied those expectations. That's essentially the same as teaching in school or assigning tasks to a child. It applies whenever someone assigns a task to another.

Ulrich's argument can be summarized with selected points from the chapter.

- The effectiveness of the process has little to do with specific policies; it's more the ability to have a candid, thorough, positive, and specific performance conversation.
- The conversations should begin with "clear standards of what makes good performance." It should be clear what is not adequate or acceptable and also what constitutes outstanding performance. People commonly want to be seen as good at what they do.
- There has to be agreement on what's expected with results "linked to consequences." That is a key to accountability. There has to be an expectation of consequences, even if it's only that proverbial "pat on the back."
- "Differentiated performance requires differentiated consequences. Consequences can be positive or negative, financial and nonfinancial." It's widely believed that hard work and good performance should be recognized.

When managers are not guided in recognizing and rewarding employees, it opens the door to favoritism and inconsistency. Relying on a stated policy and positive financial results has "the benefit of being precise, measurable and comparable across positions and people."

There are jobs where individual performance is not a relevant consideration. That's true, for example, on an assembly line. But in this era of knowledge organizations those jobs are disappearing. Individuals can make a difference, and that needs to be encouraged. When rewards are managed fairly, few people would dispute the value of the practice.

THE "WHAT AND THE HOW"—RESULTS AND COMPETENCIES

A core issue that contributes to dissatisfaction is that employers too often fail to define the purpose of performance reviews—why it's important—or what is expected of managers. The worst case is the frequently stated belief that the process is required only because of HR. Too often it's seen only as a form that has to be completed.

It's recommended that the purpose be communicated simply to improve employee performance. The criteria, possible incentives, and training for managers should be planned to support that purpose. The process should emphasize the importance of high performance but also reinforce the need for job-specific feedback and its role in improving capabilities.

The traditional role of performance standards should be addressed in system planning. The practice was originally developed by industrial engineers and used widely in manufacturing and in white-collar "factories" focused on paper processing. The argument for using performance standards continues to surface in government. An increasingly prevalent problem is that in a dynamic work environment, standards can quickly become dated.

When standards are defined at a single level, they are treated as minimally acceptable performance. Performing at standard is then all that's expected. It is effectively a pass/fail policy. It's inconsistent with the need to improve performance.

In industry, the focus is on identifying and rewarding the best performers. They generally stand out. Coworkers know and usually agree on who they are. In government too often the focus is on identifying the few poor performers, and that gives the process a negative connotation.

Where the stated purpose is to improve performance, the process has to focus on (1) what they are expected to accomplish—the "what"—and (2) feedback to help them understand their strengths as well as the competencies where improvement is needed—the "how." No one can be expected to improve their performance until they understand where they need to improve. Providing that feedback should be the central purpose in managing performance.

Improved performance requires both a new, more flexible approach to work and enhanced capabilities. The latter is focused on competencies known to be associated with high performance. For practical reasons a profile of key competencies should be defined for each job family.

To reinforce the value of exemplary performance—for both the "what" and the "how"—experience shows it is advantageous to define performance criteria at three levels: (1) the highest expected level or "role model" (a phrase used by the U.S. Government Accountability Office); (2) met expectations; and (3) failed to meet expectations. Many employees will strive to reach the highest levels.

The use of three levels is increasingly common in the private sector. The phrases "A players," "B players," and "C players" are used in workforce planning. Using levels meets an organization's need to identify its stars as well as the small number who are problems. They will also reduce the inflated rating problem. The practice is well suited to support a pay-for-performance policy. (Although it does not appear to have been studied, the distribution of ratings with a five-level scale is frequently clustered on the highest three ratings.)

This is very similar to coaching in sports. There the "what" includes team and individual goals and the "how" are the different skills needed to excel at each position. Quarterbacks obviously require different skills than tight ends or linebackers. Role model players and their skills are often identified in media reports.

Star goalies and star baseball pitchers all received feedback on needed skills as they learned their craft. Coaching is important to the development of every athlete—and every star performer.

In the same way, employee skills are important to performance at every level. Investing time to identify key skills and providing feedback are essential to improved performance.

Encouraging employees to grow and enhance their skills will help build a sense of engagement. It's reciprocal; employees will be more committed to organizational goals.

As with team sports, it is sometimes not feasible or practical to define individual performance goals. Parole Officers (POs) are an example. Hospital-based nurses are another occupation where "teamwork" and team performance are the relevant basis for goal setting. For POs, to illustrate the point, the team/group goal might be to reduce the rate of recidivism. However, since the most difficult offenders are often assigned to the best POs, everyone cannot be evaluated on the same standard for reducing recidivism.

THE ROLE OF TECHNOLOGY

Technology does not solve the perceived problems with managing performance, although it's essential in all but the smallest organizations. Its value is that it facilitates the collection and assembly of information. It also enhances consistency. The GE smartphone app, as an example, would be a valuable tool for every manager.

So many companies today have developed and marketed software for managing pay and performance; several websites claim to help evaluate the possible software providers. A search will identify the possibilities.

It needs to be emphasized that technology is only a tool. As Ulrich argues, effective performance management depends on "candid, thorough, positive and specific performance conversations."

Everyone involved will need training in using whatever system is adopted.

GETTING EMPLOYEES ON BOARD

The dissatisfaction with performance-management practices will continue to undermine support until employers adopt the strategies to address the problems, that is, until employees are convinced that management is committed to needed change.

It is solidly established that the way employees are managed is a key to their motivation and to their performance. Research shows that highly motivated employees—emotionally committed or engaged employees—can be as much as 30 percent to 40 percent more productive than those who do not share that attitude. (That depends on being both empowered and trusted.)

Contrary to the arguments of the critics, people want to know how well they are doing and are receptive to feedback—they want to grow and improve—when it is honest and constructive. That makes performance management in the broadest sense central to creating a work environment where employees share that sense of commitment. Toward that end, research confirms what is needed for most workers to make that commitment:

- They want to know what's expected, and what they need to achieve to be successful. Employees should know what is seen as outstanding performance as well as unacceptable performance.
- They want to be recognized and valued for their contribution and work effort. When their achievements are ignored or downplayed, it is unlikely the effort will be repeated. That is well established in psychology.
- For those who aspire "to be the best they can be," they want the support and the ongoing feedback to develop their capabilities and stay on track to achieve their career goals.
- They want to be treated fairly. A relatively new concept from psychologists—procedural justice—argues for making certain the decision process affecting employee careers is fair and unbiased.

It is far more likely that change will be welcomed if employees are involved in the planning and implementation. They know their jobs, the impediments to improved performance, and the changes that are needed better than any "expert." The experience years ago with reengineering confirms they are fully capable of addressing problems. That is why they are frequently asked to be subject matter experts in issues related to their jobs. When they are involved, they understand the reasons for change, are far more likely to be trusted by their coworkers, and will be effective advocates for change.

NEW BEST PRACTICE—CALIBRATION COMMITTEES

The importance of ensuring that the process is seen as fair and unbiased cannot be overstated. That is the reason the use of "calibration committees" has become an important trend in the private sector. It was on Google's list of work rules. The committees are composed of peer-level managers who react to the ratings planned by fellow managers. When managers have to explain and defend ratings, it introduces a higher level of consistency and honesty.

As with teachers and judges, individuals have different perspectives of a job, the important skills, expectations, and so on. It's the old story that some teachers are tough graders, some are easy. Asking a calibration committee to review ratings levels the playing field.

HR AS EMPLOYEE CHAMPION

HR is not accountable for the success or failure of a performance-management system and cannot solve the problems without the solid support of top management. The function has virtually no control over how the system is used—nor should it. That is management's responsibility. However, HR can and should be proactive in monitoring and initiating changes to maintain a work environment that contributes to employee engagement and that includes supporting the development of employee capabilities.

HR is the obvious choice to take the lead for defining and strengthening the employee-organization relationship. The function's role is broader than monitoring the use of the performance system. It adds more value to focus on how employees are managed. It is a sensitive role that requires HR specialists to work closely with and gain the acceptance of other executives and managers.

A concomitant responsibility is monitoring performance ratings for patterns of bias and discrimination. It would also be productive each year to use surveys and focus groups to assess how the pay and performance systems are perceived by managers and employees. It would be beneficial to commit to fine-tuning to address perceived problems. Organizational leaders will no doubt always look to HR to create and reinforce the value of these practices.

ADDITIONAL RESOURCES

Daniels, Aubrey C., and Jon S. Bailey. *Performance Management: Changing Behavior That Drives Organizational Performance.* 5th ed. Performance Management Publications, 2014. The advertising claims five hundred thousand copies of the book have been sold.

Aguinis, Herman. *Performance Management.* 3rd ed. Prentice Hall, 2012.

Ferguson, Roger. *Finally! Performance Assessment That Works: Big Five Performance Management Paperback.* CreateSpace Independent Publishing Platform, 2014.

Pulakos, Elaine D. *Performance Management: A New Approach for Driving Business Results.* Wiley, 2009.

Lawler, Dr. Edward. "Performance Management: The Three Important Features You're Forgetting." *Forbes*, April 15, 2015. Ed Lawler has been a recognized expert for three decades.

Risher, Howard. "Employers Need to Invest to Strengthen Performance Management." *Compensation & Benefits Review* 47 (2015): 55–59.

Risher, Howard. "Performance Management Needs to Be Fixed." *Compensation & Benefits Review* 46 (2014): 191–94.

Risher, Howard. "Getting Performance Management on Track." *Compensation & Benefits Review* 43 (2011): 273–81.

11

Developing an Effective Compensation Program

When the goal is to raise performance levels, it is difficult to imagine a work-management strategy that does not involve pay for performance (or performance-related pay, as it's called occasionally). Pay for performance is effectively universal in the private sector and has become an increasingly dominant practice over the past two decades. The belief that "success and hard work should be rewarded" is deeply rooted in the American culture. The best performers in virtually every field are recognized and rewarded in some way, starting in grade school.

However, the transition by public employers to a program model with salary increases linked to performance has not been smooth or easy. The switch started roughly half a century ago. When the idea is proposed, it unfortunately becomes a political hot button.

The first successful "merit pay" policy in state government dates to the late 1960s, although any documentation appears to be lost. At the federal level the first merit pay policy was adopted in 1980 as a "demonstration project" when two naval research labs merged. There have been a number of successful transition stories at the federal, state, and local levels, but the traditional step-increase program model continues to dominate.

The failed attempts in the Bush administration to switch to pay for performance in the Departments of Defense and Homeland Security continue to inhibit change at the federal level. Both initiatives started in the months after 9/11. The Homeland Security project, MaxHR, never really got started. The planning and rollout for the Defense Department's National Security Personnel System (NSPS) was a multiyear project that was finally shut down in the early years of the Obama administration. A similar but less publicized project in the intelligence community agencies was also ended. The General Schedule (GS) salary system, with its automatic step increases, has been the foundation of federal civil service and remains largely unchanged (except for the introduction of locality pay) since it was adopted in 1949.

At the state and local government levels, the experience has been far more positive. The earliest policies date to the 1960s. In the mid-1990s Charlotte, North Carolina, gained recognition as a model for city management. The city's broad management changes included a pay-for-performance salary program along with team-based bonuses. Today, several states along with a number of local jurisdictions have successful performance-based pay programs. Once a pay-for-performance policy is adopted, experience shows it soon becomes the new normal. Despite the successes, a number of the states where unions are influential have seen little change.

A SNAPSHOT OF THE PAST

Cash compensation programs include both base pay—hourly wages or salaries—and the prospect of lump-sum cash awards. In addition, to recognize employee accomplishments, employers use a panoply of reward practices, some having a financial value (e.g., dinner for two) and many that have no financial value. All should be included as elements in a "direct" compensation program.

Until the 1960s, virtually all wage and salary programs in both the public and private sectors were based on the same general principles. The framework for the program was a series of overlapping salary ranges. Jobs were classified or assigned to ranges based on an analysis and documentation of a job's duties, which was then used to classify or evaluate the job. Employee salaries started at the minimum or step 1 of their range and progressed through the range based on a schedule of step increases.

The word "schedule" was commonly used to refer to the framework of salary ranges. The word is still used where the program remains largely unchanged, as is the case with the federal GS salary system. In the private sector the word "structure" is used universally.

It was not until the 1950s that salary surveys were first conducted and used by companies in salary management. The initial surveys collected data on top management salaries.

Employees generally started and stayed with the same employer throughout their careers. There was only a loose connection to labor markets. The program focus was internal, with a classification system used to determine the appropriate salary grade and range for each job.

Looking back, the only program goal was maintaining "internal equity" as defined by the classification system. Job classification was and is a highly bureaucratic and labor-intensive process. The process to classify a job, starting with job analysis interviews with incumbents and managers, often took weeks or months. The product of the interviews was a job description summarizing job duties. For blue-collar jobs, job analysis includes the observation of incumbents, a practice that dates to the early factories.

Wage and salary programs were essentially static for years or decades (except for periodic range increases to remain competitive). An employee's job duties typically went unchanged for years. When a job vacancy occurred, the employee with the longest service was generally promoted to fill the opening. As long as an employee performed at an acceptable level and stayed out of trouble, they could expect their step increase.

Wage and salary programs in government evolved slowly. The federal government "modernized" the GS system in the 1970s when a job evaluation system, based on what is referred to as the point factor method—the Factor Evaluation System—was developed to replace the "old" classification process. That, of course, was a decade or so later than similar job evaluation systems were adopted in industry.

A common but often unrecognized problem today is the impact staff cuts have had on administering a traditional classification system. Data on head count by occupation compiled by BLS shows HR has experienced some of the most severe cuts. With pay freezes there is increased pressure to reclassify jobs to higher grades, but many jurisdictions no longer have the specialists to handle the volume of reclassification requests. At the federal level it's acknowledged that "grade creep" or overgrading has become a problem. The cost of the textbook administration of a classification system is difficult to justify.

CHANGES IN THE PRIVATE SECTOR PROGRAM MODEL

Compensation programs in the private sector also evolved slowly. The impetus for change started in the 1960s and 1970s when people began to move between employers in midcareer. That prompted employers to become more concerned about maintaining competitive salaries. Salary surveys proliferated.

Then in the 1980s, the years of high inflation triggered rapid salary increases. Cost-of-living adjustments were common. The experience made business leaders far more sensitive to labor costs.

Companies relied on job evaluation systems to assign jobs to grades. The job evaluation system marketed by Hay Associates was used widely.

"Merit pay," now pay for performance, has been the dominant salary-increase policy for half a century. Executives, managers, and many professionals also participate in incentive plans tied to company success. In addition, in publicly traded companies stock-option grants are common. At the executive level salaries are commonly a small percentage of total compensation.

Another less important but universal feature of private sector programs is related to the "exempt"/"nonexempt" distinction and the Fair Labor Standards Act. Virtually all private sector employers maintain separate pay programs for nonexempt office support and for hourly workers. Each is aligned with pay levels in relevant labor markets.

The 1990–1991 recession prompted companies to reexamine their management practices to reduce costs and make their organizations more responsive to market trends.

Companies downsized, eliminated levels of management, eliminated bureaucratic practices, and tied compensation more closely to company financial performance. Job evaluation systems were seen as bureaucratic, costly, and an impediment to change. In the early years of the decade companies dropped job evaluation systems and switched to market-based pay programs.

The program change that received the most attention was GE's adoption of a "broad band" salary program model. A number of prominent companies followed GE's lead and replaced their traditional programs with similar programs. It has not been documented, but the GE program may have been based on the salary system introduced in 1980 when two naval research labs merged. The lab's new system was based on a university faculty salary program. (The banded salary model is discussed later in this chapter.)

The corporate banded programs had a decided difference that proved to be a fatal flaw. The salary bands were 100 percent or more from lowest to highest salary. (The federal GS salary ranges, by contrast, are effectively 30 percent.) Looking back, it is clear that companies were rejecting the logic and close control along with the bureaucracy of traditional salary programs.

The new flexibility gave managers too much discretion. Salaries rose through the bands to well above market levels. With the higher labor costs, interest in the banded program model waned; many were replaced by more traditional salary grade and range programs.

Today, the dominant program model is almost identical to what companies used in the 1980s, but there is an important distinction—it has little of the bureaucracy associated with older programs.

The common framework or model for salary structures is a series of overlapping ranges. The ranges are typically 50 percent from the minimum to the maximum. New hires start at or close to the range minimum, depending on credentials. All increases are based on performance. When an incumbent is able to perform all job duties well, he or she should in theory be paid at the range midpoint, which is planned as a competitive salary. In many companies, only above-average performers can be paid by policy above the midpoint—and thus above market.

The graph that follows illustrates salary ranges with a "range spread" of 50 percent from minimum to maximum.

Grade   Salaries (000)

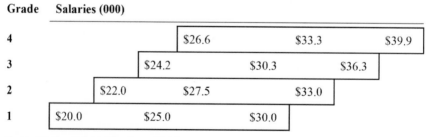

Figure 11.1. Salary Structure Graph.

The difference in today's program model is that the focus is on managing salaries relative to prevailing pay levels in relevant labor markets. Only a small percentage of companies continue to use a formal job evaluation system. "Fair pay" is now defined as a competitive, market salary; the old "internal equity" has been almost forgotten. Companies use survey data and their pay policy to determine the planned pay level for each job. It's then assigned to the range where the planned salary is closest to the range midpoint. It's a simple strategy that can be communicated easily. Jobs can be "classified" in less than an hour.

ATTRACTING TALENT IS A UNIVERSAL GOAL

Another important difference in private sector programs is the shift from thinking about employees as a cost to managing them as an asset. With costs, the common goal is to reduce them. Applying that logic to wage and salary management leads to paying as little as possible. In contrast, when employees are seen as assets, employers plan salaries to attract and retain needed talent. Maintaining a competitive compensation program is basic to that strategy. Some companies pay above-market salaries by policy to attract top talent. They see the higher pay as an investment.

To support the strategy, companies complete annual "market analyses" comparing their pay levels with the levels of other employers competing in the labor market. They budget the funds each year needed to remain competitive. That's true for hospitals, colleges, associations—every other sector.

There is, of course, the argument that compensation is less important to people interested in working in the public service. It is no doubt true for many government workers, but there is no reason to think it's limited to government. Many occupations are not considered to be high paying. Job challenge, job security, benefits, and opportunities to work on certain problems are among other reasons for career choice.

The "pay is less important" argument implicitly assumes pay levels are close to market levels, and those other factors are controlling an employee's career decisions. Studies, however, have never considered the impact on career choice if pay levels are known to be 20 to 30 percent or more below the levels paid by other employers.

There is a decided difference between a pay program where the policy is to maintain salaries broadly aligned with market and one where each year salaries fall further and further behind the pay levels in other sectors.

As the gap grows, resignations and retirements will increase, the qualifications of applicants will decline, and applications from millennials will decrease. Pay may not be the reason an employee chooses a government career, but each year with a pay freeze or pay increases below those granted by other employers will add to workforce problems.

Today, outside of government, it would be a rare employer that did not assess, formally or informally, how its pay levels compare with market levels. For larger employers of all types—those similar in size to government—the common policy is to align salary ranges with market pay levels.

An employer's "pay policy" is based on its talent strategy. In a textbook pay program, an employee who is fully competent in the job should be paid at the planned salary level. The overwhelming majority of employers plan their program to pay average market salaries.

USING MARKET SURVEY DATA

As a practical point, since the purpose is to compete in labor markets, it is important to identify the other employers competing for talent. Virtually all employers actually compete in multiple labor markets. The market for office-support personnel, for example, would typically be limited to other employers within an easy commute of the employee's home. Professionals are more likely to look for jobs across a broader region, so the market would include those who hire qualified candidates from a multistate area. At the executive level, search firms sometimes look nationally for the best applicants.

Industry is also important. Some industries pay better than others. Most of the broader surveys report data by industry. If a high-paying company is locally based, it drives up the pay levels for other employers. Public employers compete locally with all other employers for many job families. But, of course, there are occupations unique to government. There are specialized survey sources for most jobs.

It's been estimated that more than two thousand salary surveys are conducted annually across the United States. They are conducted by consulting firms, government, business/industry groups, and professional associations. The new development is the collection of individual pay data via the Internet. A quick Google search will identify the surveys for a given occupation or industry. That's true for a number of government occupations as well. For example, a search for police pay surveys produced eleven million hits. A search for teacher pay surveys found almost ninety million hits.

An important issue today is that pay information is available to anyone over the Internet. The data are of suspect validity and is not necessarily relevant to a specific job or employer, but the public may not appreciate those issues. The critics who argue that government employees are overpaid are more interested in making their point than in the validity of their claims. If for no other reason, it makes sense to assemble credible survey data confirming employees are not overpaid to be ready to refute their claims.

Surveys vary widely in quality and cost. Some professional associations compile member data and make a summary available without cost. At the other extreme, the best surveys are conducted by consulting firms for industry groups where company representatives meet to discuss the survey and the jobs to be covered. Those surveys can cost $50,000 or more, and the data are available only to participating companies.

An easy first step for public employers is to check with counterparts in other jurisdictions to learn what, if any, surveys they use for market pricing. It would also make sense to join local HR groups, since they often sponsor surveys of member employers. An Internet search would also be useful. Public employers can also, of course, conduct surveys or turn to groups like the Mountain States Employers Council to see if they conduct surveys.

There are a wealth of surveys, and assembling the data for a market analysis is straightforward for anyone with a background in basic statistics.

The goal in completing a market analysis is to determine the market pay levels consistent with the pay policy for jobs comparable to those covered in surveys. The jobs selected should be representative of the job families and job levels.

Pay freezes save money today but damage government's "brand" as an employer. That could and almost certainly has adversely affected the recruiting of young workers for years. It also contributes to increased turnover—early retirements as well as resignations. That represents a loss of job knowledge along with the direct and indirect costs of replacing an employee. In addition, the freezes (along with the criticism) adversely impact employee morale—and lower performance. Whatever the justification for a freeze, allowing pay levels to fall too far below market levels will have a cost that increases with time.

THE NEW DIRECTION IN SALARY MANAGEMENT—SALARY BANDING

When the two naval research labs in southern California merged, the naval commander in charge was told by his HR staff that it would take two years to classify all the jobs in the new organization. He told them that was unacceptable, and that they had to find a better answer. Fortunately, the then recently enacted Civil Service Reform Act of 1978 allowed federal agencies to experiment with new ideas in salary management (known as "demonstration" projects).

The HR staff suggested adopting the program model commonly used for faculty in higher education (e.g., salary bands for Professors, Assistant Professors, etc.). The lab workforce included a number of highly educated scientists and engineers. The Commanding Officer accepted the proposal. In a meeting to discuss the planned program with his direct reports, he is reported to have said, "If you have any questions, ask them now. But when you leave this room, you will be supportive of our plans." The new program was a success and became the model for several federal "demo" projects.

The National Academy of Public Administration has recommended the banded salary model to replace the GS system in three reports starting as far back as 1991. The Department of Defense adopted the idea for its failed NSPS program. When the GS system is eventually replaced, it's very likely it will be based on a banded model. The Charlotte, North Carolina, pay program was based on a banded model. The state of South Carolina adopted a banded salary program in the mid-1990s. Banded salary programs are now used by several states.

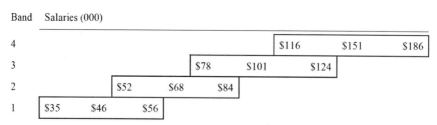

Figure 11.2.   Salary Bands.

The phrase "broad banding" was adopted to refer to the new program model. Today, "salary banding" is a more commonly used phrase.

Banding is a simple framework for managing salaries. There is no standard format. A common banded program has a band for each of the three or four levels in a career ladder. A distinguishing feature is the minimal overlap from one band to the next. The bands are based on market data. Employees progress from one band to the next when there is an opening and they are ready for promotion to the next level. Figure 11.2 illustrates salary bands.

When employees make lateral job changes, it's generally to broaden their job skills or to take advantage of proven skills. Some companies recognize the value to the organization and then give a small increase, such as 3 percent, to recognize the increased value.

Banding has several decided advantages. It shifts the focus from the job to the employee and their career progress. It minimizes the time and resources to classify jobs. A job can be classified in minutes. For an organization that wants to move from one traditional grade and range structure to another (the new structure would typically involve an increase or decrease in the number of grades), it would take an extended period to classify jobs in the new structure—which was the reason the Commanding Officer declined to accept the delay. That inevitably produces "winners and losers." With a banded program, jobs are simply slid horizontally to the new bands. The cost to maintain a banded program is dramatically less.

Perhaps the most important advantage compared to a traditional government program is the flexibility to respond to market dynamics, organizational changes, and individual growth and development. The rigidity of those old government pay programs like the federal GS system made them part of the problem. At the federal level, the GS salary system has become a barrier to modernizing government.

PAY DISCRIMINATION

Concern about pay discrimination gained national prominence in the 1980s when women advocated pay equity or comparable worth. It prompted consulting firms to rethink job evaluation practices that dated to the post–World War II era and that clearly devalued what were then jobs traditionally held by women. However, it was largely forgotten in the 1990–1991 recession and never gained a foothold in business.

Despite dramatic movement of women into male-dominated jobs over the years, women on average are still paid 79 percent of what men are paid.[1] A number of conflicting "macro" statistical analyses over the years have attempted to study what factors contribute to the pay gap. They have compared male and female pay levels, taking into account education level, years of experience, and so on. Over the years the differential has declined, but all have found an unexplained gap. It's assumed that the remaining gap is discrimination.

Those analyses are based on multivariate statistical methods that are understood by relatively few people. They also fail to take into account all factors known to explain pay differentials. They are certainly useful to keep the issue before the public. As discussed in this chapter, employers have largely moved away from job evaluation systems that claim to determine the relative value of jobs.

However, federal law applies to men and women performing essentially the same job. Comparative starting salaries and salary increases are clearly important and need to be monitored closely. The HR office should be proactive in looking for possible discrimination. The role of calibration committees (discussed later in this chapter) is a way to minimize manager bias.

Perhaps more important are federal and state actions making pay more transparent and protecting employees who question pay practices and who discuss pay with colleagues. That has always been true in government, of course. Until men and women are no longer channeled into separate "male" and "female" job categories, there will be a pay gap.

THE ARGUMENTS FOR AND AGAINST PAY FOR PERFORMANCE

Plans to switch to pay for performance can be contentious. It represents a significant change in the role of managers and in their relationship with employees. For employees it represents a significant change in the psychological contract. Announced plans to switch to pay for performance frequently trigger a time of uncertainty and anxiety, especially when management is widely distrusted.

A decided difference between the public and private sectors is that in business the focus is on rewarding the best performers. That gives the policy a positive connotation. The policies have been in place for years and are accepted as the norm by new hires. Another important difference is that individual salaries and salary increases are confidential. A few employees are denied an increase, but aside from close friends their situation is not widely known.

In government, the focus, as one union spokesperson stated in a congressional hearing, "is all on the negative, the threat of punishment for poor performance.

This is all stick and no carrot." Other union leaders would no doubt voice a similar argument.

The statement may have been triggered as a reaction to politicians who in some cases support the change to deny increases to poor performers. Unions use that to build resistance.

Academics sometimes voice opposition, but a version of pay for performance is the standard policy for faculty pay in universities. It's doubtful the best-performing faculty would want to revert to step increases.

Critics have argued that research does not confirm that pay for performance actually improves performance. One of the most frequently cited sources is the best-selling book by Daniel Pink, *Drive: The Surprising Truth about What Motivates Us* (2011). His argument is based on research related to the theory of intrinsic satisfaction and studies from the 1960s that had students rewarded for performing small tasks. The flaw in his argument is that salary increases are once a year and, in contrast to the student tasks, the increases are not tied to specific tasks. The increases should be communicated as recognition of learning and accomplishments throughout the year.

Pink's alternative—paying employees above market levels—is very unlikely to gain acceptance. It means higher costs, no assurance performance will improve, and for some he must assume employees will no longer compare their salary with the pay of their peers. Throughout his career he has not had the learning experience that comes from managing groups of employees.

Other researchers have looked at performance ratings before and after a performance pay policy was adopted. When the ratings did not improve, they concluded that the policy had no impact on performance. That assumes that the ratings are a valid measure of performance.

Despite the arguments of Daniel Pink and others, the business community is solidly committed to pay for performance. Business leaders would resist any proposed policy that guarantees pay increases. That's true even for the smallest mom-and-pop businesses. The philosophy that hard work and accomplishment should be rewarded is broadly accepted by employees at all levels. Employees understand that they benefit, if only in job security, when their company is successful.

It's also important to appreciate that a salary increase policy does not exist in a vacuum. An often-overlooked aspect of a performance pay policy is that the assessment of performance is also important as a determinant of employee career progress. For executives and managers, cash incentives and stock ownership plans represent far larger financial reward opportunities. Plus, multiple management practices reinforce the importance of performance throughout the year. In that environment ongoing successes are celebrated.

In a work environment or culture where performance is understood to be tied to organization success, pay for performance and the small differences in the increases are not a powerful motivator. But the increase policy along with the performance ratings reinforce the focus on business goals and the importance of performance. The recognition value in rewarding high performers is possibly more important than the

WHY PERFORMANCE PAY IS JUST THE BEGINNING

Plenty more could be done to transform public workforces into meritocracies.

by Charles Chieppo | Posted previously on Governing.com, January 5, 2016

Indiana governor Mike Pence's recent decision to dole out $42 million in performance-based pay raises to state employees is the latest milestone in a slow march toward using incentives to increase the productivity of government workforces. Employees who meet expectations will get 3 percent raises, those who exceed them will reap 4 percent increases, and outstanding performers will see their salaries jump by 6 percent.

Although Pence's action is a step in the right direction, much more should be done to transform state and local governments into meritocracies. While some of the Indiana employees who will receive raises are unionized, collective bargaining agreements often make it difficult to expend pay for performance to union employees. Instead of mandating that each worker is treated the same, collective bargaining agreements could specify annual increases for the bargaining unit as a whole but give managers flexibility to allocate individual raises based on merit.

State and local governments also should have the ability to raise salaries for workers in high-demand fields. When Google and Facebook moved in offices near an important state data center, North Carolina responded in 2014 by putting $7.5 million into a fund to retain not only state employees those companies might want to hire but also other workers with in-demand skills such as nurses. Such a program could also be used to attract teachers in subject areas where there is a shortage, such as math, science, and special education.

As some states and a few local governments experience surpluses for the first time since the Great Recession, public officials would do well to learn from the example of Pence's predecessor, Mitch Daniels. When Indiana found itself with an unexpected $1.18 billion surplus in 2011, Daniels shared part of the bounty with the highest-performing state employees.

Of course, the success of performance pay depends on the competence of government managers. Public employee unions take a lot of heat—some of it justified—for public sector labor practices such as pension spiking and abuse of sick-time and overtime rules, but managers must also step up if state and local governments are to use incentives to improve productivity.

There is a strong temptation for managers to take the path of least resistance and treat all employees the same. But any short-term gain from that approach is fraught with long-term consequences. Productive workers leave; after a time, generous pension incentives make it hard for others to go, and the result is an older workforce that values job security over advancement—not exactly a recipe for efficiency and productivity.

In the final analysis, transforming state and local governments into meritocracies requires changing the culture. It is almost by definition a slow and painful process, but one that could ultimately pay handsome rewards.

Charles Chieppo is a Research Fellow at the Ash Center of the Harvard Kennedy School and the Principal of Chieppo Strategies, a public policy writing and advocacy firm. He frequently posts a column on Governing.com.

added dollars. Employees want, possibly need, to have their value recognized. It's important to employee engagement.

In contrast, the message with a step increase policy is that performance is not important. When increases are essentially automatic and promotions are based on seniority, the importance of performance is downplayed. Both practices undercut efforts to create a culture where performance is a shared focus.

Two psychological theories support pay for performance. Equity theory argues that an employee's motivation is linked to his/her perception of equity, fairness, and justice practiced by the management. The best performers want to be recognized for their contribution. Expectancy theory argues that workers are likely to repeat or continue desired behavior if they can expect it to be recognized or rewarded. If extra effort is not recognized, it's not likely to be repeated. Both were discussed in chapter 3.

STRATEGIES TO SWITCH TO PAY FOR PERFORMANCE

The textbook pay-for-performance policy is based on increase percentages specified in a "merit matrix," which is defined on one side by performance rating levels and on the other by what compensation specialists refer to as "compa-ratios." Compa-ratios are simply an employee's salary divided by the salary range midpoint. With 50 percent min-to-max ranges the ratios range from .80 to 1.20.

To reiterate, the common policy in developing salary structures and in planning pay-for-performance policies is that when an employee is fully competent in a job, he should be paid the planned salary. That is to say, their compa-ratio should be close to 1.00.

A typical merit matrix might look like figure 11.3.

The matrix and the percentages are to some degree arbitrary. The planning starts by determining an average performance rating from the prior year or two along with the average compa-ratio—the combination for this purpose is the average employee.

A core assumption is that an average performer is to be granted an average increase. Another assumption is that the distribution of ratings will not change significantly from year to year (i.e., the percentage of the workforce at each rating level will not change significantly).

Currently, employers are budgeting roughly 3.0 percent for increases. Employee data and their salaries make it possible to determine the aggregate payroll dollars in each cell of the matrix, and the totals then can be used to estimate the increase dollars in each cell. The designated percentage increases in each cell usually have to be adjusted, often several times, so the total increases across all cells is equal to the overall budget. An important point is that every dollar awarded to a poor performer (the lower cells) means fewer dollars will be available for the high performers.

Compa-Ratio

Performance Rating		.80 -.90	.90- 1.0	1.0 – 1.1	1.1 – 1.2
	5	5.5%	4.5%	3.0%	1.5%
	4	4.5%	3.5%	2.5%	1.0%
	3	3.0%	2.5%	1.5%	0.5%
	2	2.0%	1.5%	1.0%	0
	1	1.5%	1.0%	0	0

Figure 11.3.

The matrix reflects the usual pattern of a learning curve. That is, an employee's job knowledge increases rapidly in the first year or two and eventually flattens. The assumption is that their value and contribution will follow their learning curve.

Note that the emphasis is on the employee's "value" and the salary level, not the increase.

Organizations with step-increase pay programs rarely have strong performance-management systems. Badly inflated ratings are common. But ratings that lack credibility undermine the perceived fairness of the pay increases.

Top management has to make the switch an organizational priority. The early strategy should be twofold: to invest in improving the performance system (see chapter 10) and to initiate the planning for pay for performance for executives and managers. If the policy is not seen as "working" at the senior levels, it's unlikely to be successful at lower levels. They should be accountable for the success of the new policy.

Pay for performance is a zero-sum problem. That is to say, granting larger increases for the best performers means fewer dollars are available for other employees. That is a core issue.

In the private sector the funds budgeted for increases are allocated pro rata to managers, and they are then responsible for deciding individual increases, usually within guidelines specifying the increases at each rating level.

A simple transition policy is to set aside a small percentage of the increase budget (e.g., 0.5 percent) as a separate fund for rewarding high performers. The balance of the budget can then be granted as a general increase to all employees. The "bonus" awards, if limited to 20 percent of the workforce, for example, would give each recipient an added 2.5 percent of salary, and for a midlevel employee that's roughly $1,500. It introduces and reinforces the idea of rewarding top performers. After a year or two it should make the transition easier to accept.

Pay for performance requires a commitment to performance management. It will be important to monitor increases to avoid charges of discrimination and favoritism. It should be reinforced by periodic messages from top management confirming the importance of performance.

BONUSES AND INCENTIVES

For the purpose of this discussion, cash awards can be paid as either a "bonus" or an "incentive." The two terms are often used interchangeably, but in the jargon used by compensation specialists, bonus awards are largely subjective and decided after an accomplishment or event. Bonuses are sometimes paid as a gesture of goodwill (e.g., a Christmas bonus). Incentives, in contrast, are based on a formula that specifies the amounts that can be earned and the linkage to specific results. (See the discussion in chapter 9.)

Cash bonus awards are used widely to recognize performance. The amounts should be budgeted and made available pro rata so that the reward opportunities are similar across the organization. There should also be a common set of rules for governing the amounts (e.g., no larger than $100), the possible forms other than cash, and the review and approval process. The HR office should review awards, looking for patterns related to fairness.

The decisions to award bonuses are generally made by managers and supervisors to recognize an employee's "special" achievement. The usual argument is that awards should be made shortly after an accomplishment. When bonuses are paid at year end, they're likely to be too far removed to be motivational. An idea is to ask a group of employees to develop the rules for bonus awards. That will avoid claims of unfairness. It is probably better to make a number of small bonus awards rather than a few larger awards. The public recognition is possibly more important than the money for many employees.

There are also opportunities to introduce group or team incentives. "Gain sharing" plans with payouts tied to savings were introduced by a union leader in the 1930s. More recently, similar plans with payouts linked to achieving goals—"goal sharing"—have proven to be an effective way to raise performance levels. Charlotte, North Carolina, as long ago as the 1990s had incentives in each department with payouts based on goals and metrics relevant to each department. Incentives are a proven strategy to improve performance.

THE KEY IS PERFORMANCE MANAGEMENT

In practice the difference in the salary increase to reward the best performers is rarely more than 2 to 3 percent. If the budget for increases is 3 percent, an average performer might expect 2.5 percent and the best 5 percent. In a weekly paycheck the difference after taxes would be barely be enough to buy lunch for a family at a fast-food restaurant. The dollar differences may be small, but it would be difficult to convince an employee an average increase is fair, especially if they believe they are better than "average."

The critics normally focus on the salary policy, but the dollars are governed by performance ratings. If the ratings are not credible, it's unlikely employees will be satisfied with their increases. The core concern with ratings credibility is a strong argument for relying on calibration committees to review ratings. The increases should be reviewed for possible bias and discrimination.

The message that performance is a priority is essential and has to come from top management. This is not an HR problem; it's a management issue. With a step increase policy, performance management is often seen by managers as an HR annoyance. Pay for performance makes the management of performance an immediate concern. Employers should invest the time to confirm that the process is viewed positively as an early step in transitioning to performance pay.

There is solid evidence that workers want to have their value recognized, but surveys of employees frequently show they are dissatisfied with reward and recognition practices. That problem can be addressed if top management makes it a priority. A number of public employers have made the transition successfully. It may not be the textbook reason for pay for performance, but it will be viewed more positively by high performers.

This is central to the management of all rewards, financial and nonfinancial. The rewards have to be consistent with relevant psychological theory and be seen as fair and consistent with employee views of comparative performance. In other words, rewards have to go to the best performers (as defined by the performance-management process). Then rewards will strengthen motivation.

ADDITIONAL RESOURCES

Risher, Howard, and Adam Reese. *Primer on Total Compensation in Government.* IPMA.HR, 2016.

Risher, Howard. *Planning Wage and Salary Programs.* WorldatWork, 2009.

Berger, Lance, and Dorothy Berger. *The Compensation Handbook, Sixth Edition: A State-of-the-Art Guide to Compensation Strategy and Design.* McGraw Hill Education, 2015.

Nelson, Bob. *1501 Ways to Reward Employees.* Workman Publishing, 2012. This book is a classic. It was first published as *1001 Ways to Reward Employees* in 1994 and is still available in bookstores.

"The Gender Pay Gap on the Anniversary of the Lilly Ledbetter Fair Pay Act," an Issue Brief released by the Council of Economic Advisers, January 2016.

NOTE

1. The most recent report on the gender pay gap is Council of Economic Advisers Issue Brief, "The Gender Pay Gap on the Anniversary of the Lilly Ledbetter Fair Pay Act," January 2016.

12

Cash + Benefits = Total Compensation

The sum of cash compensation and the net cost of benefits is "total compensation"; it's the single largest discretionary budget item at all levels of government. A problem today is that the typical government benefits package—including retirement income/savings benefits, health/medical benefits, death and disability benefits, and paid time off—is configured differently, involves a different pattern of employee contributions, and is typically funded in a different pattern than is common in the private sector.

In comparisons of the cost of benefits, the critics usually rely on broad data for all private sector employers. That ignores the fact that the millions of small, mom-and-pop businesses often provide only legally required benefits, which holds down the average private sector cost of benefits. (Of the total 5.7 million employers in the United States, 5.1 million have twenty employees or fewer.) The older workers in government agencies push up the costs.

Realistically, comparisons of government pay and benefits with levels in the private sector should be limited to employers competing for talent and should reflect the differences in workforce demographics.

But the appropriateness of the comparisons is never discussed in the reports released by the critics of government. In 2014, for example, the American Economic Institute released an eighty-seven-page report, "Overpaid or Underpaid? A State-by-State Ranking of Public-Employee Compensation," which compared the total compensation of state employees with the averages in the private sector. Another conservative think tank, the Cato Institute, has released a number of reports claiming public employees have "excessive retirement benefits," "excessive and fraudulent disability claims," and higher percentages of benefits. The Heritage Foundation, another conservative group, claims government employees work fewer hours, totaling a month less per year, to support their contention that public employees are overpaid.

The media also carry frequent critical articles. Public pension benefits and their funding have been a recent legislative and judicial focus in several states, and those stories receive extensive local coverage.

In this era of economic and job uncertainty, staff reductions, and frozen wages, the benefits provided to public employees appear—without adequate background information—to be overly generous. The level of benefits is significantly better than what an "average" U.S. worker enjoys. That is especially true for benefits provided to retired workers. The critics have learned this is a winning political argument with conservatives. The phrase "pension envy" has surfaced in media reports.

The fact is that private employers have reduced benefits and require increased employee contributions that make government benefits look richer by comparison.

Total compensation needs to be understood as more than a line in the budget. The components need to be justified separately, but more importantly in combination they are a so-called zero-sum problem. The pressure to reduce or control government costs means no component can be increased significantly unless there is a decrease in one or more other components. That makes it important to plan and manage the mix of pay and benefits to support good government.

The components are more or less universal across larger employers in both the private and public sectors. It's the mix or relative value that varies. The required level of employee contributions is another important difference. Public employers allocate more of the total compensation package to benefits and specifically to retirement benefits. That reflects historical patterns that are now difficult to change. The use of supplemental cash payments as a percentage of the total is higher in the private sector because of the cash incentives/bonuses and profit-sharing plans.

The relative breakdown of the compensation package, based on data compiled by the U.S. Bureau of Labor Statistics (BLS), is summarized in table 12.1.

Table 12.1. Comparative Total Compensation Costs

	Private Sector	State and Local Government	Federal Government
Wages and Salaries	69.3%	64.0%	68.8%
Benefits	30.7%	36.0%	31.2%
Paid Leave	6.9%	7.3%	
Supplemental Pay	3.0%	0.8%	
Insurance[1]	8.2%	11.9%	
Health Benefits	7.7%	11.6%	
Retirement and Savings	4.1%	10.2%	
Defined Benefit	1.9%	9.3%	
Defined Contribution	2.2%	0.9%	
Legally Required	7.9%	5.9%	

Source: U.S. Bureau of Labor Statistics.

[1]Insured benefits can include medical/health, dental, vision, and life and disability insurance.

The data are based on averages across the entire U.S. workforce from executives to janitors. Digging deeper in the private sector data, there are significant differences by company size—larger companies that are more comparable to government provide better pay and benefits—by industry and by job level.

THE DIFFERENCES BETWEEN
THE PRIVATE AND PUBLIC SECTORS

The difference in the cost of retirement income/savings plans is a core issue. Over the last thirty years traditional defined-benefit (DB) pension plans (where the benefits are defined by formula and take into account final earnings and years of service) have virtually disappeared in the private sector, except for a few plans with frozen benefits. Companies have replaced the DB plans with defined-contribution (DC) or savings plans to reduce costs.

The important distinction that controls the cost of DB plans is that the employer is liable for the accrued benefits, and if investment values plummet, as exemplified by the 2008–2009 recession, the employer has to increase contributions to make up for the loss. With DC plans the value of an employee's account depends on their voluntary contributions and their investment decisions. (Small companies sometimes use profit-sharing plans to fund retirement benefits.)

Plan funding is a problem in some jurisdictions for three different reasons that are not common to private sector employers. For a company, the ERISA law sets forth requirements for minimum annual funding, but the law does not apply to government. Government employers do not have to keep a DB plan fully funded. When the recession triggered a steep drop in stock prices, jurisdictions found they no longer had adequate funds to pay future benefits. As this is written, more than five years later, the unfunded deficits are still a serious problem in several states. In addition, cost of living adjustments for retirees mean the liability keeps increasing. Similar adjustments are very rare in the private sector. Another difference is that early retirement benefits are more generous than an actuarial equivalent. These factors drive up the cost and in an era of tight budgets make it difficult, if not impossible, to grant competitive salary increases.

The demographics are another important difference. Employees in the public sector are older and tend to spend far longer with an employer than is typical in the private sector. Many spend their career with the same agency. With DB plans each year of service drives up the costs. By comparison, a young workforce with heavy turnover holds down benefit costs.

Recent surveys conducted by the BLS show that 90 percent of state and local workers have access to a retirement plan, while 66 percent of the workers in the private sector can participate in a plan of some type.

However, among private sector workers participating in retirement plans, estimates show 70 percent participate only in a defined-contribution plan. Three decades ago roughly the same percentage of private sector workers participated only in a defined-benefit plan. That trend accounts for most of the difference in the benefit packages between the public and private sectors.

In government the dominance of DB plans along with benefit levels were established years ago, often with little concern for future costs (which was sometimes seen as a problem for future elected leaders). It was easier to promise future benefit increases than current salary increases. Life expectancy is longer now, which adds to the costs. As this is written, in some jurisdictions it is still not clear how or when the funding will "satisfy" the pension benefits for all covered employees.

The problem, however, is not limited to the differences between DB and DC plans. Companies account for the cost of benefits as a business expense, which means they are deducted in financial statements and reduce companies' tax liability. The tax savings reduces the net cost.

THE IMPLICATIONS FOR STAFFING AND PERFORMANCE

All of this contributes to a workforce problem that impacts many public employers. The concern is related to the demographics of the workforce. Large numbers of public employees are expected to retire in the near future. Their retirements will trigger a serious loss of job knowledge. The management of older workers was the subject of chapter 8.

For employees approaching retirement, the typical public pension has been high on their list of reasons for continuing to work in government. The more years they continue in their careers, the higher the benefit and the stronger the motivation is to stay.

When plans are announced to modify or even terminate a DB pension plan, older workers are the first to express their anger. Even if the planned changes do not affect them personally, they are likely to resist. And there are always elected officials who support their position.

The past few years, of course, have seen morale plummet in some financially hard-hit jurisdictions. However, older workers are likely to stay regardless of how discontented they become. There are stories of people "retiring on the job," and to use the Gallup phrase, "becoming actively disengaged." Their behavior affects the morale of other employees.

But the story is very different for young workers. A pension to anyone under, to pick a number, age thirty-five, is less important than other job attributes. When they become dissatisfied, they know their prospects for finding a better, more satisfying job are good. At their age many would be receptive to replacing a DB plan with a DC plan. Other benefits—medical, vision, life insurance, and so on—are also less important to them.

They also have to be aware that the pension funding problems make it difficult to grant competitive salary increases or to support additional training or education.

Young employees will have their own idea of what's important, what they look for in a compensation package, and what the deficiencies are in the current package. Periodic focus groups would be useful to understand concerns. It's a good practice to

WHY WE NEED TO RETHINK
PUBLIC EMPLOYEES' COMPENSATION

Traditional public pensions widen the public-private pay gap, and they aren't a good fit for a younger government workforce.

by Thom Reilly, Director of the Morrison Institute for Public Policy

Pensions—except for one's own, of course—seldom rank high on Americans' list of hot topics. But the Great Recession and the huge debt surrounding public employees' pensions have thrust this complex and rather arcane issue into the spotlight.

Which is where it belongs. Nationwide, unfunded liabilities for public sector pensions and retiree health care range anywhere from $1.4 trillion to more than $4 trillion, depending on the assumptions used. And looking ahead, there's good reason to conclude that current public pension plans will not fit the needs of younger generations of public workers.

The national debate over public pensions raises a number of key issues, including fairness, transparency, the proper role of government, and the sanctity of the free market. The bottom line, however, is the bottom line: Are public sector workers making out better than their private sector counterparts? The answer, according to a new model of private-versus-public-sector lifetime compensation, is yes.

Taking a new approach to the ongoing debate, I constructed a public-versus-private-sector model to gauge the cost of lifetime compensation. The model, measuring total wealth accumulated during both active-employment and retirement years, includes three types of workers:

- A private sector employee with a typical 401(k) retirement package
- A public sector employee with a defined-benefit pension plan plus Social Security income
- A public sector worker with a defined-benefit plan but no Social Security income

Two sample occupations were reviewed: administrative assistants (white-collar workers) and engineers (professionals).

The results: for both occupations, total lifetime compensation of an average public employee was higher than that of the private sector counterpart. While preretirement compensation levels were comparable between the two sectors for the administrative assistant and higher for the private sector engineer, the retirement benefits of public sector employees for both occupations were far greater than those of their private sector counterparts. This was not only because public sector retirement payouts are more generous but also because public employees can retire on average five years earlier than private sector workers.

Over the years, benefits have become a growing portion of total compensation for public employees. Elected officials have often favored more-enhanced benefits packages in lieu of salary increases because it has been politically easier: benefit-package increases are less visible to the public, and the costs can be spread out over time.

But there is a growing conviction among policy experts that it may be time to re-evaluate how we compensate public employees—that public pay is too heavily skewed toward deferred compensation, which can hide a full accounting of the costs from the public while pushing a significant portion of those costs onto future generations.

In addition, these plans may no longer be the best choice for today's younger and more mobile workforce. Most defined-benefit plans, for example, are not portable. Thus, many workers feel constrained to remain with one employer, no matter how unhappy or unproductive they are. Other types of plans—such as defined contribution, cash balance, and hybrid—may be much more appealing to workers who desire more flexibility with their retirement accounts.

The model described here clearly does not end the debate on comparative compensation. But it does offer a different perspective on the growing disparity between the retirement costs associated with public sector workers and those of their private sector counterparts at a time when there is growing political resistance to preserving retirement benefits for public employees that are far more generous than most private sector workers can ever hope to enjoy.

The paramount challenge for policy makers is to design sustainable compensation systems that ensure recruitment and retention of quality public workforces while providing protection for retirees. Some hard choices are certainly ahead. But it's time—if not well past time—to take them on.

Thom Reilly is the Director of the Morrison Institute for Public Policy and a professor in the Arizona State University School of Public Affairs. He previously served as county manager of Clark County, Nevada. He is a Fellow of the National Academy of Public Administration.

monitor changes in the benefits provided by relevant other employers to learn where future adjustments may be necessary.

Benefits do not contribute to job satisfaction—research confirmed that years ago—but when an employee feels he has been unfairly treated by management decisions, it can trigger dissatisfaction. And that can undermine an employee's commitment and his/her performance.

All of this has important implications for recruiting and staffing. Where the media focus on what the critics are saying about a jurisdiction's HR practices, pension problems, or wage freezes, it has to adversely impact the "brand" or reputation of the organization as an employer.

That has to make it even more difficult to recruit and retain high-caliber young employees.

TOTAL COMPENSATION STATEMENTS

A straightforward step would be to create individual total compensation statements to make certain employees understand the value of the components and what they can expect.

Ideally, the first step would be drafting (or revising) a compensation philosophy statement. An Internet search will find examples, including several from government organizations.

Another useful step is helping senior leaders to understand the compensation program so they can explain and discuss pay issues with staff. It's not helpful if they respond frequently with, "You better ask HR." This communicates a clear lack of interest.

Employees want to understand how their pay is determined. It's a given that they would like a higher salary, but they are adults, and even more basically, they want to feel they have been treated fairly. "Fair" in this context is consistent with the stated philosophy and method for classifying jobs and determining adjustments over time. That makes the process and adherence to the process a key.

If survey data were a factor, and it's used in a credible manner, there is no compelling reason to refrain from sharing the results. Too much data are readily available on websites. Employees will be interested in the comparative conclusions.

It's often forgotten that employees are naturally interested in their future prospects. Government workforces are not growing and are not likely to grow for the foreseeable future. Employees need to have a general understanding of what they can expect.

Employees also need to understand the goals of benefit plans along with the mechanics of how individual benefits will be determined. Where costs are a concern, employees should be aware of the possible ramifications. If the need to fund a pension means there will be less money available for other benefits or for pay increases, the facts should be communicated to both employees and the public.

It would be highly advantageous to remind employees of all their benefits, including those that are a convenience but have little financial value. Recent reports in the business media suggest companies are adding benefits like on-site dry-cleaning services that are intended to minimize time on personal errands.

Those subjects can be discussed in an annual statement as well as occasional brief reminders on an intranet or newsletter. The practice is common and has been proven to increase employee appreciation for the full value of their entire package. There are many vendors today, but if costs make it necessary, in-house staff could develop a simple version.

A website compensation information list of the possible items includes:

1. Leave Benefits
   o Holidays / x Days
   o Sick Leave / x Days Available
   o Personal / x Days
   o Bereavement / x days available
   o Vacation/PTO / x days
   o Jury Leave / x days available
2. Insurance Benefits—Employee Cost/Employer Cost
   o Medical Insurance
   o Basic Life Insurance & AD&D
   o Dental Insurance

    o Supplemental/Dependent Life
    o Vision Insurance
    o Short-Term Disability
    o Long-Term Disability
    o Flexible Spending/Cafeteria Plan
    o Long-Term Disability
    o Health Care Spending Account
    o Business Travel Accident

3. Financial Security—Employee/Employer Cost
    o Retirement Plan—Defined Benefit/401(k)
    o Workers' Compensation
    o Social Security
    o Federal Unemployment Insurance
    o Medicare
    o State Unemployment Insurance

4. Additional Benefits
    o Adoption Assistance
    o Health Club Membership Discount
    o Child Care
    o Paid Parking/Commutation Allowance

ADDITIONAL RESOURCES

Ellis, Charles D., Alicia H. Munnell, and Andrew D. Eschtruth. *Falling Short: The Coming Retirement Crisis and What to Do About It.* Oxford University Press, 2014.

Mitchell, Olivia S., and Gary Anderson, eds. *The Future of Public Employee Retirement Systems.* Oxford University Press, 2009. This is a managed book with chapters by a number of academic researchers.

Munnell, Alicia H. *State and Local Pensions: What Now?* Brookings Institution, 2012.

Munnell, Alicia H., Jean-Pierre Aubry, Anek Belbase, and Josh Hurwitz. "State and Local Pension Costs: Pre-Crisis, Post-Crisis, and Post-Reform." Center for Retirement Research, Boston College, 2013.

Kellar, Elizabeth. "Retirement Security: A Moving Target." *Public Management* (November 2015). The author is president/CEO, Center for State and Local Government Excellence, Washington, DC.

13

Developing Productive Labor-Management Partnerships

This book is purposely neutral on the role of unions. That is an issue for elected officials to decide. Existing public employee labor laws were enacted starting in the 1960s, a time when unions still flourished in the private sector. (Wisconsin was the earliest state in 1959.) The laws allowing government employees to form unions were and are strongest in what were then heavily industrialized states. The public's view of unions in those years was different than it is today. If the recent events in Wisconsin and other states are meaningful, efforts to weaken unions are likely to continue for years.

It's unfortunate when the politics become acrimonious. While political battles can damage labor-management relations, the battles are largely independent of the potential value of unions when there is agreement to work together for reform. Where unions do not exist, employee groups can work as partners with management to improve the functioning of their organization. The word "potential" should be emphasized. Politicians who denigrate the value of the workforce undermine public service and trigger (or strengthen) the resistance to change. Successful reform cannot be mandated. Employers and, in government, the public never benefit when labor and management are adversaries.

The public sector has still not recovered from the Great Recession. Government employment as a percentage of the U.S. workforce has actually fallen steadily from a peak of roughly 19 percent in the mid-1970s to 16 percent today. That is the same percentage when John Kennedy took office. In several states the pension crisis is a barrier to moving forward. Local government is hiring again, but the budget deficits continue to make it difficult for state and federal agencies to add workers. In under-staffed agencies, when there is little expectation that the deficits will end soon, they contribute to lower morale and unfortunately to an "us versus them" mind-set that is antithetical to the idea of partnership.

KEY SUPREME COURT DECISION

In March 2016, the U.S. Supreme Court deadlocked four to four in the case *Friedrichs v. California Teachers Association*, which affirmed a lower court decision. The case was brought by a group of public school teachers who as nonunion members are required by state law to contribute to fees supporting the union's collective bargaining efforts. Their lawyer argued that the distinction between permissible fees to support bargaining and impermissible fees that go to political initiatives is "unworkable" in the public sector.

In the oral arguments in January court observers voiced the belief that the conservative justices would rule against the union. But the death of Justice Scalia changed the balance.

Unions cannot compel nonmembers to support their political activities, and unions must send annual notices to nonmembers itemizing the union fees. Under California law, a nonmember must affirmatively opt out yearly to avoid giving the portion of the fees they cannot be compelled to pay.

Currently, twenty-five states forbid mandatory union fees. "Fair-share" fees are permitted in twenty-three states and the District of Columbia. The precedent for the payment of required fees was established forty years ago. If the union had lost, it would have undermined union finances.

In April, the lawyers for the teachers requested that the Supreme Court rehear the case when the ninth justice is appointed. This issue may be reexamined in the future.

The budget crises at every level of government have forced unions into a defensive posture, working to save jobs and avoid pay and benefit cuts. In the current environment there are no winners, only losers, including the public. In the private sector labor can be more aggressive; striking is an accepted tactic (although used far less frequently today). For workers it's all too natural when one's job and income security are threatened to pull back and resist changes that threaten working relationships and careers. It should not be surprising that the interest in creating labor-management partnerships has declined since the Great Recession.

This is a time when government would benefit from changes in the work-management paradigm that reduce costs and increase productivity. In business, history shows tough times are a period of change. Change is sometimes necessary for the survival of a business. Public agencies may not have to worry about survival, but everyone would benefit if labor groups were to partner with management to improve agency performance. The changes in the work-management paradigm are likely to contribute to a more satisfying work experience. Looking back, if government had followed the evolution in the management of work that has transformed business organizations, government would have its own list of the "best places to work."

WORKS COUNCILS IN EUROPE

The idea of labor-management partnerships is certainly not new. In Germany, so-called works councils with elected worker representatives became accepted early in the last century. The Nazis abolished the councils and unions, but they were started again after the war. Today, the word "codetermination" is used to describe the partnership between labor and management.

The German system recognizes worker rights. German labor law requires consultation and collaboration with workers in a works council. At a minimum, the councils guarantee workers a voice in corporate decision making.

A resurgence of works councils in other European countries dates to the 1970s. At first, the idea of authorizing works councils was unpopular, but by the mid-1980s the European Commission (EC) began to facilitate discussions between labor and corporate representatives. In 1994, following the creation of the European Union, the Directive on European Works Councils (EWCs) required multinational firms with at least one thousand employees in EU countries to form works councils. The directive called for covered firms to create EWCs or "a procedure for informing and consulting employees" that would transcend national boundaries. The requirement affected some fifteen million workers in about 1,500 companies, including a number of U.S. firms with large European operations.

Since the 1994 initiative, the number of active works councils has steadily risen. As of June 2015, a total of 1,071 are running. While this number continues to increase, the rate of increase has slowed. Over the last five years, some twenty-five new EWCs have been started each year. For the five years prior to the recession, the average was about forty-two per year.

In 2016, the EC is planning an evaluation of the EWC directive that will undoubtedly lead to debate on the need for further review of European regulation of EWCs.

Research provides some support for the claim that works councils improve labor-management relations, at least as each side views the other. Surveys of European business executives and managers show that they are more receptive to works councils today than they were in the 1970s.

However, the claim that works councils contribute to improved company performance is not well supported by research. Actually, studies in the early to mid-1990s found, if anything, the opposite. Those studies suggested that works councils have at best no significant effect on company performance. Some studies indicate that councils might have negative implications for company profitability.

LABOR-MANAGEMENT PARTNERSHIPS

The United States has stayed away from the works council model with its requirement that management accept the role of unions (or worker representatives) in corporate decision making. The alternative is a negotiated agreement to create labor-management partnerships.

Virtually every union with labor agreements in the public sector has stories of partnerships on their websites. However, the fact that the information is not displayed prominently suggests most of the activity is at the local work site level, and (not surprisingly) secondary to national union priorities. Furthermore, the combination of Republican majorities at the state level and in Congress is not a sympathetic or supportive climate. Plus, the budget problems have contributed to increased friction that undermines interest in cooperation. Partnerships that existed in the years before the recession may not have survived.

At the federal level, the partnership idea has had support from Presidents Clinton and Obama. Clinton issued Executive Order 12871 in 1993, creating the National Partnership Council that was (1) to support "the creation of labor-management partnerships and promoting partnership efforts in the executive branch, to the extent permitted by law"; which was (2) to propose "to the President by January 1994 statutory changes necessary to achieve the objectives of this order, including legislation consistent with the National Performance Review's recommendations for the creation of a flexible, responsive hiring system and the reform of the General Schedule classification system." Looking back, however, there were no meaningful changes in the hiring system or the GS system.

Within a month of his inauguration, President Bush signed Executive Order (EO) 13203, revoking EO 12871 and rescinding "any orders, rules, regulations, guidelines, or policies implementing or enforcing E.O. 12871." Through the years of the Bush presidency, unions had limited access and minimal dialogue with agency leaders. When Democrats won a majority in Congress in the 2006 elections, the unions regained their influence and responded by working successfully to kill major Bush workforce initiatives, including a multiyear project to switch to pay for performance.

In President Obama's first year in office, he issued Executive Order 13522, which created the National Council on Federal Labor-Management Relations. In its first year it created a "strong framework of principles, guidelines and metrics, which individual labor-management forums have used to become established and effective." There have been regular Council meetings. Unfortunately, to date there have been few significant success stories. One reported in 2014 is the gains made by the U.S. Patent and Trademark Office, which rose somewhat dramatically from one of the lowest-ranked to one of the best places to work.

The most useful discussion of labor-management partnerships in government was the report "Working Together for Public Service." It was based on a study of labor and management collaboration in fifty workplaces and issued in May 1996 by the Task Force on Excellence in State and Local Government through Labor-Management Cooperation. It was commissioned by the Secretary of Labor.

The Task Force was unanimous in the view that public workplaces must change from traditional, top-down management and move toward workplace cooperation and employee empowerment. Further, the Task Force concluded that public agencies offer significant opportunities for productive labor-management partnerships. Both union and government leaders voiced strong support for increased collaboration.

Despite the support for partnerships, the report acknowledged that barriers to new working relationships include:

- "Public pensions and financial security"—This was more than a decade before the Bush presidency and the recession, but money was already an issue that constrained innovative workforce practices.
- "Difficulty in convincing everyone of the need to change"—This includes middle managers, shop stewards, senior managers, elected officials, and union leaders.
- "Mistrust and difficulty in beginning new relationships"—The old attitudes need to be set aside, however difficult that may be.
- "Must learn to work together; cannot impose cooperation"—This is likely to be much more difficult than creating effective working relationships between new hires.
- "Over reliance on legalisms and formalities; formalistic traditions of personnel practices and labor relations"—They could have added the formal, highly structured practices in a bureaucracy.
- "Intent to contract out 'no matter what'"—The Task Force found managers who saw relying on contractors as an easier way to hold individuals accountable.
- "Political considerations or forces"—Obviously political differences are not set aside after an election.

The report also listed the "key ingredients to begin cooperative relationships," which if absent would be added barriers:

- "Top leadership support"—The report makes the point that "Without top leadership on both sides, it's difficult to get started, convince others to take a new approach, allocate resources, and . . . guide the process through the inevitable problems in the early going."
- "Commitment to real and responsible decision-making"—"Employees . . . must be committed to responsible participation and managers must be committed to real involvement and power sharing."
- "Program managers directly involved in labor relations"—This is not an HR or labor relations problem. Managers "must be involved in order to help share the authority . . ."
- "Acceptance of union presence and role"—Unions can only be comfortable and commit to the partnership when they do not have to be defensive.

The report includes several additional "key ingredients"—training, manager accountability, communications, and so on—but suffice it to say that creating a productive labor-management partnership is not a simple problem. The report, of course, was issued twenty years ago in an era of prosperity and before unions were attacked at the state level. If the barriers were important then, they would be higher today.

Three of the ingredients listed would contribute to a more productive workplace independent of the partnership idea. One is the flattening of organizations and eliminating layers of management. That was important to the changes adopted by businesses following the 1990–1991 recession. It imposes a broader span of control and makes more employee autonomy unavoidable. It should be part of any strategy to improve performance.

A second ingredient is "interest-based bargaining," a negotiating strategy in which both sides start with declarations of their interests instead of putting forward proposals, and work to develop agreements that satisfy common interests and balance opposing interests. Interest-based bargaining is also called integrative or "win-win" bargaining. The report provided a side-by-side comparison of traditional and interest-based bargaining. Interest-based bargaining is well suited to local agreements. The idea assumes it's advantageous to start with the issues where the interests of the two sides are complementary.

The third ingredient is an increase in the prevalence of team and group incentives. Group incentives are usually very effective at increasing teamwork and improving performance. Incentives are discussed in the following section. The savings from increased productivity can be shared as cash awards for plan participants or used, as examples, for additional training or for improved equipment.

LINKING GROUP INCENTIVES TO IMPROVED PERFORMANCE

Employees want their organization to be seen as a success and highly regarded. Unfortunately, the public does not universally have a positive view of government. There are a number of reasons for that, including media attention to performance problems, but with effective leadership employees and their unions can play a vital role in quieting the critics. Performance can be improved, and with changes in the work-management paradigm, the improvements can be significant. Research confirms the potential.

It is all too obvious that public employers cannot delay increasing worker compensation for too many more years. An alternative to wage and salary increases is to introduce group/team incentives *with* payouts linked to improved results. That's a proven alternative in the private sector.

Those who have studied successful efforts to create productive labor-management partnerships have commented on the frequent reliance on team- or group-based incentive schemes. They provide a proven reason for people to work together to solve problems.

In the 1930s, a union leader, Joe Scanlon, conceived the idea of gain-sharing plans as a way to save companies experiencing severe financial problems in the Great Depression. Simply stated, when employees suggest innovative operational ideas that result in reduced labor costs, the "gains" are shared with employees. The idea has been used and proven successful by this point in thousands of companies.

In concept it's simple and logical. A core element that marked a significant change in the working environment in that era is the idea that employees need to feel empowered to voice their suggestions. As powerful as the concept is, it is likely to be viable for only a few years, since with each performance period the potential for future savings diminishes. An important element of the plan today is that new technology and systems are introduced frequently. Those gains are in concept attributable to technology, not employees. But the idea should be considered.

A variation is the goal-sharing concept (discussed briefly in chapter 9). Goal-sharing plans are very similar to executive incentive plans, with payouts based on performance relative to goals. The amounts are, of course, considerably smaller. These plans should include savings as one of the goals. It's always important with incentives that the plan won't increase costs.

In the private sector, goal-sharing plans typically pay out 5 percent or so of aggregate salaries for achieving goals. In government the planned payout might be 3 percent— similar to the target awards at the executive level—which would be the amount paid for achieving defined goals. Each goal is weighted (so the total equals 100 percent), and performance is calculated separately, usually within a minimum (or threshold) to a maximum range. Actual payouts might range from 1 percent to 5 percent.

Charlotte, North Carolina, had a version of a goal-sharing plan for a number of years, with payouts in each department linked to achieving goals. The city combined savings goals and departmental operating goals. An example of the latter would be reducing lost-time accidents. It was the 1990s, so the payouts were smaller, less than $500, but the city's manager of compensation once stated, "I am always surprised by how excited employees are when they get the checks." The explanation perhaps is that they liked the idea that working together as a team and earning the money was evidence of their value to the city. Charlotte was then seen as one of the best-managed cities. They adopted the phrase "manage like a business."

A similar plan was adopted by a unit of the federal General Services Administration (GSA). The organization had a number of units handling different federal contracts, and separate goals were developed to support each unit. When it was first proposed, the GSA unions pushed back, and it was taken before an arbitrator, who ruled that management could introduce the plan. A year later it was so popular that the union wanted the concept extended to all of GSA. Performance had improved significantly; the plan worked and employees earned awards. After a couple of years GSA was reorganized, a new Administrator was named, and the plan was terminated. That, unfortunately, is not unusual.

THE KEY IS A COLLABORATIVE WORK ENVIRONMENT

As a prominent consultant once wrote in a long client report, "for those who have read thus far," it may be apparent that changes in working relationships that contribute to successful partnerships are consistent with arguments throughout this book. Formal agency-level agreements would certainly be useful, but collaboration rides on individual supervisors who empower their people to make job-related decisions.

When the relationship is negotiated at a high level, it ideally should impact the way people interact at lower levels, but it does not follow that the agreement will prompt supervisors and workers to collaborate effectively. That's been proven by the research on works councils.

For people working at the front-line level, collaboration means they have to discard old biases and beliefs and redefine their working relationships. Of course, both "sides" need to do that. That is always difficult. It will not happen simply because of a formalized agreement.

There is a need for leadership, on both sides. Top management cannot stamp it as "an HR initiative" and ignore it. Unions need to "sell" the importance of change and their commitment to worker interests. Any initiatives should have "PR" people to publicize the success stories. Meetings between HR heads and union leaders do not change front-line working relationships.

The impetus for collaboration could come from either side, but someone has to take the lead. Two other "game changers"—quality management and business process reengineering—were backroom engineering concerns for decades. Quality management was far from new when a book, *Out of the Crisis*, was published, and its author, Dr. W. Edwards Deming, was anointed as the father of total quality management (TQM). Michael Hammer is now credited with introducing reengineering in a 1990 *Harvard Business Review* article followed by a best-selling book, *Reengineering the Corporation*. Both men emphasized the need for change and the value of relying on front-line workers to address problems. Both men provided the leadership needed to build support for change.

Over the decades, long before those books were published, many supervisors undoubtedly asked their people to help solve problems. HR used to talk about "participative management," but it never had much impact. It was not until Deming and TQM gained media attention and highlighted the real potential for workers to contribute that these ideas gained broad acceptance. Today, "empowerment" and involving workers in problem solving are "business as usual," at least in the private sector. But it took leadership.

The collaboration of labor and management to improve government performance warrants the same level of attention. The parties involved in the success stories as well as government would benefit from media coverage. The public should know that government is making progress. The positive recognition would make it easier for others to get on board. Collaborative working relationships need a champion at the start.

In business, stories of collaborative working relationships are prominent in the reports of the "best places to work." Collaboration is an often-told theme of reports on employers like Google, Southwest Airlines, and the Mayo Clinic. These and other employers on those lists expect a lot from their people and have adopted people-management practices that recognize the value of the capabilities employees bring to the job. They empower and trust employees to make decisions that benefit the organization along with those individuals served by the organization.

The real impact of the change in working relationships will unfold and be realized "where the work happens," on the front lines. That's possible in every organization, organized and unorganized. Unions can play an important role in building support for change. Of course, not all workers agree with the positon of a union designated as their representative. A union can marshal coordinated leadership at the local level to push its members forward, or unfortunately it can make change more difficult. Management, of course, can do the same.

There are reasons why companies rely almost universally on incentives and pay for performance. In addition, as discussed in chapter 9, a number of management practices reinforce the focus on performance. Those practices combined with incentives play an important role in helping employees focus on current priorities.

Companies also have the advantage of a shared focus on the goal of continued profitability. Everyone understands the "bottom line" is a key to job security and increased personal income. Over time while leaders change, the focus on the goal of profitability never changes. The commitment to success is central to the business culture, and employees live with it throughout their careers. In recent years the transition to increased flexibility and empowerment has enhanced their work experience.

Scholars argue that government employees are motivated by "Public Service Motivation," but that does not supplant the importance of effective people management. There is a significant potential to raise performance levels, and labor-management partnerships could play an important, lead role in initiatives that generate savings and related results. Where unions do not exist, it would make sense to bring together a committee of workers to play a similar role. Their meetings would provide a focus and a conduit of communication. This would be a win-win for everyone.

ADDITIONAL RESOURCES

DiSalvo, Daniel. *Government against Itself: Public Union Power and Its Consequences*. 1st ed. New York: Oxford University Press, 2015.

Najita, Joyce M., and James L. Stern. *Collective Bargaining in the Public Sector: The Experience of Eight States*. New York: Routledge, 2015, Kindle edition.

Stein, Jason, and Patrick Marley. *More Than They Bargained For: Scott Walker, Unions, and the Fight for Wisconsin*. Madison: University of Wisconsin Press, 2013, Kindle edition.

Masters, Marick F., Christina Sickles Merchant, and Robert Tobias. "Engaging Federal Employees through Their Union Representatives to Improve Agency Performance." http://www.govexec.com/pdfs/021010ar1.pdf.

Sherk, James, Research Fellow in Labor Economics. "How Collective Bargaining Affects Government Compensation and Total Spending." The Heritage Foundation, Testimony before Committee on Government Affairs, Nevada Assembly, April 7, 2015. A conservative's comment on the role of unions in government.

LMP LABOR MANAGEMENT PARTNERSHIP—The partnership between Kaiser Permanente and twenty-eight local unions could be a model for government.

"The Labor Management Partnership is the largest and longest-lasting partnership of its kind in the country. Created in 1997, it is based on a series of agreements between the Coalition of Kaiser Permanente Unions, made up of 28 union locals, Kaiser Permanente and the Permanente medical groups in each region. Today, it covers more than 100,000 union members and tens of thousands of managers and physicians" (copied from the website).

14

Communication Is the Foundation for Improved Performance

One of the very real but often unrecognized differences between government and successful companies concerns the importance of internal and external communications in each sector. Publicly traded companies are required to report their financial results quarterly. Their annual reports have pages of financial data, but the early pages in those reports tout the company's achievements and plans for the future. Their goal is to convince current and potential customers that they are a great company. They invest heavily to convince the world they are successful and have a bright future.

Companies are good at "blowing their own horn." They need to attract and satisfy customers as well as investors. It's for that reason that large companies have three separate communications groups—a public relations office, a marketing office, and an investor relations office. The leaders of public companies devote considerable time to communicating with the media. Employees in successful companies take pride in their reputation.

That's also true for hospitals and universities. They compete for "customers" and for prestige. Virtually everyone working at a great hospital, for example, feels good about their jobs, and that influences their job performance. The reputation or "brand" helps to attract highly qualified job applicants.

Employees are aware that public relations statements sometimes exaggerate their employer's achievements, but they benefit when their family and their friends believe they work for a highly regarded company. Press releases sometimes recognize the accomplishments of prominent employees. When a company is highly regarded, everyone benefits. NASA stands out as a government agency that publicizes its accomplishments—and it's consistently ranked as the best place to work in the federal government.

Agencies as well as their employees would benefit from promotional campaigns to convince the public that government is not "part of the problem." Existing agency websites are typically planned to be useful to people seeking information but until recently provided little performance information. Providing access to performance data would help the public appreciate the value of government and its efforts to improve performance.

Communication today takes many forms. Technology had all the attention, but now GE, Google, and other leading companies show clearly that discussions between managers and their people are essential for high performance. In successful companies performance is a common subject of conversations at all levels. Communication of results is a key to creating a culture where performance is a shared priority.

KEEPING EMPLOYEES INFORMED

Roughly two decades ago the phrase "open-book management" was introduced to refer to the philosophy that argues for keeping employees informed. Its most ardent advocate is probably Jack Stack, who has been called "the father of open-book management." Stack argues, "The best, most efficient, most profitable way to operate a business is to give everybody in the company a voice in saying how the company is run and a stake in the financial outcome, good or bad."

Stack argues for sharing financial results but also wants employees to see themselves as partners in the business. His book, *The Great Game of Business*, is in its twentieth edition.

His basic rules for open-book management are:

- "Know and teach the rules: Every employee should be given the measures of business success and taught to understand them."
- "Follow the action and keep score: Every employee should be expected and enabled to use their knowledge to improve performance."
- "Provide a stake in the outcome: Every employee should have a direct stake in the company's success—and in the risk of failure."

A very similar practice was widely adopted a decade earlier as an element of total quality management (TQM). Organizations committed to the principles of TQM kept employees aware of the metrics associated with product/service quality. The practice often included posting the operating data on the 1980s equivalent of a whiteboard.

The experience with quality management confirmed that employees who have access to performance data will naturally work to realize improvement. People feel good when others are aware of their improved performance.

A related practice is the use of performance dashboards or balanced scorecards. The purpose is very similar, but the information generally is at a higher level—to communicate important performance metrics so leaders can track progress.

The benefits attributed to the use of dashboards are consistent with the argument for open-book management and include:

- Provide a consistent view of results—"to keep score."
- Monitor the performance of business processes and activities to track progress.
- Analyze the cause of problems by exploring relevant and timely information.
- Manage people and processes to improve decisions, modify strategies, and steer the organization to achieve planned results.
- Increase employee coordination, motivation, and focus.

In Boston, the mayor's office in early 2016 launched CityScore, a dashboard that shows how well the city is performing on everything from fire department response time to school attendance to fixing potholes. The platform—which resembles Fenway Park's Green Monster scoreboard—is designed to provide a "nearly real-time" indication of what's happening in the city across areas such as public safety, education, constituent satisfaction, health and human services, and basic city services.

Multiple examples of the many dashboards developed by public entities can be found on the Internet. The value is as much internal, keeping employees focused on performance results, as with city residents.

At lower levels in organizations, significant investment has gone into developing and refining key performance indicators (KPIs). Thousands of books now discuss the practice in all sectors, including government at the federal, state, and local levels.

Long before the acronym KPI gained wide usage, companies tracked performance data in every department. That's been true for years. Dependence on data is universal in finance, manufacturing, and marketing/sales. It may well be true that every corporate employee in a white-collar job has data of some type crossing their desk every week, in some cases every day. Business is obviously about competition, so the metrics focus on what competitors are achieving and on comparative data versus a prior time period (week, month, or year).

The tracking and monitoring of performance data may have had more attention and a greater investment of time over the past decade than any other management idea.

A thread running through all the books and practices is that the communication of performance results sends a powerful message to keep employees focused on desired results. Research, as well as experience, confirms they want to know what's happening and what they can expect. All but the most actively disengaged want their organization to be successful and highly regarded, and they want to feel that their efforts are contributing to that success.

Another difference between the private and public sectors is that performance data was originally collected for use by elected officials and agency executives. That's a narrow reporting and communication purpose, and it's reflective of the practice in business half a century or more ago when top executives controlled everything. Businesses today tend to disseminate data to the managers and employees where it will be best used to make operational decisions. For metrics to be truly useful, they have to be made available to employees empowered to address operating problems. Professor Ammons at the University of North Carolina recently published an article confirming that a problem in government is that data are commonly not used in the same way to guide day-to-day operations. (See chapter 9.)

INVOLVING MANAGERS AND EMPLOYEES IN PLANNING

It was in the 1970s that Volvo was credited with first relying on autonomous, now self-managed teams. A year or two later Scott Paper opened a new plant in Dover, Delaware, where the plan was eventually to eliminate all professionals except the plant manager along with accounting and purchasing specialists. Employees loved working there. In an interview one thanked God for the chance to work there. Another said, "There is no way we'll let a union in to screw this up." It was more successful than expected until problems with new equipment forced Scott to bring in engineers from the corporate office. With the involvement of the engineers, workers lost day-to-day control, but they proved they could function nicely without an immediate "boss."

In the early 1990s, the experience with reengineering once again proved that workers in all fields could work together to solve problems. Over the decade a word used by psychologists, "empowerment," gained wide usage. Now companies commonly have employees who function independently and rarely see their manager. Managers rely on performance tracking systems and videoconferencing systems to manage staff. The close, over-the-shoulder style of supervision has essentially disappeared in the most successful companies. The key is the ready availability of performance data—and trust.

This book emphasizes the value of involving managers and employees in planning the policies, systems, and programs used to manage the workforce. Google's Project Oxygen highlights how important this highly successful company believes employee involvement is in driving its success.

The answers have to be practical, "fit" the culture of the organization, and gain broad acceptance. As the saying goes, it's not brain surgery. With guidance, managers and employees have proven they can develop effective answers. It's HR's responsibility to develop the action plans to coordinate and guide the projects giving employees a broader role in decision making.

Relying on employees for planning new programs is a common approach in higher education, where the collegial culture makes it almost mandatory. Managers and employees routinely play a role as members of committees asked to rethink people programs. That's also true in health care.

It's a strategy that has been used successfully in government as well. One of the most successful federal HR programs was developed by the National Geospatial-Intelligence Agency (NGA), which is an agency in the intelligence community. The agency has won awards as a "best place to work." When NGA was created by merging two agencies, they decided to start by studying best practices and relied on a number of committees to develop their HR policies and programs.

EMPLOYEE COMMUNICATIONS SUGGESTIONS

- Include questions in employee surveys related to their understanding of the pay and benefits programs.
- Follow up with focus groups to discuss the survey results and to learn if employees understand current policies and practices. Use the information and the groups to discuss possible changes to minimize problems.
- Check with local highly regarded companies to learn how they handle employee communications of pay and benefits.
- When changes in pay or benefits are introduced, develop a multimedia campaign that includes town-hall meetings where employees can ask questions.
- Ask senior leaders to attend meetings to reinforce the goals and the importance of program changes.
- Check the website of IPMA-HR, the Society for Human Resource Management, and WorldatWork for ideas on communicating policies, planned changes, and pay and benefits.

NGA made a commitment to employees that their program will be managed fairly. Each year the agency solicits feedback from employees to identify perceived problems, which are then addressed, primarily by employee task forces. This sends the invaluable message that management respects employees and is committed to collaborative decision making.

RECONFIRMING HR'S RESPONSIBILITY FOR EMPLOYEE COMMUNICATIONS

In the same way that a marketing function has the lead in all advertising, HR traditionally has been responsible for delivering normal communications with employees. In HR textbooks, organizations are advised to develop an overall communications plan and strategy to manage the messages, the schedule, the media to be used, and plans for auditing the effectiveness of employee communications.

When the plan is developed, it's the basis for developing a budget and confirming that the staff has the needed skills.

HR's responsibility for communication should encompass all media—paper, Internet, video, training, all-hands meetings, as well as coaching executives and managers on face-to-face discussions. An HR website can serve as a conduit for disseminating information and soliciting feedback. HR's responsibility should include everything generated by the HR office, from job descriptions to surveys to policy communications to performance reviews. Vendors frequently play a role, particularly in producing individualized statements, but they should work under HR's direction.

A good plan helps to insure a consistent message to all employees and helps to prevent unnecessary misunderstandings and conflict. In avoiding misunderstandings, the plan assures compliance with federal, state, and local labor and employment laws.

All employees require up-to-date information about policy changes and about changes in benefits, along with timely details about deadlines for applications and submissions.

Possibly the most important message is what senior leaders say about pay and benefits as well as what they do not say. In a political climate with an uncertain economy, no one perhaps can say definitively what will happen. Employees certainly understand current budget problems. They do want to know their pay and benefits have not been forgotten. Silence sends an unfortunate message. There is another old saying: "If you don't have anything good to say . . ." Where trust is low, people can make erroneous assumptions. A simple statement explaining what is unfolding and why it will be important is rarely a mistake.

An emerging issue is the availability of individual pay information on websites. The public's access to pay data makes it even more important for public employers to have a solidly conceived and credible logic behind their pay programs. The websites provide the media with easy access to individual pay information as well as the names of key people they may want to contact. Information related to trends for employees in other sectors can also be obtained readily from the Internet. That makes it important to help employees understand how their pay and their colleagues' pay are determined. All pay is relative, so the ease of access makes the explanation that much more important.

Drafting (or revising) a compensation philosophy statement is the best starting point. That communicates the organization's commitment to a well-managed program.

Another priority for HR is helping senior leaders along with managers and supervisors to understand HR policies well enough to discuss pay issues with members of their staff. They should understand the benefits and the basic reasons for recent changes, and they should have a sense of the impact of those changes on employees.

The communications plan should include a schedule so the HR staff who will play a role in producing materials or responding to questions know what's ahead. They can also take time to pull together relevant materials.

It would be useful to conduct an audit of employee communications each year to evaluate their effectiveness. Focus groups are a good way to understand the best way to communicate and where employee knowledge is inadequate or misguided. The feedback can provide guidance for future communication initiatives.

A NEW ROLE FOR HR—"SELLING" THE ORGANIZATION AS AN EMPLOYER OF CHOICE

Job seekers first learn about an organization even before they apply for a job. Today, websites like Glassdoor.com post information from employees describing a company's "warts." Those reports are never verified but can influence future job seekers.

Recruiting, hiring, and onboarding is best managed as a communications problem, and HR has to take the lead.

The "brand" of government as an employer has been adversely affected by media reports of performance problems, the criticism of government (and government employees) by elected leaders and pundits, and by the workforce actions triggered by the Great Recession and budget crises. The brand is also affected by what job seekers learn about an employer's people-management practices.

As used here, "brand" is a construct that refers to an employer's reputation in the labor market. It evolves over a period of years. If it's largely negative, because it's amorphous, it is difficult both to study and to correct. Regardless, a negative brand can create problems that hurt staffing for years.

Every employer has to address the question, why would a well-qualified person apply for a job? Government still presumably has the attraction of Public Service Motivation, but research has not shown how applicants, especially millennials, balance that with other brand considerations. With anticipated retirements and an increasingly tight labor market, government's brand will be an important factor in replenishing the workforce with young talent.

Becoming an "employer of choice" is a recently introduced goal and an element of a staffing strategy. Today, job seekers have access to websites that provide a picture of an employer's culture, its reputation in the community, snapshots of how it treats employees, its pay and benefits—as well as reports from disgruntled former employees. For government the problem is complicated by the many different employment experiences in different agencies. That makes it important for each agency to become aware of its reputation as an employer through social networks and soliciting feedback from current employees.

The ringmaster for managing this collage of information has to be the HR office. The basic goal is to create an image in the labor market that the organization is a good place to build a career. A public employer with a recent layoff or pay freeze is analogous to a manufacturer with a recent recall of defective products.

Since an organization's brand is a product of media reports as well as the comments of current and past employees, it cannot be directly controlled or managed. The best strategy, perhaps the only realistic strategy, is to learn how employees view the organization and to initiate the internal changes to make certain employees believe it's a good place to work.

For organizations that anticipate heavy near-term retirements or that are experiencing heavy turnover, a negative brand can cause serious staffing problems. It should not be ignored.

THE CONTINUED IMPORTANCE
OF VERBAL COMMUNICATION

A thread running through this book is the importance of ongoing performance discussions between managers and their people. The Gallup Q[12] questions highlight the importance of those interactions to employee engagement. The new GE approach to performance management also highlights the importance of regular exchanges to coach and collaborate on operational issues. And of course Google's eight "Rules for Managers" are each related to advice or information managers should communicate to staff.

Managers are key. Trust is an issue, and it can only be built through honest, meaningful dialogue between managers and their people. Those who are not good at communicating with staff are unlikely to succeed. One of the primary reasons executive coaches are brought in is to address ineffective/damaging behavior.

Everything leaders do, including body language and silence, sends a message, so they better concentrate on what they communicate. There is also an old saying about great leaders being great communicators.

HR can be a valuable resource to executives and managers if they develop a relationship where their advice is welcomed by organizational leaders.

ADDITIONAL RESOURCES

Reiman, Joey. *The Story of Purpose: The Path to Creating a Brighter Brand, a Greater Company, and a Lasting Legacy*. John Wiley & Sons, 2013.

Cowan, David. *Strategic Internal Communication: How to Build Employee Engagement and Performance*. Kogan Page, 2014.

Barton, Paul. *Maximizing Internal Communication*. Aviva Publishing, 2014.

LeMenager, Jack. *Inside The Organization: Perspectives on Employee Communications*. Create Space Independent Publishing Platform, 2011.

15

Managing Special Government Occupations

The breadth of government operations requires a far more diverse range of knowledge and occupational specialties than in the typical company. At one time the federal classification system recognized four-hundred-plus job series or occupational specialties. With the growing list of specialized jobs and certifications in technology, the list today is longer. For many occupations, public employers are competing for talent with employers in other sectors. For those jobs, businesses, hospitals, and private universities have the lead in defining wage levels and terms of employment.

But for a long list of occupations and specialties, government is the only employer—park ranger, police, border patrol, social worker, mine safety, and so on. Those agencies have to be able to attract adequately qualified talent, provide career opportunities where employees can grow, and create a work environment where employees are committed to high performance.

Agencies with missions and jobs unique to government cannot readily argue that they need to be competitive in talent markets or that their best people are leaving for similar jobs in the private sector. But they are confronted with the same aging workforce concerns. They also have to deal with employee reactions to pay freezes and layoffs, and to the pressure to perform better. This makes it that much more important for each agency to anticipate its specialized talent needs and to maintain a brand as an employer that continues to attract an adequate pool of qualified applicants.

The job families unique to government often are organized and managed in separate agencies. Law enforcement is the most prominent example. But there are a number of others—corrections, natural resources, family services, forestry, education, and so on. Courts are, of course, a separate branch of government.

A central question is: Is a uniform civil service system the best approach to managing diverse occupations? When the civil service model originated in the 1800s, there was no meaningful recognition of labor markets or the issues related to competing for talent. Many of today's occupations did not exist. The first personnel offices were created years later. Few of the hottest issues affecting workforce management today would have been contemplated when merit systems were first adopted.

Effectively managing operations and people requires knowledge and skills appropriate for the work situation. Certain management systems (e.g., budgeting, procurement) can and should be uniform—but the approach to supervision that is effective in a social work agency is not likely to be equally effective along the U.S.-Mexico border or in a banking and securities agency. Each agency has to be accountable for its performance and for developing a work environment that brings out the best from its workforce.

Efforts to improve workforce performance have only recently recognized the importance of managers and supervisors; traditionally a promotion to a supervisory position was a reward for service and based on seniority and/or technical job skills. Now overlaying the differences in agency operations and in the importance of the supervisory role makes it clear that a uniform approach to the selection and training of supervisors and managers is not the best strategy. Added to that, far too many supervisors have not had adequate basic training.

Performance problems generally start from one or more of four common reasons: the organization not thoroughly understanding the job or the skills needed for success, failure to conduct a recruitment process focused on needed skills, poor evaluation of candidates, and/or inadequately preparing new hires to be solid performers. Rigid, antiquated civil service processes also contribute to early performance problems. And, of course, political affiliations continue to be in some situations the reason for the selection.

Regardless of the mission and the nature of the work, there are core practices known to be important to employee engagement and high performance.

- Have an updated and well-thought-out mission statement and core values for the organization. These should be communicated to all personnel and periodically discussed by leaders to emphasize their importance. All employees should understand the commitment of top management and elected officials to the success of the organization. People want to hear their work is important.
- Have the right employees, in the right place, at the right time. This is critical to the success of the organization. In an era of limited resources, it increases the prospects for high performance and contributes to workforce morale and continued commitment. This makes the staffing strategy a key concern.
- Develop trust within the organization. Trust has to be earned and can be easily lost. Management has to treat all employees honestly and fairly, deal with them the way they would want to be treated, and not discriminate or show bias in any way. Employees need to know what they can expect and what's expected of them.
- Place a high priority on inclusion and diversity. In today's climate, the workforce needs to be representative of the public served.

- Ensure that employees understand their jobs and performance expectations, have adequate training and development opportunities, and are given regular feedback to help them grow and succeed. That's known to be important to employee engagement.
- Make competitive pay and benefits a high priority. Employees want to know they will be treated fairly.
- Recognize good performance, whether it is in a monetary or nonmonetary form. Even small monetary or nonmonetary incentives can go a long way in recognizing employee contributions and improving morale in an organization. Ignoring good performance or treating everyone the same sends an unfortunate message.
- Conduct periodic employee surveys followed by focus groups to determine how all employees feel about the organization, their management, and the policies that affect them. Group discussions can be productive in soliciting ideas for improvement.
- Empower employees to give them opportunities to succeed and fail. Sometimes failure is necessary in order to learn and do better in the future. Feedback is important to help them understand how they could have performed better. Of course, it is important that failure not occur on a continuing basis.
- Where possible, employees should be able to have fun at work. Providing public service is multifaceted and important and is sometimes stressful and dangerous. There are, to be certain, situations where fun would be completely inappropriate. But people enjoy opportunities to socialize, celebrate achievements, and make friends. Management should indicate that they want employees to enjoy their work.
- Have open and regular communications. Effective communication is a two-way street and has to be demonstrated on an ongoing basis. Communications, whether positive or negative, should be done on a proactive and timely basis. When employees are kept informed, they will feel better about the organization and their jobs. (Communication was the subject of chapter 14.)

Beyond the core practices, there remains the fundamental question: Do circumstances exist where jobs and employees in certain occupations need to be organized and managed differently? That is a practical, not a rhetorical question. If the high performers in different occupations were asked to rethink the way they and their coworkers are managed, their conclusions would no doubt reflect the core practices, but it's very unlikely their lists would be the same—and that argues for civil service reform.

THE UNIQUE NEEDS OF LAW ENFORCEMENT

As a leading example, the management of law enforcement personnel needs to include the core practices, but the essential point is that the nature of the work mandates more disciplined supervision than in other government operations (e.g., public works, parks and recreation, social services, etc.). In other words, a "one-size-fits-all" management philosophy is inconsistent with the reality of diverse government workforce needs.

The broad law-enforcement field—public safety—is one of the unique government occupations that stands out for its special mission. The primary role is "to protect and serve," and the nature of the jobs, including fire services, makes it essential to be trained to react with discipline. In dealing with critical and often life-threatening situations, where decisions often have to be made quickly and decisively, well-defined departmental standard operating procedures are imperative. Employees have to know what's expected and be able to take and carry out orders. That is uniquely important to the jobs in this field and makes it fully appropriate to operate in a paramilitary environment that follows a well-defined hierarchy. Given the dynamics facing the law enforcement profession throughout the country, certain unique management concepts need to be included if success is to be achieved.

Recently, the media have focused on allegations of excessive force by law enforcement officers, including officer-involved deaths of citizens. There have also been riots and other tense situations where citizens expressed concerns about excessive force by law enforcement. Respect for law enforcement officers has diminished in many parts of the country. Murders of law enforcement officers as well as other forms of assaults by citizens have become common occurrences. Law enforcement officers—the "last line of defense" for society—are grappling with these issues as well as battling continued high crime rates. Everyone working in law enforcement needs to stay abreast of what unfolds.

Also at play is that in many jurisdictions, law enforcement agencies are experiencing significant turnover and increased difficulty in hiring new officers. The reasons include the heightened focus on the dangers of being a law enforcement officer and relative low pay.

The management of law enforcement personnel should clearly include the eleven practices discussed earlier in this chapter. In addition, the following points should be included to enhance officer commitment. It's noted that several are extensions of the core practices.

- As part of the recruitment process, applicants should be provided information about the "philosophy and form" of service delivery by the law enforcement agency. Over the years, agencies used what is referred to as a "traditional" form of law enforcement, which essentially was a reactive way of providing service. The primary emphasis was on reacting to crimes, with a lesser emphasis on prevention, including limited involvement on the part of the public. Over the past several years, many law enforcement agencies have transitioned to what is known as "community-oriented policing," which places far more emphasis on prevention and involves police entering into a strong partnership with the community in order to identify criminal activity, including crimes being committed, and then working together to find solutions. The new approach requires officers to get out of their vehicles more than in the past and engage with citizens and community and business leaders and participate in the development of strategic action plans to prevent and combat crime. Whatever the method of service delivery, it's important for applicants to understand what will be expected, since their success rides on their commitment, and a "square peg in a round hole" is likely to result in performance problems.

- Hire personnel who are honest, intelligent, have common sense, and are physically fit and emotionally stable. It's important in the selection process to emphasize the ability to react well under pressure, including in life-threatening situations.
- The probationary period for law enforcement personnel is critical. Each new employee should be assigned to a field training officers (FTO) who will assign and monitor their work, and give feedback. The FTO should have a strong background in law enforcement, clearly understand and support the agency's mission and core values, and demonstrate behaviors expected from officers.
- Provide an open-door policy for new officers to be able to talk with higher-ranking personnel about training, personal concerns, and other matters without fear of intimidating reactions or ridicule.
- Ensure that shift and geographical assignments are handled fairly.
- Insist that supervisors and command staff periodically ride or otherwise work with officers.
- Ensure that discipline and grievance processes are fair and handled on a timely basis.

In January 2016, approximately two hundred of the nation's most prominent police chiefs, Justice Department and White House officials, and police training personnel met in Washington to discuss ideas regarding possible police reforms. Some of the subjects discussed included the need to develop new training and law enforcement departmental polices in order to attempt to decrease officer-involved shootings. Reform will make workforce management an even higher priority.

ANOTHER UNIQUE OCCUPATION—SOCIAL WORKER

Another prominent but very different occupation that's also unique to government is that of social workers. Employees need the skills to work with families and individuals to solve and cope with difficult problems faced on a daily basis. Social workers provide support in order for those served to try to improve their lives. Employees performing this work have to work within legal boundaries and are required to be extremely ethical. The work at times can be hazardous and stressful.

Social workers are generally found in agencies operated by local government (usually counties) or in social service agencies operated by state government. They also work in hospitals and hospices, nursing homes, and voluntary agencies.

Few occupations place such a heavy emphasis on the ability to understand complex interpersonal situations and help clients address difficult life problems. Very few other jobs involve daily interaction with emotionally troubled people.

Work is often conducted in offices, but field visits are a standard and required part of the job, frequently in less desirable neighborhoods. The work can be psychologically rewarding, but also stressful.

In addition to the core practices outlined previously that are known to be universally effective, the following points are applicable and critical to managing social workers.

- Managers need to have frequent contact with social workers to monitor workloads, answer questions, offer guidance, and watch for high levels of stress. Where stress is observed that appears to adversely impact the employee and/or the delivery of social services, the employee should be referred to appropriate support organizations for assistance.
- Particularly with newer social workers, pair them up with longer-term employees who have experienced the positive and negative aspects of social services delivery. This is a form of a "buddy system" and can be highly effective in the transition of new employees. It also provides recognition to the longer-term employee.
- Administrative methods and processes need to be established that enable employees to provide appropriate, ethical, and timely services to clients.
- Ensure there is a support system of other related agencies to provide assistance when needed. Those agencies should include the courts, law enforcement, emergency medical services, and health providers.
- With changes that occur in the field of social service delivery, in the understanding of client behavior, and in laws and policies, employees need ongoing and timely training and development.
- Employees should be encouraged to pursue additional formal education. Human behavior is complex, and our understanding is constantly evolving. Employees will be better prepared to assist clients if their knowledge is expanded by ongoing exposure to new developments. Their participation typically increases when their employer provides some level of reimbursement for tuition and books.

FOCUSING ON UNIQUE OCCUPATIONAL NEEDS

The unique demands of these two occupations highlight the essential importance understanding the characteristics of individuals likely to be successful in a specialized field. The demands also make it important to understand the approach to supervision and the supervisory skills proven to be effective in each field. The needs are not likely to be completely unique, but it will be advantageous periodically to consider if current practices are meeting an agency's needs. It is highly unlikely that a uniform civil service system is the best answer.

There are, of course, many other job specialties where specific management techniques are known to contribute to high performance. Generally, professional associations maintain a library of the best resources. New developments are discussed regularly at meetings. Their members would be eager to play a role in rethinking people-management practices. A core purpose of most professional associations, of course, is advancing the careers of members along with the public's view of the profession.

A simple strategy is to assign one or more employees in each field to stay abreast of developments that should be considered to improve the functioning of the agency. It should be very clear that they are answerable to their coworkers to make leaders aware of developments in other jurisdictions that can be expected to improve agency and individual success.

It takes support from top management and HR specialists, and an open mind, but a goal of improved performance makes it essential that occupational differences be reflected in the way employees are managed. The strategy most likely to generate credible, widely accepted "answers" is to involve managers and incumbents known to be high performers. A simple step is to invite feedback annually on ways to improve performance. In contrast to business, where cultures, values, and priorities tend to be more consistent across industries, any attempt to impose a "one-size-fits-all" approach to workforce management is never going to be fully successful.

ADDITIONAL RESOURCES

Whisenand, Paul M. *Managing Police Organizations.* 8th ed. Prentice Hall, 2013.

Ash, Ruth C., and Pat H. Hodge. *Five Critical Leadership Practices: The Secret to High-Performing Schools.* Routledge, January 2016.

Most occupations have professional associations that maintain resources useful in reviewing the people-management practices known to contribute to success in the field.

Handbook of Occupations, U.S. Bureau of Labor Statistics (http://www.bls.gov/ooh). This book is a useful resource with basic job family information. There are a number of similar but not as all-encompassing handbooks of defined groups of occupations.

16

Redefining the Role of HR

The HR function is entering a future that has yet to be fully defined. For years, occasional articles have been critical of the function. If there is a cult classic, it would have to be the caustic 2005 cover-story article, "Why We Hate HR," in *Fast Company* that began,

> After close to 20 years of hopeful rhetoric about becoming "strategic partners" with a "seat at the table" where the business decisions that matter are made, most human-resources professionals aren't nearly there. They have no seat, and the table is locked inside a conference room to which they have no key. HR people are, for most practical purposes, neither strategic nor leaders.

More serious discussions recently have floated ideas for redefining the role of what has been the Human Resource function. A thread in the broader discussion was expressed in two recent *Harvard Business Review* articles where a prominent business consultant, Ram Charan, was an author. The first of the two articles, "It's Time to Split HR," was published in 2014.

Then he was joined for a second article in 2015, "People Before Strategy: A New Role for the CHRO," by Dominic Barton, Global Managing Director of the consulting firm McKinsey & Company, and Dennis Carey, Vice Chairman of the executive search firm Korn Ferry. In the community of business advisors, it would be difficult to assemble a more prominent trio. The second article subtly refined but strengthened the "split HR" argument. It started by making the case for a more important role for HR.

> It's time for HR to make the same leap that the finance function has made in recent decades and become a true partner to the CEO. Just as the CFO helps the CEO lead the business by raising and allocating financial resources, the CHRO should help the

174

CEO by building and assigning talent, especially key people, and working to unleash the organization's energy. Managing human capital must be accorded the same priority that managing financial capital came to have in the 1980s, when the era of the "super CFO" and serious competitive restructuring began.

They argue for forming a triumvirate at the top of organizations comprised of the CEO, the CFO, and the CHRO. This three-person team will form a "core decision-making body" for the organization in which *"the CHRO will be the trusted advisor in all things people-related"* (italics added, of course). Articles critical of HR are not new, but this perhaps is the first to argue for elevating the function to the level of finance. Not too many years ago that would have been inconceivable.

The role and evolution of the CFO would be a good model. At one time they were glorified bookkeepers. Their staff still keeps the financial records, but today the CFO reports to the CEO and the board. They are responsible for a company's past and present financial situation but do not directly control the spending of budgeted funds. In the same way the CHRO should be responsible for planning, acquiring, and developing talent but would not directly manage the talent.

In government a similar idea was proposed in a 2012 report prepared jointly by the National Academy of Public Administration and the American Society for Public Administration. They proposed structuring an agency's management team to include the CFO, CHRO, along with the CIO, and to be led by a Chief Management Officer. Management and administration are often used interchangeably, but the issue here is the responsibility for initiating change. The team allows elected and appointed officials to focus on policy and programmatic issues. The CMO would be similar to a Chief Operating Officer in a company.

It's important to keep in mind that HR's stature and role are controlled not by the HR community, but by business and government leaders. To borrow from the *HBR* articles, HR leaders will need to convince those leaders that HR should have the lead in *"building and assigning talent, especially key people, and working to unleash the organization's energy"* (italics added for emphasis). That is important to government as well as the private sector. It's the purpose of developing this book.

The goal is to insure that HR is recognized internally as a valued resource and advisor in applying best-practice expertise in workforce management known to contribute to high performance and agency success. HR can and should be the catalyst for the strategies discussed throughout this book.

Charan is correct, of course, that HR plays two very different roles. The most visible one is the ongoing, day-to-day responsibility for maintaining personnel records and administering HR activities. The second involves advising executives and managers on workforce concerns and, to use his words, focuses on "improving the people capabilities." It's the second that is central to elevating the function.

David Ulrich, a prominent HR thought leader, responded to Charan's first article in a letter that was also published in *HBR*. He made the point that the split "has been underway [within central HR offices] for over 20 years." The emerging HR organization is reflected in the concept of *service centers* to handle the administrative

work, and *centers of excellence* as a resource for HR and people-management expertise. At the agency (or in a company, the business unit) level the HR offices are led by
generalists who work with managers and employees to address day-to-day problems.
Ulrich contends, "All of these parts of HR need to work together to offer integrated
solutions to talent, leadership and culture."

The split may not make sense or even be feasible in small HR offices. However, it
would be useful to identify one or more staff members who demonstrate the interest
and the interpersonal skills to be an effective advisor. Someone in addition to the HR
director should prepare for that role.

Employers of all types, public as well as private, can expect to benefit if elected
officials and executives know they can turn for advice to a group with recognized expertise in workforce management. They should also be confident that all HR administrative responsibilities are managed efficiently and that managers and employees are
satisfied with their experience in dealing with issues related to HR policies and plans.
The service center idea is the answer.

The head of HR is the natural leader of both groups. There should be a single
contact to initiate discussions and studies to address workforce concerns. Charan and
his coauthors were correct that the head of HR should be "the trusted advisor in all
things people-related."

THE CASE FOR HR SERVICE CENTERS

The articles critical of HR generally focus on HR's administrative responsibilities.
Of course, that's not all HR does. If Charan had focused on government, he might
have added

- HR's role in labor relations—rare today in the private sector,
- the political sensitivity in being accountable to the spectrum of elected officials,
  and
- operating in an environment where individual personnel actions are far more
  likely to be scrutinized by everyone.

Government employees are not hesitant to complain, and HR is expected to resolve employee problems. There is always the possibility that a disgruntled employee
will take his or her complaint to an official more important than HR. This work is
necessary, but avoiding or minimizing problems does not earn a seat at the executive
table.

Unfortunately, the administrative responsibilities have dominated how the function is viewed. Ulrich is correct, of course; the service idea is not new. HR departments now frequently use a phrase like "center for service excellence," but it's not
clear if that represents meaningful change. The critics' argument is reinforced each
time an employee is not satisfied with the way their request is handled.

In the classic HR department, individuals serve as both administrators and advisors. As administrators, HR specialists sometimes have to deny a request, and that can undermine their acceptance as "business partners" and advisors.

Benefit, payroll, and attendance administration have been the focus of outsourcing, but administrative capabilities are relevant to the full panoply of other HR responsibilities—salary management, training, recruiting, performance management, grievance handling, and of course, record keeping. As an example, the distribution of performance review forms with necessary follow-ups would be best handled by a service center. The individuals working as administrators in these areas develop skills that have value wherever administration is ongoing.

The performance and rewards for leaders in an HR service center should be based in part on "customer" satisfaction as it would be for any group serving customers.

HR's experience is valuable in planning for and evaluating proposals from outsourcing service providers. They know better than anyone what the internal customers expect, especially where "high touch" personalized and/or twenty-four-hour service is important. In addition, the HR office needs to have the in-house expertise to manage vendors.

And, of course, the organization of HR's administrative activities will continue to be impacted by technology. Vendors are now marketing human resource management systems that handle multiple HR responsibilities. That opens the door to organizing staff under a broader service-center model.

There are also opportunities for public employers to take advantage of the gains from shared-service models, but they will need to overcome issues like differences in the benefits provided, workforce demographics, funding strategies, and so on. The success of a shared-service arrangement depends on the commitment of all parties. The value of a shared-service model can be undermined by a member employer that is not committed to its success.

Finally, all HR activities need to comply with federal, state, and local employment laws and regulations as well as in-house policies. This is likely to be handled best in partnership with the organization's legal department. They may decide to outsource, since hopefully these problems arise only occasionally.

NEW CENTER OF EXCELLENCE— WORKFORCE MANAGEMENT

Charan's argument highlights an important point—the organization would benefit if executives and managers had access to advisors who could help in "building and assigning talent, especially key people, and working to unleash the organization's energy."

That is essentially a consulting approach to introducing and managing change. Advisors need to understand how emerging knowledge of the work environment, assembling and building talent, and an employee's work experience influence their performance.

They have to combine knowledge of best practices, the organization's HR policies and programs, any recent workforce challenges, and coaching skills to help managers supervise staff.

Advisors also need to be able to quickly develop a basic understanding of the mission and operating strategies of an agency. Not having an adequate understanding of the "business" has long been a criticism of HRM.

These are different skills from the ones needed in program administration. Individuals who are good in one role are unlikely to be successful in the other.

The initial step would be to identify the individuals currently on the HR staff who have demonstrated both an interest and the skills associated with effectively "selling" their expertise and providing advice. They should be asked to "think outside the box," become familiar with the arguments of thought leaders like Dave Ulrich, and develop plans to create a team with the credibility to function as a center of excellence. They may want to test their conclusions with key people outside of HR.

At some point they will need to gain the support of agency leaders. That is likely to follow from early success stories. It's better to start small and build credibility. Leaders need to understand the goal in forming the center along with an idea of expected gains and costs.

An early step for the team should be a survey to assess current employee attitudes on issues known to be associated with employee engagement. The purpose is twofold: to understand strengths and weaknesses in current practices and to identify the work units where serious problems indicate change is needed most. If the workforce is large enough, it would be advantageous to complete analyses similar to those in research studies to confirm the interactions between work-management practices, current engagement levels, and performance measures. The evidence would help to convince leaders.

Since engagement is almost always going to be a core issue, the individuals identified as in-house consultants should have a solid understanding of the factors known to influence employee commitment. One or more members of the team should have experience facilitating change.

The team should also include or have access to individuals designated as go-to resources for performance management, rewards and recognition, and career management. As resources, they should need to develop an understanding of best practices, monitor new developments, and be effective advisors as projects go forward. They can be external experts initially, but the long-term goal should be to develop internal specialists with credibility as resources.

Technology will be a consideration, so the team should establish a partnership with the IT specialists who have experience evaluating and addressing technology concerns.

Finally, the center of excellence team needs to be capable of working with managers to improve their effectiveness. That will often be more important than any other issue. A suggested strategy is to identify the most effective managers and ask them to develop an action plan to help other managers improve their supervisory skills. The team is then responsible for developing a strategy to assist less effective managers. The Google "Better Bosses" project is worth considering.

At the end of the chapter is the story of reform in the state of Tennessee as told by its HR director, Rebecca Hunter. Her team has played the lead role in driving significant changes in the way employees and their performance are managed. The state's reform is now in its fourth year.

HR IN A LARGE, MULTIUNIT, MULTILOCATION ORGANIZATION

The argument has been made in prior chapters that government is best understood as a conglomerate. In a business conglomerate, the business units typically have different business strategies; serve different customers; and have different histories as organizations, different cultures, and different talent needs. It would be rare to find a business conglomerate that relies on one-size-fits-all HR policies and programs. It would far more typical to see each business unit with its own internally developed programs planned to support and advance local people-management considerations.

In business the single HR program that is frequently mandated across diverse business units is executive talent management. Executives are managed as a "corporate asset." The federal Senior Executive Service is consistent with that operating strategy.

Below that, with agencies as diverse as public health, corrections, banking, and agriculture, a one-size-fits-all HR system is not compatible with effective people management. These agencies have to compete for specialized talent in very different labor markets. Some public employers have taken the initial steps to decentralize HR management. Agency HR offices should be led by generalists who have the skills to work as partners with line managers and with easy access to leading-edge thinking.

The HR staff in each agency should be able to consult and bring in the resource specialists associated with the center for excellence as well as other resources.

ANNUAL "AUDIT" OF PEOPLE-MANAGEMENT PRACTICES

It's common today for employers to conduct an annual employee survey. The Internet makes it relatively easy to solicit feedback. An emerging trend is conducting brief "pulse" surveys focused on specific issues throughout the year.

Surveys are best understood as tools to assess employee views. The results provide a snapshot of employee thinking. The survey results should be discussed in follow-up focus groups to gain employee ideas for addressing problems. Those discussions can go further and develop specific recommendations for change. Conducting surveys without a commitment to address problems only makes them worse.

Using employee feedback to plan change was the strategy followed by the National Geospatial-Intelligence Agency (NGA; discussed in chapter 10). NGA overcame early concerns by planning broad employee involvement to develop the people-management policies and programs when the agency was formed by merging two organizations. They also adopted an annual process that includes surveys, targeted interviews, and focus groups to audit the effectiveness of the practices, and have worked to improve system processes and develop solutions to issues that surface.

As a result, the agency workforce has repeatedly expressed support in surveys, where NGA scores high among federal agencies. The program has contributed to employee engagement across the agency. It has fully met the original objectives of increased flexibility to assign work and support high performance.

HR NEEDS TO EMBRACE CHANGE

The HR function will almost certainly undergo significant change within the fore-seeable future. Change is under way in the private sector. A 2015 research report released by the Korn Ferry Institute made the point that HR executives in larger companies are now paid only slightly less than finance executives but more than the heads of marketing and information technology. In the most successful companies HR executives commonly report to the CEO.

Government HR directors have not risen to a comparable level. Unfortunately, few of the thought leaders defining the HR of the future in either the academic community or in the leading consulting firms appear to have much interest in government. Leadership is needed both within organizations and in the broader HR community.

The heightened interest in employee engagement and high-performance work teams opens the door to individuals who can lead or support change initiatives. Government sometimes takes a few years to adopt change, but delaying only pro-longs problems.

Here, however, since HR offices often have few advocates, initiatives to consider new or modified practices that promise to improve performance could gain the support of leaders.

Outsourcing will undoubtedly become increasingly important, but there will always be a need for in-house advisors to leaders and managers, and for someone ready to respond to questions throughout the day. Outsourcing might reduce costs, but broadening the evaluation of service-provider proposals could be an opportunity to assess and take steps to improve "customer" service.

The center of excellence concept represents an opportunity for HR to work pro-actively to contribute to a positive employee experience. That is a key to improved performance. Change, of course, is frequently resisted, but here the focus is on modifying HR policies and practices to positively impact working lives. It's about helping employees to realize their potential. Creating forums where managers and employees can voice their ideas for enhancing HR's service would generate valuable

TENNESSEE'S STORY OF CIVIL SERVICE REFORM

by Rebecca Hunter, Tennessee's Commissioner, Department of Human Resources

The State of Tennessee passed legislation, known as the Tennessee Excellence, Accountability and Management (TEAM) Act, in 2012 to transform its employment practices from a focus on seniority to a focus on performance. The foundation of the act was to establish a system to recruit, retain, and reward a talented workforce, while increasing customer-focused effectiveness and efficiency within a best-practice environment. Beginning with the hiring process, a focus was placed on knowledge, skills, abilities, and competencies of the applicants, rather than testing and scoring. A new emphasis was placed on recruiting a high-performing workforce, including using behavioral-based interviewing for key positions.

Prior to the act, employee performance goals were not written objectively, resulting in 85 percent of employees receiving scores in the top two tiers of a five-tier rating scale, often for simply showing up to work timely. Some employees had never received an evaluation, and employees had not received a salary increase in three years, so there was no incentive attached to high performance, which caused low morale and lack of desire to achieve. We felt this was *the* area to drive performance excellence. The act allowed for merit pay to recognize above-average performance and specified that individual performance plans be specific, measurable, achievable, relevant, and time sensitive (SMART).

Because we knew creating SMART performance goals can be challenging, we put a concentrated effort into training all eight-thousand-plus supervisors in understanding SMART goals. We then randomly audited the performance plans and provided additional training and resources to assist agencies in assuring that their plans were SMART. We trained over three thousand supervisors in performance coaching to assist them in reinforcing positive behavior and equip them to coach employees who are displaying negative behavior. Our goal is to teach supervisors how to create a culture of continuous feedback instead of having an event-driven performance discussion at defined points in a year.

Because it was clear that we needed a culture change, we converted from a numerical rating system to definitions that more clearly describe performance expectations. The most challenging area here has been to help supervisors understand that employees who are doing the job they were hired to do are considered valued, they must go above and beyond to be rated advanced, and they must effect measurable improvements in organizational performance to be rated outstanding.

To continue the focus on objective performance standards, the system was changed to require that a reviewer approve the initial performance plan, both interim review discussions, and the final evaluation. This assists in minimizing favoritism or bias on the part of the supervisor. In addition, the department head must approve all unacceptable or outstanding ratings, and documentation or justification must be provided for each.

The good news is that we're beginning to see the impact of the work that has gone into changing the culture to focus on performance. After training in SMART performance planning and introducing the new rating scale, 2.26 percent were rated as outstanding, 24 percent as advanced, and 71.53 percent as valued contributors, which is reflective of the fact that the majority of state employees are doing the jobs they were hired to do, and we have our share of high performers.

As we continue to develop our employees, our goal is to have more high performers. We don't want to limit people at the top of the scale—we're trying to build more of them through focusing on collaboration, professional development, coaching, and empowering people to do great things.

Our research indicates that for a pay-for-performance plan to be successful, it should occur in phases. The first year must provide employees with line of sight of the overall organization to the individual's performance goals. So to reflect that performance management starts at the top, the governor's vision and top priorities, along with the agency's goals, are available in the performance-management system, which enables employees to see how their work contributes to the bigger picture. Departmental goals are tied to the governor's priorities, and those goals are then cascaded down to each employee. Each employee in the executive branch now has a SMART performance plan, which is aligned with the agency's goals and the governor's priorities. All cabinet members receive an annual review from the governor on their SMART goals, and the cabinet meets twice a month to work collaboratively across the enterprise to solve problems.

We recently completed our third year of performance planning under the SMART model. Our most recent audit indicates 92 percent of the audited goals comply with the SMART principles; but because we want to champion high performers, we launched a new curriculum called Get SMARTer. The focus of the course is to continue to minimize the subjectivity of performance ratings by continuing to equip supervisors with the knowledge of how to differentiate between the job the employee was hired to do and exceeding performance expectations. Supervisors go through an interactive learning experience to help employees think beyond valued performance and understand how to strive to achieve higher performance.

The state's market- and performance-based compensation philosophy is that the citizens of Tennessee deserve the best possible service from employees. The state must provide equitable and adequate compensation based on merit, performance, job value, and competitiveness in the labor market. Moving forward, employees will be compensated based on performance, but also continue to remain competitive in the marketplace by continuing to move salaries toward market value. We've learned that performance management, when practiced continuously, will result in more accountability, objective measures, increased collaboration, and opportunities for development.

The state has placed an enormous emphasis on developing employees through a comprehensive talent-management strategy that encompasses the following ten talent-management practices: employee career planning, competency management, high-potential employee development, learning and development for all employees, performance management, leadership development, succession planning, professional development through continued education, recruitment, and retention.

Our ultimate goal is to become a learning organization and become the employer of choice by recruiting, retaining, and rewarding a talented workforce.

Rebecca Hunter has been the Commissioner of Human Resources for the state of Tennessee since 2011. Prior to that she was Director of Human Resources for Hamilton County. She also served as the county's Director of Financial Management. Hunter is a Certified Public Accountant and also holds the IPMA-CP and SPHR certifications.

feedback—with the caveat that HR needs to be ready to explain why some changes are not possible.

Recent attention has been paid to the "red team" idea. These independent teams challenge an organization to improve its effectiveness. They gained prominence in national intelligence and war gaming and take the use of focus groups to a higher level. The NGA experience confirms that groups of employees can, with guidance, plan solidly successful HR policies and practices.

A number of HR consulting firms would, of course, be ready to develop recommendations. However, the question is how HR can help an organization improve, and that necessarily encompasses HR's relationship with executives and managers. It would be easier and far less costly to create teams of managers and employees and ask them to work with HR specialists to evaluate current and alternative practices, and develop recommendations. That is the best strategy to "unleash the organization's energy."

The message is clear. HR has to find ways to reaffirm its value. The past few years make it very clear that there is a need for "trusted advisor[s] in all things people-related."

ADDITIONAL RESOURCES

Ulrich, Dave, Bill Schiemann, and Libby Sartain, eds. *The Rise of HR: Wisdom from 73 Thought Leaders.* HR Certification Institute, 2015, e-book. This is a 550-plus-page book with chapters by a number of prominent names.

Losey, Mike, Sue Meisinger, and Dave Ulrich, eds. *Future of Human Resource Management: 64 Thought Leaders Explore the Critical HR Issues of Today and Tomorrow.* SHRM, 2005.

"How Close Is Human Resources to Becoming a Strategic Business Partner?" An IPMA report, 2015.

"Deloitte's High-Impact HR Operating Model: Business HR." A Deloitte report, 2015.

"How Close Is Human Resources to Becoming a Strategic Business Partner?" A Mercer report, 2011.

A highly regarded HR expert, Dr. John Sullivan, posted a column in 2011 that discusses how HR can work with managers to improve performance. The title is "Increasing Employee Productivity: The Strategic Role That HR Essentially Ignores" (http://www.eremedia.com/ere/increasing-employee-productivity-the-strategic-role-that-hr-essentially-ignores/). It's been reprinted or referenced thousands of times. He lists "22 factors, broken into six categories that significantly influence (positive/negative) individual/team productivity" that he identified in his "30 years of observational research." The list that follows includes nineteen of the factors in his list where HR working with managers and supervisors can expect to improve performance. His column discusses each briefly.

Staffing
- High-performing and innovative employees
- Effective managers and leaders

Resources
- Budget resources
- Technology, tools, and equipment

Direction and Guidance Factors
- Action plans to build commitment
- A defined and communicated purpose
- Team and individual goals
- Priority-driven resource allocation
- Performance metrics for improvement
- Effective monetary rewards

Support Factors
- Best-practice sharing
- Compatible team composition
- Balanced empowerment with control
- Nonmonetary recognition and rewards
- Support for innovation
- Elimination of organizational barriers

Skills, Communications, and Information Factors
- Employee skills and knowledge
- Effective communications and feedback
- Information and data related to productivity

17

Good Government and Reform

"Good government," based on a statement ascribed to Thomas Jefferson, *"should be judged by how well it meets its legitimate objectives."*

The presidential campaigns leading to the 2016 national elections have refocused the public's concern with government. After two terms of a Democratic president, it is not at all surprising to learn that Republicans disagree with the direction of government. Their criticism of government has been ongoing. In addition, the Tea Party movement has become a fragmented but still influential voice advocating a significant reduction in the size and scope of government. There is broad support for change. The role of government is very likely to be an issue in campaigns at all levels.

Public opinion surveys have confirmed a steady decline in support for government. The Pew Research Center provides the most comprehensive understanding of public opinion. Their surveys conducted in late 2015 found that:

> "Currently, just 19% say they can trust the government always or most of the time, among the lowest levels in the past half century." "At a general level, the public finds the government frustrating and badly managed. Just 20% say the federal government runs its programs well, and 59% say it is in need of 'very major reform,' up 22 percentage points since 1997." "Fewer than three-in-ten Americans have expressed trust in the federal government in every major national poll conducted since July 2007—the longest period of low trust in government in more than 50 years."[1]

The most recent Pew survey of the public's view of state and local government was in 2013. Then 57 percent had "a favorable view of their state government" and 63 percent felt favorably about local government. Both were lower than in 2001. (In 2013, 28 percent reported favorable views of the federal government; pewresearch.org.)

This book is silent on the "legitimate objectives" of government. That is for the public to decide in elections. Instead, the focus is on strategies to improve "how well

185

it meets" those objectives. Government should not be seen as "frustrating and badly managed."

Public support began to decline shortly after 9/11 and has continued through two very different presidencies. Nothing on the horizon suggests it will change direction unless concerted actions are taken.

NATIONAL PERFORMANCE REVIEW

When President Clinton was inaugurated, he was confronted with a similar decline in public trust dating from the final years of the Reagan administration. His response in March 1993 was to initiate the National Performance Review (NPR), led by Vice President Gore, with the goal of reinventing government.

The initial report, *From Red Tape to Results: Creating a Government That Works Better and Costs Less,* was released in September 1993. David Osborne, coauthor of the landmark book *Reinventing Government,* served as a key advisor along with about 250 career civil servants and interns, state and local government employees on loan, and a few consultants.

The NPR mission was intended to appeal to the public's distrust—"In time for the 21st century, reinvent government to work better, cost less, and get results Americans care about." That was to be accomplished by operationalizing four general principles: "putting customers first," "cutting red tape," "empowering employees to get results," and "cutting back to basics." Of course, it had the support of the White House.

A month later, in October 1993, Clinton issued Executive Order 12871 (discussed in chapter 13) creating the National Partnership Council with union and management members, and charged it with developing recommendations for changes that in combination capture what at any level of government would be broad civil service reform:

- "Form labor-management partnerships for success"
- "Create a flexible and responsive hiring system"
- "Reform the General Schedule classifications system"
- "Improve individual and organizational performance"

The council's recommendations were set forth in a January 1994 report, "A Report to the President on Implementing Recommendations of the National Performance Review." Unfortunately, meaningful reform never happened.

Books and articles discussing the NPR published in the 1990s were largely positive if not laudatory. However, looking back, this high-level, national effort accomplished little if any systemic change. No major human capital legislation was enacted. The labor-management partnership failed to secure support from either Democrats or Republicans to enact the laws needed for civil service reform. The many initiatives that won Hammer Awards remained local, and today it would no doubt be difficult to find many of the award plaques. NPR effectively ended with the Bush inauguration.

A couple of statements from the reports are worth highlighting. In *From Red Tape to Results*, NPR defined the *"basic ingredients of a healthy, productive work environment"* as *"managers who innovate and motivate, and workers who are free to improvise and make decisions."* That undoubtedly happened in isolated units, but it's as central to broad reform in government as it has been in every successful knowledge organization. The 1994 report from the National Partnership Council argued that the four operating principles *"could be incorporated into the cultures of Federal agencies only by reinventing human resource management throughout the Federal government."* The individuals involved in drafting the report clearly understood the importance of workforce support. They knew what was needed.

The NPR is relevant not because of what it accomplished—none of the HR reinvention goals were realized—but because it exemplifies how difficult systemic reform can be. The NPR had momentum. It was an initiative of a newly elected president, the unions signed off on a report discussing the planned changes, but in the end the efforts to achieve government-wide reform failed. Looking back, the NPR mandate was a few years ahead of the revolution in the way work is managed that gained momentum later in the decade. Today, a similar initiative would be planned and managed differently.

By the time Clinton left office, the public's trust of government, as tracked in Pew surveys, had more than doubled. However, that may have little to do with NPR. The country's economy had experienced the longest period of growth in history, 116 consecutive months, and averaged 4 percent expansion a year. At the end of the Clinton presidency, his approval rating was in the 60 percent range. Reform was no longer a high priority.

THE NATIONAL PERFORMANCE MANAGEMENT ADVISORY COMMISSION

To repeat a quote from chapter 2, taken from the foreword of a 2010 report prepared by the National Performance Management Advisory Commission:

> At no time in modern history have state, local, and provincial governments been under greater pressure to provide results that matter to the public, often within severe resource constraints. At the same time, government officials and managers are challenged to overcome the public's lack of trust in government at all levels.

The report provided a model for public sector performance management based on seven basic principles, applicable to state and local government performance planning, budgeting, and management, intended to lead to improved performance. The thread running through the seven principles is the importance of goals, data, and processes. As solid as the report is, it intentionally added little that is new. As stated in the conclusions

> This framework was developed in response to the demand from governments for more information about performance management practices, the benefits of implementing performance management systems, and what constitutes performance management. The framework was created to focus attention on performance management as a way of addressing the critical challenges confronting governments today . . . and to persuade leaders to adopt performance management to deal with these challenges.

It's worth noting that the authors recognize that "*the emphasis on process and compliance that has typified traditional public-sector management has not been sufficient to make this happen*" (i.e., producing results that benefit the public). Something has to change.

The report highlights the importance of systems and performance measures. Those words—"system" and "measure" (or measurement)—appear on virtually every page, often two or more times. On the few pages where the words "employee" or "union" are found, their involvement is clearly passive.

The authors further contend, "Leaders must instill a sense of urgency about improving performance in their governments, build performance-based organizational cultures and management structures, continuously communicate the necessity of listening to the public, and provide resources to assure that a performance-based culture and related practices are initiated and sustained."

That statement captures the goal of this book. The authors clearly appreciate what is needed but also acknowledge that what has unfolded to date has failed to satisfy fully the needs of society.

Significantly, Dr. David Ammons, a member of the commission, recently reported that his research shows metrics have been used for reporting, but not used in the day-to-day decisions that differentiate management from administration. His column, "Getting Real about Performance Management," was cited in chapter 9. That is a key to understanding why performance management initiatives have frequently been disappointing. His conclusion makes this a people problem, not a systems problem.

THE TWO WORLDS OF PERFORMANCE MANAGEMENT

The experience with NPR and Government Performance and Results Act as well as the commission report highlights a core weakness in the management of performance in government. The expertise on performance in government has been split between two largely separate groups. One group has focused on technology and has been responsible for developing the management systems and more recently the applications using performance data. These "answers" have the advantage that they can be adopted with little impact on organizations, reporting relationships, or on the majority of jobs. The systems and enhancements have been implemented by contractors and advocated in the marketing of both technology firms and consulting firms.

The second group focuses on "people management" and has its own theories and best practices. The group unfortunately works under the "HR" banner and has never been able to gain the same attention as the "system" advocates. Initiatives to change work-management practices tend to be "messy" and contentious. When employees are not involved in the planning, they tend to resist change; that's human nature. Unions voicing the concerns of members often take the lead in resisting change.

The two groups have their own experts, researchers, literature, professional groups, and theories. Unfortunately, there has been little overlap. Despite the split, prominent, highly successful organizations in every sector demonstrate the impressive gains when the two groups collaborate.

There is compelling evidence that in a supportive work environment, employees at all levels have job knowledge that would enable them to perform at higher levels. If asked, job incumbents are fully qualified to contribute their ideas. That's widely accepted and is reflected in the management philosophies of many successful companies. The Google story highlights that point. Employee empowerment is no longer questioned.

This is not to deny the importance of management systems, but technology has always been a tool; it's not the solution. Ammons's research confirms that point. Individuals ultimately make the decisions that govern performance; the only issue is the level where those decisions should be made. Today, high-performing companies routinely trust employees on the "front line." It's now common to find workers who function with virtually no direct supervision. Delegating decision-making responsibility to the lowest possible level is a proven strategy to raise performance levels.

Looking to the future, public officials who want to improve performance and restore the public's trust of government should not downplay the importance of a strategy that fully taps the potential for employees to perform at higher levels. Government should have its own models of high performance.

FOCUSING ON REFORM

This book is about reform. The scope encompasses but is broader than what is commonly referred to as "civil service reform." That phrase emerged in the late 1800s and referred to efforts to correct truly ugly and indefensible employment practices. Reform too often is narrowly focused on the laws and rules related to hiring and firing. Even within the past few years, some "reform" efforts have triggered images of the 1930s labor-management clashes.

There is no intent to ignore the lessons of the past century, but reform as discussed throughout this book is wider ranging and more positive. Yes, hiring should be based on merit. And poor performance should not be tolerated. There is little disagreement. All employees should have a guarantee that they will be treated fairly.

Bureaucratic and inflexible HR programs need to be replaced. The basic reforms do not have to be contentious.

The lessons that should guide reform are those from the private sector. Nothing would preclude government agencies from adopting the people-management policies and practices proven in the "best places to work." Those lists are not limited to leading-edge, high-paying companies. One company that is annually close to the top is Wegmans Food Markets, a regional supermarket chain. In 2015, the company was number seven on the *Fortune* magazine list. The "answer," as Wegmans and other companies on those lists have learned, is the underlying belief in the value of workers and an appreciation for how they will respond when they and their abilities are respected.

People-management reform is badly needed. The goal is or should be to create a healthy, more productive work environment. The NPR reforms focused on the right issues. This is about reinventing "human resource management," but that phrase should be replaced with "people management." The needed changes are broader than HR policies. The HR function will have to play a lead role, but only because no other function has the requisite focus or expertise. This, however, involves a re-defined role for HR. Managers have to be accountable for employee performance; HR has been on the sidelines with the towels and Gatorade but now will be involved in the coaching for a new game. This could just as easily be called management re-form, since it should contribute to more productive working relationships between managers and the employees they manage. It is based squarely on a management philosophy that sees employees as valued assets.

A core assumption is that when people start their work lives, they expect that they will be successful; they do not start that first job expecting to fail or to be categorized as a problem employee. Under the right circumstances, new hires—and that includes virtually everyone—should become valued team members who look forward to coming to work each day and contributing to making their organization a success. Of course, that will be seen by some as idealistic, but it's likely that even today's cynics approached their first job with similar career aspirations.

At some point, possibly beginning as early as the onboarding process, traditional management practices fail employees and consequently organizations, and in the case of government, the public. Ineffective management, unthinking leaders, and poorly conceived policies that should have been scrapped decades ago undermine morale and frustrate workers to the point that they adopt an "us versus them" attitude.

Poor supervision is not the only reason people fail, of course. It happens when employees are slotted in jobs that are simply not a good fit, it happens when they do not receive adequate training, and it can happen when they do not have the tools or resources to perform at a higher level. It can also be triggered by personal problems at home. All but the latter can and should be corrected. Understanding and support can help with personal problems.

Those problems are not unique to government. Until the past decade or two there was a "that's just the way it is" mind-set. Work was work, and it was not expected to be rewarding, at least not for those who were in the "them" category. Long ago Karl Marx argued in essence that work is bad, and an inevitable gulf separates management and workers. For years the phrase "labor peace" was intended as a positive comment on what was assumed to be the natural tension between management and workers. It's only recently that employers have developed strategies to close the breach. In a well-managed organization, the interests of workers are best served when they contribute to their employer's success. A collaborative work environment makes the work experience more satisfactory to everyone.

The Google story is relevant to government. The company recognized that their cadre of managers and supervisors was inhibiting workforce performance. They invested the time to learn what behaviors would be better suited to improving performance in this knowledge organization, and redefined the policies and programs to reinforce and reward the transition to more effective people management.

Employees want to know that management is concerned and willing to invest in developing a fully productive work environment. They look forward to providing feedback. That's true of "workers" at all levels, including managers and supervisors. Surveys and focus groups are basic methods to both gather ideas to address problems and test reactions to possible policy changes. They want to be involved. Their involvement contributes to a sense of ownership and acceptance.

The story of the NGA is also relevant. When this federal agency was created in 2003, top management committed to adopting "best practice" HR policies and programs. They created a series of employee groups to develop those programs. Today, the agency regularly asks for employee input to assess how well the programs are working, and commits to fine-tuning to address any problems. The agency has since been recognized as a best place to work several times.

NGA's strategy is consistent with the common practice in colleges and universities where the culture places a high value on collegiality. Wage and salary programs tend to be the most sensitive, and when college leaders conclude that a program needs to be replaced or modified, they commonly rely on committees composed of representatives of the groups that will be affected to plan the changes. The employees involved take their role very seriously, agonize over difficult decisions, and with guidance are fully capable of developing programs that will be accepted by their colleagues. They rely on the same approach that would be followed by consultants but also bring their knowledge of the organization to the planning.

Managers and employees are in the best position to know what's working and what's not working. With the Internet, it's easy for them today to learn what other employers are doing. Initiatives to improve performance are intended to influence decisions and change behavior. It's important that everyone view planned changes as necessary, solidly conceived, in line with best practices, and fair.

An important lesson from reform initiatives in other sectors is that when HR policies and programs are modified or replaced, it is very important to gain acceptance of the program changes by managers and employees. The phrases "buy-in" or "ownership" describe the goal. For employees to feel that the decisions affecting their careers are fair, they need to understand why the changes were necessary, how the decisions were made, the issues that were considered, and the reasoning behind decisions. They want assurance that decisions are without bias or discrimination. Their buy-in assures they will work to make change a success.

Tennessee is, of course, not the only state to undertake reform. Reform initiatives in Georgia, Colorado, Indiana, and Arizona have been reported by the media. Other states have decentralized or deregulated HR policies in a way that could be called reform. South Carolina was one of the earliest two decades ago. Florida, Texas, and Montana have deregulated workforce management. Wisconsin, of course, has been in the headlines.

Some reform efforts have failed. The most prominent is the Defense Department's National Security Personnel System. Unfortunately, the failures are often not studied adequately to understand where they went off the track. Those lessons could be invaluable.

It's probable that every public employer has adopted new policies or installed new HR systems in the past decade. But for reasons that have not been explored (or at least not reported), the announcements have not emphasized the creation of a more positive work environment. In "best practice" companies that strategy is now commonly proven to contribute to success.

THE NUMBER-ONE CHALLENGE FOR GOVERNMENT— HUMAN CAPITAL AND WORKFORCE ISSUES

In late 2015, the website Route Fifty partnered with the Government Business Council to survey leaders in state and local government to understand their most important challenges.[2] They received over nine hundred responses representing all fifty states and numerous counties and municipalities.

The overwhelming majority—90 percent—indicated human capital and workforce issues are challenges for their organization. That was checked as the most important challenge (of six alternatives) by 37 percent of the respondents. This is central to the reason for developing this book.

Only 41 percent believe their organization is prepared for the anticipated wave of retirements. As one respondent stated, "the brain drain and loss of institutional memory is critical." Only two out of five believe their organization is competitive with the private sector in its ability to recruit and hire talent. Among state respondents, the number who believe their organization is competitive with the private sector drops to less than one out of five.

Wage and salary levels are known to be low in many jurisdictions, but respondents from rural areas have also learned that it is "hard to attract professionals" for rural or suburban government jobs, due to "isolation, lack of urban amenities, and lower wages." That is a special problem for prisons, which have to provide medical care to inmates at a time when there is a projected shortage of health care specialists, especially in rural areas.

Budget problems and IT/technology management are the second and third most pressing challenges. Both are interrelated with the workforce challenge. Respondents believe their in-house IT specialists do not have the expertise to procure and manage new technologies. They also find it difficult to attract and retain qualified IT talent.

The survey questions did not focus on the reasons for the recruiting and retention problems, but it's known that the brand of government as an employer has deteriorated since the Great Depression. The reasons are well documented: wage and salary levels have declined relative to market levels; with retirements and layoffs, workloads have increased; job vacancies have gone unfilled for extended periods; training budgets have been cut; service levels have been cut; and criticism of government and its employees has increased.

Government agencies that accept the challenge will need well-thought-out human-capital and workforce-management practices. An employer's reputation cannot be redefined overnight. Unfortunately, there are agencies where an "us-versus-them" mind-set is a barrier to collaboration and rebuilding employee commitment. That mind-set is sometimes deeply entrenched, but it has to be overcome to realize meaningful reform. An old saying makes the point clearly: everyone has to be on the same page.

In a television show, *Undercover Boss*, the "boss" has an opportunity to observe employees at work. As in the show, it would be advantageous for elected leaders to have opportunities to work with employees for a day. It would be especially valuable for leaders who have never managed large groups of employees. Those who have seen the show have seen the revelatory impact on "bosses" when they realize how important it can be for workers to perform at high levels. People even in the most menial jobs want to feel they are doing a good job. Leaders need to understand how employees feel about their jobs and the harm that has transpired over the past several years. They also need to understand the importance of being valued and respected.

Workforce issues are a challenge that should be a priority. With projected retirements, agencies should anticipate losing additional job knowledge, especially among managers and supervisors. That comes together with the problems government is having at all levels attracting, hiring, and retaining young, qualified workers.

For employers that recognize the importance of the challenge, and the importance of reform, possible steps to consider include:

- Undertake an assessment of the brand or reputation as an employer
- Complete an analysis to identify the jobs where near-term retirements and loss of talent could be problematic
- Assess recent turnover experience to understand why employees resign
- Conduct focus groups with managers and employees to assess the work environment and identify the impediments to improved performance
- Complete a market analysis to determine if pay levels are competitive

- Assign a small team the task of researching the reports of "best places to work" employers to understand the differences in their practices, especially those that have a nominal cost
- Contact leaders in organizations that have initiated reform to understand lessons learned

The goals are straightforward: good government, meeting and exceeding the expectations of the public, and creating a work environment that provides employees with rewarding, satisfying careers. When the assessments are complete, senior management should take a day or more behind closed doors to evaluate the situation and develop a game plan for reform. There will then be a need for a champion to promote and guide needed change. Success will not be realized overnight. With progress, people are likely to get on board. They will come to understand that this is a win-win for everyone.

NOTES

1. Pew Research Center, "6 Key Takeaways about How Americans View Their Government," November 23, 2015.
2. Route Fifty and Government Business Council, "2016 Top Management Challenges for State & Local Government," an annual study of public sector employers, 2015.

Index

128; coaching, importance of in, 54–55; performance-development system, 111; "rank and yank" policy of, 109–10; real-time performance development, 110; touchpoint conversations, 110

General Schedule (GS), 6, 35, 125–27, 131–32, 152

General Services Administration (GSA), 155

generation X, 86

Georgia, 66, 192

Germany, 103, 150–51

Glassdoor.com, 61, 65, 164

Global Workforce Study (2012), 53

goal power, 96–97

Goldsmith, Marshall, 42

Google, 84, 113, 123, 135, 156, 160, 189, 191; "Better Bosses" project of, 51–52, 54–56, 179; Project Oxygen, 162; Rules for Managers, 52, 166; work philosophy of, 112

Gore, Al, 1–2; National Performance Review, 5, 10, 94, 186

government: public trust, increase in, 187

Government Accountability Office (GAO), 12, 41

government agency: purpose, importance of, 12–13

government brand, 22; problem of, 60–62, 159

Government Business Council, 192

government employment practices: General Schedule (GS) pay system, 4; as outdated, 4

government executives, 36; "amateur managers," 33; "best practice" program, lack of, 34, 38; coaching, 43; compensation model of, 34–35; competency profiles, 37–38; executive compensation, 44–46; executive development, 40–41, 43–44; executive positions, documenting of, 38–39; executive review boards, 46–47; executive selection, managing of, 39–40; executive succession planning, 40, 60; executive talent management system, 36–41, 43–44; high-potential employees (HIPOs), 40–41; honest feedback, 41; mentoring, 43

Government Performance and Results Act (GPRA), 10, 94, 188; Modernization Act, 11, 15

Graduate School USA, 41

Great Depression, 154

The Great Game of Business (Stack), 160

Great Recession, 2, 5, 44, 135, 145, 149–50, 165

Hammer, Michael, 156

Harding, Stephen, 53

Hay Associates, 127

health care, 3, 59

Heritage Foundation, 141

Herzberg, Frederick, 23

Hitler, Adolf, 13

Human Resources (HR), 33, 37, 64, 67–68, 78, 81, 102, 120, 127, 130, 131, 138, 146–47, 156, 166, 173, 187, 191–92; as catalyst for change, 8; center of excellence concept, 180; change, need to embrace, 180, 183; employee communication, 163–64; employer branding, 61; employer of choice, 164–65; Enterprise Social Networks (ESNs), effect of on, 75–76; high performance, role of, 7–8; human resource management systems (HRMs), 177; managers, as partner to, 8; outsourcing, 180; participative management, 156; pay discrimination, 133; performance improvement factors, 183–84; performance-management practices, 123, 139, 189; redefining role of, 174–83, 190; red team idea, 183; responsibilities, 7, 27, 162; service centers, 175–76; training, 84–85

Hunter, Rebecca, 179

IBM Center for the Business of Government, 104

improved performance: subject matter experts (SMEs), 79; training, impact of, 78

"Increasing Employee Productivity: The Strategic Role That HR Essentially Ignores" (Sullivan), 183

About the Authors

Howard Risher is a private consultant who focuses on compensation and performance issues. Creating high-performance work environments has been a focus throughout his 40-year career. He has a reputation for developing innovative practices that are now widely used. He has worked with clients in every sector and level of government. Risher previously managed consulting practices for two national consulting firms, and also worked as director of compensation for two large corporations—a global conglomerate and a for-profit hospital management company. He has developed five prior books; the most recent is *Primer on Total Compensation in Government* (IPMA.HR). He earned a BA in psychology from Penn State and an MBA and PhD in business from the Wharton School, University of Pennsylvania.

William Wilder is a human resources and management consultant, and owner of Wilder Consulting in Charlotte, North Carolina. The services provided include executive search, development and administration of applicant assessment/selection processes, strategic compensation, performance management, succession planning, organizational studies, administrative reviews/investigations, and mediation services. He was formerly human resources director for the City of Charlotte, North Carolina. The HR Department received several awards from national and state organizations for their strategic approach to a wide range of HR services. Wilder was previously the chief of classification and pay for the State of Florida. He has co-authored several articles with Howard Risher for professional publications. He earned a BA in business from Florida State University and an MBA from Queens University of Charlotte.